BISHOP'S UNIVERSITY
LIBRARY
LENNOXVILLE

A Garland Series

The English Stage

Attack and Defense 1577 - 1730

A collection of 90 important works
reprinted in photo-facsimile in 50 volumes

edited by

Arthur Freeman

Boston University

The Antient and Modern Stages Survey'd

by

James Drake

with a preface
for the Garland Edition by

Arthur Freeman

Garland Publishing, Inc., New York & London

1972

Library of Congress Cataloging in Publication Data

Drake, James, 1667-1707.
The antient and modern stages survey'd.

(The English stage: attack and defense, 1577-1730)
Reprint of the 1699 ed.
"Wing D2123."
1. Collier, Jeremy, 1650-1726. A short view of The immorality and profaneness of The English state. 2. Theater--Moral and religious aspects. 3. Theater--England. I. Title. II. Series.
PN2047.C62D7 1972 792'.013 70-170446
ISBN 0-8240-0615-1

Printed in the United States of America

Preface

Among the longer replies to Collier's Short View *is* The Antient and Modern Stages Survey'd, *now generally attributed to James Drake (1667-1707), the Tory writer whose experience with the theatre comprehended a comedy,* The Sham Lawyer *(1697), based upon Fletcher's* Spanish Curate *and* Wit without Money, *which its title page asserts "was damnably acted at Drury Lane." If comedy is to instruct by example, argues Drake, it need not do other than show what is to "be avoided rather than what should be imitated. And there must be no examples except for caution" (Krutch,* Conscience and Comedy *[1949], p. 243).* The Antient and Modern Stages *was advertised in the Tory* Post Boy *for 11-14 March as "this day is published . . . ," and its publisher was Abel Roper, the editor of the periodical and principal antagonist of George Ridpath, author of the pro-Collier* Stage Condemn'd *some six months earlier.*

Our reprint is prepared from a copy of the original edition in the possession of the Publishers, collating $A^8\, a^8\, B\text{-}Z^8\, Aa^8$ *(Aa8*^{v} *blank), partly uncut. Lowe-Arnott-Robinson 324; Hooker 23; Wing D 2123.* DNB *(sv. "Drake") gives "1700," presumably a ghost-date, and I find no record of any reprint.*

July, 1972 A. F.

The Antient and Modern Stages survey'd.

OR,

Mr *COLLIER*'s View OF THE Immorality and Profaneſs OF THE *Engliſh* Stage Set in a TRUE LIGHT.

Wherein ſome of Mr *Collier*'s Miſtakes are rectified, and the comparative Morality of the *Engliſh* Stage is aſſerted upon the Parallel.

Rode Caper *Vitem, tamen hinc cum ſtabis ad Aram,*
In tua quod fundi Cornua *poſſit, erit.* Ov.

LONDON,
Printed for *Abel Roper*, at the *Black Boy* over againſt St. *Dunſtans* Church in *Fleetſtreet*. 1699.

TO THE
Right Honourable
CHARLES
Earl of *Dorset*, and *Middlesex*,

Baron *Buckhurst*, one of the Lords of His Majesty's Most Honourable Privy Council, Lord Lieutenant of the County of *Sussex*, and Knight of the most Noble Order of the Garter, *&c.*

My Lord,

IN addressing to Your Lordship, tho I betray my Ambition, I shall strengthen the opinion of my Integrity. For bv appealing to so great, and so impartial a Judge, I give the World sufficient demonstration, that I trust more to the Merit of my Cause, than of my Performance, and depend rather upon the matter, than the manner of what I deliver, for my Justification.

The Tyde of Prejudice runs high for my Adversary, and the less discerning part of the Town are so prepossess'd with the Specious Title, and the Plausible Pretence of Mr *Collier*'s Book, that they think the whole Interest of Virtue and Religion embark'd on that Bottom. Immorality and Prophaness are things so justly abhorr'd, that whoever enters the Lists against 'em, has all Good Men for his Seconds. And their

zeal

zeal for the Cauſe ſo far blinds many of 'em, that they neither ſee, nor ſuſpect any Defect or Treachery in their Champion. For men are very unwilling to hear Truth, againſt Prejudice, and ſuffer Reaſon to triumph over Inclination.

The Town is divided in its Judgment of the Piece, and the whole Conteſt lies betwixt thoſe that are Judges, and thoſe that are not, as Cardinal *Richlieu* ſaid upon another occaſion. The latter are of the Oppoſite Faction, and are as much more numerous than the former; as Vanity and Preſumption are more Univerſal, than Underſtanding.

This makes the Prefixing your Lordſhips name, by your own Permiſſion, whoſe Judgment is as little to be byaſs'd, as 'tis to be queſtion'd, not only matter of Honour to me, but of neceſſary Defence. Not that I expect any Protection for thoſe Errors which I may have committed. They muſt be left to the mercy of Readers of far leſs Judgment and Candour, than *Your Honour*. To be tried by ſuch a Grand Jury, is a happineſs I am ſo far from expecting, that I know it impoſſible. But the Deference due to ſo great a Name may procure me a fair hearing amongſt ſome, upon whom a bare regard to Juſtice wou'd hardly prevail ſo far.

Did Mr *Collier* contend only for the better Eſtabliſhment of Virtue, and Reformation of Manners, I ſhou'd be aſham'd to appear againſt him. But there is a Snake in the Graſs. Mr *Collier* under-

undertakes the Patronage of Virtue, as Cunning Men do the Guardianſhip of rich Orphans, only to make his Markets of it. That this is his caſe, the following Sheets will, I hope, ſufficiently demonſtrate. His Vehemence gives us juſt ground to ſuſpect his Integrity, and to believe that he has ſome conceal'd Intereſt, or Pique at the bottom. The diſintereſted enquiry after Truth is always accompany'd with Candour; where that is wanting, there is juſt reaſon to ſuſpect ſome further deſign. In Mr *Collier's* management, the Heat and Smoke are too great and apparent for the Fire to be long conceal'd. His Deſign is manifeſtly not to argue the Poets out of their Faults, but to bully his Readers out of their Underſtandings, and by violence to alter the Impreſſions already receiv'd of thoſe matters, which he treats of. His Style is adapted to his purpoſe, fierce and bold, full of vehement exaggerations, and haughty menaces, he racks Sentences, and tortures Expreſſions, to extort a Confeſſion from 'em of things to which they are abſolute Strangers. The conſequence of this way of writing is, that Women, and Weak Men, whoſe Fears are ſtronger than their Judgments, will be aw'd into a Perſwaſion before they are convinc'd of the Truth of it. For ſuch People in moſt caſes meaſure the certainty of Aſſertions by the Confidence of him that pronounces 'em, and the Importance by the falſe weight that is laid upon 'em.

'Twas

'Twas this consideration, not any extraordinary Affection for the Stage, that engag'd me in this Argument. I look upon it as an attempt towards usurping the Soveraignty of Men's Understandings, and restoring the Tyranny of Bigottry, whose Yoak we have scarce yet sufficiently shaken off. My Reason is the dearest, and freest part of me, or at least it ought to be so, and he that puts the Dice upon that, affronts me in the most sensible manner. I had rather be bubbled of my Money than my Intellects, and shou'd chuse rather to be thought his Cully, than his Fool. 'Tis true, these tricks are not to be put upon a man that is aware of 'em, and consequently I might have secur'd my self without making a publick

disco-

diſcovery. But I think it a Cowardly piece of Caution, a ſort of Criminal Miſpriſion to connive at the cheating of others; and while I am able to inform 'em, the Clamour of Knaves or Fools ſhall never awe me to Silence.

That this is no extravagant Surmiſe, no Hypochondriacal Fancy, is evident from the Tenour of the whole Book, eſpecially the third Chapter. Every thing is deliver'd with an air ſo haughty, ſo magiſterial, ſo deciſive, that he ſeems rather to ſerve us with an Injunction to believe him, than an Argument. That this Impoſition may be the more tamely ſubmitted to, he palms the Authority of the Church upon us, and pretends her Commiſſion to make Fools of the Laity.

The Church is by no means oblig'd to him, for endeavouring to caſt the *Odium* of his own Arrogance and Ambition upon her. How great ſoever his Zeal for her ſervice may be, his Indiſcretion in it does not come a whit behind it. For to extend the Power and Authority of the Prieſt, he curtails the Articles of the Church, and denies the King's Supremacy, which ſhe has already oblig'd him to ſwear to the belief of.

I ſhall not treſpaſs ſo far upon Your Honour's patience, as to recapitulate the ſeveral Invidious things, which he fathers upon the Church. I will hope well of his Deſign, tho I fear the effects of his Performance will not turn to her Service. And I cou'd wiſh his Motives were better,

or

or not ſo apparent. If *Demetrius* was a Stickler for the honour of *Diana*, 'twas becauſe he made Shrines for her, the intereſt of his trade engag'd him in her Party. Mr *Collier*'s Caſe is not much different. The Poets had ſometimes made bold to diſplay a vicious, or a fooliſh Prieſt, and thoſe that were Knaves in the World, and Drolls in the Pulpit, had been made Cheats and Buffoons upon the Stage. The Mask of Formality and Sanctity was pull'd off, and the Blockhead and the Hypocrite ſhewn bare-fac'd. Thus the Profane Vulgar were ſuffer'd to peep, and pry into Myſteries. This Mr *Collier* reſents as if he were perſonally concern'd, and wou'd perſwade the world, that to expoſe Hypocriſie is to affront the

Church,

Church, than which her Enemies cou'd not have ſuggeſted any thing more malicious. However, this miſtaken Injury has rais'd a Flame, which will coſt the effuſion of abundance of Ink before it is extinguiſh'd. *Manet alta Mente repoſtum*, and is never to be forgiven while Mr *Collier* can wag a Gooſe-quill.

Our *Clergy* deſervedly have both at home and abroad the reputation of the moſt learned *Clergy* in the World, and I ſhall venture to affirm, that they are the Beſt in the World. Their Candour towards thoſe that differ from 'em in Opinion, their Modeſty in aſſerting their own, and their ſober Conduct in the diſcharge of their own Conſciences, and not aſſuming the dominion of thoſe of other men,

will

will prove what I say to to be no Paradox. And therefore Mr *Collier*, in making so large a demand in their names, has obliquely traduc'd 'em, by giving occasion to those that don't sufficiently know 'em, to suspect that he acts by their Approbation and Authority.

But I forget, that while I talk to Your Lordship, I wrong the Publick, which claims so great a share in your thoughts and time. I shall not attempt the Character of Your Lordship: For, to write of you, as I ought, to do you Justice, I must write like you, which I hope I shall never have the vanity to pretend to. But the Name of *My Lord Dorset* alone carries more Panegyrick than the fruitfullest Invention can furnish. Those Adventurous

Gentlemen, that have already tried their Strength at it, have by their foils taught me caution. Their Performances fall ſo extreamly ſhort of the Merit of their Subject, that when they have exhauſted their Fancies, their whole ſtock of Rhetorick looks like an Oſtentation of Beggery. This conſideration alone is ſufficient to deter me from preſuming further upon Your Lordſhip's Goodneſs, except to ask Pardon for my Ambition of taking this Publick Occaſion to declare with what profound Reſpect I am

My Lord,

Your Honour's Moſt humble

and devoted Servant.

THE
TABLE.

a Clemens

The

The

Love,

The Table.

Moral

Mr

Poetical

A

Loose

Anti

The

ER-

ERRATA.

PAge 28.l.7.r. *'em off* : p.52.l.ult.add *in* : p.68.l.22.r. *Mulciber* : p.73.l.5.dele *not* : p.74.l.5.r.*Infancy* : p.76. l.11.r.*of* : p.86.l.8.r.*for* : p. 101.l.ult.r.*possibly* : p.132.l.5 for ἐκεῖσεην r. ἐκείνην : p.173.l.25.r.*proud* : p.190.l.11.r. *disengage* : p.235.l.25.dele *not* : p.255.l.23.r.*waving particular* : p.302 .l.2.r.*shewn. She was* : p.306.l.17. r. *push her* : p.306.l.19.r. γάμοις :ibid.l.20.for γῆ r γ' ἦ p.308 l.2.r *Indignation* :3p.11..l.7.r. νυκτέρων : p. 313.l. 2. add *made* : p.315.l.18.for *guge* r. *jugi* : p.339.l.1.r.*conspexeris*: p.341.l.19.r.*dare*.

Errata in the Margine.

P.23.for *se de* r.*sed &*: p.29.for *Verundia* r.*Verecundia*. p.57.for *ictæo* r.*dictæo* : p.69.r *ac*.for *relicta* r.*relicto* : for *tribi* r.*tribu*: p.71.for *victus* r. *victis* : p.113 .for *Dio* r.*Dii* : p.169.r.ἄχρηστ : p.126.dele *and* : p.192.dele *The Moral*: p.226.r.δυστυχίαν p.317.r. *Mr Collier's instances*.

Mr

Mr. COLLIER's *View* OF THE *English Stage,* &c. Set in a TRUE LIGHT.

THe aim of all Writers is, or ought to be, to maintain or propagate *Truth*, to inform the *Judgment*, improve the *Understanding*, and rectifie the *Mistakes* of others. *Introduction.*

others. Where this is the real end and design of a Writer, no Itch of *Popularity*, or Awe of *Faction* ought to bear him from his Byass, or make him give an inch to his *Hopes*, or *Fears*; and the more Universal and Important the Truths are, which he discovers, or defends, the greater in proportion ought to be the Zeal and Application.

Were these rules constantly, and prudently pursued, we might hope for an honester, as well as wiser world, than it has been my fortune yet to find any Memoirs of, since the multiplication of Mankind. For tho the *Declaimers* of all *Ages* have inveighed with great bitterness against their own times, and extoll'd the antecedent; yet even hence we are furnish'd with an argument, that all have been equally culpable, since those times, which we, to humble our own, affect so zealously to commend, our *Fore-fathers* did as vehemently condemn; and if we do not find the *Topicks* of *Satyr* to be in every *Age* the same; we can only from thence conclude, that the *Mode, and not the Measure of Iniquity is alter'd.*

But

But whether the rules be ſtrictly obſervable, or not, may be matter of doubt. For, beſides that grand Seducer *Intereſt*, which few withſtand, *Paſſion*, *Prejudice*, and *Inclination*, have an almoſt irreſiſtible Influence over us; and even in the cooleſt, and ſevereſt of our deliberations, we are apt to give too much to *Prejudice*, and to humour *Appetite* and *Paſſion* beyond Reaſon.

That this is no uncommon caſe, moſt of the preſent *Paper-Combats* demonſtrate, in which the War on both ſides is carry'd on with an obſtinacy and fury, very diſproportionate to the trifles generally contended for. The Combatants enter the liſts againſt Chimerical Gyants of their own raiſing, and lay about 'em like *Ajax*, or *Cervantes*'s *Hero*, amongſt the Sheep, Gyants, or Windmills, 'tis all one, if they ſtand in their way they muſt be encounter'd.

The moſt formidable of theſe, is the Author of the *Short View of the Immorality and Profaneneſs of the* Engliſh *Stage*. This Gentleman, ſome time or other, between ſleeping and waking, had happen'd to hear ſome of Mr *Durfy*'s

Rattles, and perhaps ſome ſaucy *Jack* or other of the Stage diſcharge an Oath or two, and preſently miſtaking 'em for a noiſe of Drums, and volley of Shot, falls to dreaming of Invaſions and Revolutions, that the Church Artillery was ſeiz'd, and turn'd upon it; of a terrible Stage Plot, and a huge Army in Ambuſcade behind the Play-houſe Scenes; and therefore he cries out to have the Beacons lighted, and the Bells rung backward in every Pariſh, to raiſe the *Poſſe* of Fathers, Councils, Synods, School-men, and the reſt of the Church Militia, and caſt up Retrenchments, for the Vanguard of *Parnaſſus* are upon 'em. Then he calls for his *Durindana* of a Gooſe-quill, and thunders out *Anathema*'s as thick as Hail ſhot.

Thus inſtructed and appointed, he draws out his forces, and charges with ſuch violence and fury upon the Forlorn-Hope of the Stage, that it had been impoſſible for 'em to have ſuſtain'd the ſhock, if *Pegaſus* had not been train'd of old to the ſervice, and very well acquainted with the temper of the Enemies Fire.

This Anti-poetick War has been carry'd on with abundance of heat at divers times and in divers Countries; it broke out first in *Spain*, about the close of the last Century, under *Mariana* a Jesuit, who publish'd a Book *Contra Spectacula*; and after that another, by the Special Approbation of the Visitor, and the Provincial of the Jesuits of the Province of *Toledo*; from thence it travell'd into *Italy*, where it was fomented by *Francisco Maria*, a *Sicilian* Monk, and *P. Ottonelli*, a Jesuit; and was thence translated into *England*, about sixty years ago, by Dr *Reynolds* and Mr *Prynne*; to *France*, about thirty years ago, by the Prince of *Conti*, the Sieur *de Voisin*, *&c.* and tho bury'd for some years in its embers, broke out again there not many years ago into a flame; at which Mr *Collier* took fire, and reviv'd the quarrel in *England*.

The quarrel to the modern Stage first formally commenc'd in Spain.

All these disputes have been manag'd with great vehemence and fierceness on the Agressor's parts, and had the success been answerable to their Resolution, the scatter'd rout of *Parnassus* had been never able to have rally'd,

 or

or made head again; but their Onſet was like that of the *Turks* and *Tartars*, the Noiſe was much greater than the Execution. I cou'd never find that the Muſes were famous for Martial Exploits, or that their Votaries e're ſignaliz'd themſelves by any extraordinary atchievements in the Polemicks. How comes it then, that ſuch impetuous Aſſailants have gain'd no more upon 'em? For as yet the very Outworks of *Parnaſſus* ſeem to be in no danger. Is it the natural ſtrength of the Place, or Reſolution of the Defendants that Protects 'em?

Before I give a direct anſwer to theſe queſtions, it will be neceſſary to premiſe a ſhort account of the occaſion, ſtate, and progreſs of the Controverſie, in, and from the time of the Primitive Fathers down to our own Times; by which we may be enabled to make a right Judgment, how far the preſent Stage is affected by the Authorities, and Arguments urg'd from 'em.

Shows among the Heathens of Religious Parentage.

It is on all hands agreed, that the *Ludi* and *Spectacula* of the *Greeks* and *Romans*, were a great part of the Solemn and Publick Worſhip of their Gods,

Gods, inſtituted on purpoſe to commemorate, or expiate ſome ſignal Benefit, or Calamity, of which thoſe Gods were the ſuppoſed Authors, or Inſtruments: Theſe Plays or Shows were uſually preceeded by a Solemn Proceſſion of the Gods to whom they were dedicated, and the Prieſts and Sacrificers in their Formalities, with the Victim in all its Religious Pomp, (much after the manner of the Solemn Proceſſions in uſe amongſt the *Roman* Catholicks to this day) this was ſucceeded by Vows made, and Sacrifice perform'd upon the ſpot, whether it were Theatre, *Circus*, or any other place of publick Shows, or Games. After all theſe were perform'd, or finiſh'd, the Play or Show was order'd to begin, which was alſo a principal part of the Religious Worſhip, and concluded the Solemnity of the day.

The Drama of the ſame extraction.

The Dramatick Repreſentations ſpring both from one Original, and were inſtituted for the ſame general end and purpoſe with the reſt of the Heathen Games, that is, for Religious Worſhip. Theſe (if I may be allow'd to uſe the plural number, for that which in the Original, was but one

 thing)

thing) were invented in honour to *Bacchus*, and conſiſted of Songs in his praiſe, Muſick, and Dancing about a Sacrific'd Goat, intermixt with ruſtick raillery, ſuitable to the Genius and Temper of the Boors, and Villagers, that were the performers. Tragedy and Comedy were not yet become Separate Provinces in Poetry, but either name indifferently ſignify'd the ſame thing, the firſt being taken from the Sacrifice, which was a Goat, the other from the Performers, which were the Peaſants, or Villagers, or from the nature of the Entertainment itſelf, which was compos'd of Rural Muſick, Songs, and Dances. By what ſteps and gradations the improvements were made, how the decorations of the Stage were introduc'd, and when the Drama firſt branch'd into Tragedy and Comedy, as diſtinct members, are pretty ſpeculations, and afford an occaſion, which one, that like Mr. *Collier*, affected to ſhew much reading to little purpoſe, wou'd not let ſlip; but not being to my purpoſe, I ſhall not proſecute 'em any farther.

Tragedy & Comedy originally one thing.

'Tis

'Tis probable the partition of Tragedy and Comedy was first made, when the Poets, quitting the *Dithyrambi*, or Hymns to *Bacchus*, betook themselves to the representation of Stories or Fables of their own invention; the nature of the subjects then becoming different, according to the Poets choice, the names were divided betwixt 'em. Or perhaps, that part which we now in a restrain'd sense call Tragedy, being first refin'd and improv'd, and becoming the study and diversion of more Polite Men, the other continuing longer in the Possession of the Villagers, retain'd the name of Comedy for distinction sake, even after its utmost improvements. *When first distinguisht*

But when, or howsoever this was, tho the Sacrifice of the Goat at Plays was left off, the *Satyri* in praise of *Bacchus* discontinued, and the Plays appointed indifferently in honour of any of the Gods, as occasion directed, that they were, as the Auditors rightly observed, *Nihil ad Bacchum*, yet the Stage remain'd sacred to and under the Protection of its old Patron, who had amongst the *Romans* his Altar on the *The Stage under the Patronage of Bacchus.*

Right

Right hand of the Stage, and the particular God to whom the Play was for that time directed, on the Left. This was the Posture and Condition of the Stage in the time of the Fathers.

This being the case, a Christian cou'd not be present, or assist at these representations, without openly countenancing or conforming to the Idolatrous Worship of the Heathens; which the Fathers, as became careful and pious Pastors, were extremely solicitous to prevent. They were sensible of the difficulties they had to encounter, and the obstacles they had to surmount. The Christian Religion was yet but newly planted, and therefore till it had taken sufficient Root was carefully to be cover'd and defended from the injuries of rude Blasts, and the contagion of those rank superstitious Weeds that grew about it, by which the Root might be kill'd, or the Soil infected, and the Sap withdrawn.

Paganism a Religion contriv'd for popularity.

Paganism was a Religion, invented at first to oblige and captivate the people, and gain'd its Credit and Authority among 'em by indulging their Sensuality, and even gratifying their Lusts; it was

aug

augmented by degrees, by ambitious, cunning men, who, to render themselves more popular, and gain an interest among the multitude, recommended to 'em, under the notion of Religion, what they found most acceptable to the humour and palate of the populace. By this means, the various Processions, Games, and Shows were introduc'd, and became the most formal part of their Solemnities, men being easily perswaded to like what was so conformable to their inclinations, that in the exercise and discharge of their Duties, their Senses were entertain'd, and their Appetites flatter'd.

Against a Superstition thus fram'd for Luxury, and contriv'd to cajole the Sences, Christianity was to make its way, and to drive out those Rites, and destroy a Title founded upon the prescription of many ages, supported by the authority of the Civil Government, and fortify'd in its Possession by Prejudice, Inclination and Interest; and all this to be done with the assistance only of Truth, and Simplicity of Doctrine and Manners; the Pomp, and Magnificence of their Solemn Worship

ſhip was abſolutely to be taken away, and their licentious practices to be reſtrain'd, and reform'd; and inſtead of 'em ſevere Principles, and an auſtere courſe of Life were to be eſtabliſh'd, in an Age, and amongſt a People, whom the Submiſſion and Tribute of all the World for ſome ages, had made wealthy, proud and wanton.

Heathen Religion all Ceremony.

It is not therefore to be wonder'd, if thoſe early Champions of the Goſpel proportion'd their Zeal and Vigilance to the preſſingneſs of the occaſion, and the ſtrength of the oppoſition. The Games and Shows of the antient Heathens were the parts of their Religion the moſt generally engaging, that attracted moſt, and kept the Multitude firmeſt to 'em. The reſt of their Religion ſat but looſely about 'em, they had no fixt, or neceſſary Faith, aud their devotion conſiſted only in a frigid compliance with thoſe Forms and Ceremonies, which were purely matters of Worſhip; their Zeal appear'd for nothing ſo much as their Games and Shows. For as *Varro* * and *Seneca* † informs us, the preparatory Solemnities were ungrateful to the ſpectators, who im-

* Pompa populo ingrata fuit, quia ludis mora. Varro de Ling. Lat. Lib. 4.

† Non ignoras quam ſit odioſa Circenſibus Pompa.

impatiently expected the Show. The Fathers, who knew where their ſtrength lay, have employ'd all their Artillery againſt theſe Shows, their Batteries have play'd inceſſantly upon 'em, as the only Forts that were capable of making reſiſtance, and ſtopping their Progreſs.

Idolatry of the Stage, the principal argument of the Fathers againſt it.

Tho the antient Fathers bent their Rhetorick, with all its Force, and in all its Forms and Figures, againſt the Heathen Shows; tho they declaim'd with all their Nerves, and Vehemence, and diſplay'd all their Arguments with the utmoſt ſtrength of Colour and Proportion, yet there was nothing in which they ſo much confided, in which they ſo unanimouſly agreed, as the objection drawn from the Idolatrous inſtitution and end of 'em. They were unwarrantable, becauſe Idolatrous. It was (in their opinion) impoſſible for a Chriſtian, how well principled, or diſpos'd however, to partake of the Entertainment, without ſharing the Pollution, or to abſtract the Diverſion from the Guilt. They thought it dangerous to truſt their Converts, however fortify'd, to the tempta-

temptations of ſo jolly a Religion, which was ſo far from curbing the appetites, and laying any reſtraint upon the deſires of its Proſelytes, that many of its duties were but Pimps to their Luſts, and almoſt all its acts of Devotion but ſo many entertainments of their Sences. They knew the frailty of humane Nature right well, and were aware, that tho Faith might in ſome be ſo ſtrong as to triumph over all temptation, yet that Multitudes wou'd fall before it, if they were permitted to run the riſque.

The portion of thoſe that embrac'd Chriſtianity was Mortification, and ſuffering, perpetual diſcouragement, and frequent Perſecutions (till the time of *Conſtantine*) their Reward was in Reverſion; their Expectation indeed was large, but the Proſpect was diſtant. Now preſent Eaſe and Enjoyment are very apt to prevail againſt a remote Hope. In our common affairs of the world, Futurity maintains itſelf but ill againſt the Preſent, and neither the greatneſs, nor the certainty of the Reverſion, make good head againſt immediate Poſſeſſion.

This

This was the caſe of Chriſtianity in its Infancy. The Heathen Prieſthood was contented with the Countenance and Encouragement of the State, and ſubmitted to the directions and appointment of it, even in matters relating to their own Myſteries; they aſſum'd no Dominion, or Juriſdiction over private Conſciences, either in point of Principle or Practice; but left thoſe matters wholly to the Civil Government, which made Laws for the regulation, and appointed Magiſtrates for the inſpection of Men's Manners; in which regard was had chiefly, if not only, to the Publick Quiet and Security, to the Preſervation and Augmentation of the State. If a ſcrutiny was made into the Conduct and Behaviour of particular perſons, 'twas as they were ſubordinate to the Publick, and might be inſtrumental or prejudicial to the common welfare, either immediately, by their practices, in wronging the State, or thoſe under the Protection of it; or by withdrawing themſelves from, or incapacitating themſelves for its ſervice; or conſequently by debauching, and corrupting others by their Examples.

In

In all theſe matters the Prieſt had no concern ; and therefore 'twas no wonder, if the People receiv'd ſo eaſily, and liv'd ſo contentedly under a Religion, which, tho falſe, gave 'em ſo little diſturbance, and ſo much ſatisfaction: For, as for the Multitude, their Theology was like their Worſhip, ſuited and adapted to their capacities, the one conſiſting of ſurprizing Fables, the other of delightful Solemnities. Thoſe that were wiſer among 'em, and ſaw thro their Myſteries, (who were not a few) were many of 'em *Sacris initiati*, and engaged in their ſupport ; the reſt having no higher warrant than their own Reaſon, and nothing more certain to ſubſtitute in the room of 'em, were perhaps unwilling to unſettle matters, and paying a languid Complacence, ſuffer'd things to run on in the old Channel ; whoſe Banks ſhou'd they break down, they knew not what courſe the Stream wou'd take, nor how far the Confuſion might ſpread.

But the Goſpel had none of theſe advantages, it was not contriv'd and modell'd for Popularity, it did not humour the Inclinations, and indulge the

the Appetites of the People. To the Purity of its Doctrine, a Conformity of Life, and Manners were requir'd, the Passions were to be curb'd, and the Desires moderated ; instead of Pomp and Ceremony, Simplicity and Sobriety were to be their Entertainments: their rampant Gods, whose fabulous Histories gave countenance to Men's Lusts, and encouragement to their Debaucheries, were to be cashier'd, and the knowledge and worship of the True One to be introduc'd, whose Majesty was as awful, as the other was represented frolicksome.

These were the conditions of Conversion from Heathenism, and the change must needs appear disadvantageous to meer Flesh and Blood The Fathers therefore, who knew how hard it was to keep the Appetites in entire subjection, took care to fortifie as strongly as possible those parts, in which they expected the Rebellion shou'd first break out. The Plays, of all the Heathen Solemnities, were those that gave the strongest temptation to the new Converts; they had so little of

Heathen Plays dangerous temptations to the new Christian Converts.

of the Air of Religion, that they thought if they did not approve of the end and design of 'em, they might, without imputation, partake of the Diversion, in which they met with frequent Examples of Innocence and Virtue. This alarm'd the Fathers, who knew that *the transition from one Religion to another* (as Mr *Collier* observes) *was natural*; and justly apprehended, that from a liking of the Entertainments themselves, they might proceed to approve the occasion of 'em; that the seeming Innocence and Virtue of 'em might reconcile 'em to a Superstition which recommended those excellent Gifts after so easie and agreeable a manner, or that perhaps the delights of those places might soften the temper of their mind, and relax the nerves of their zeal, and so unqualifie and indispose 'em for those Austerities, which the Posture and Circumstances of the Christian Religion at that time requir'd.

Zeal of the Fathers against 'em not unnecessary.

To obviate these dangers, they summon'd all their Prudence, and all their Art; they omitted no Topick which Rhetorick or Satyr cou'd supply, to fright or perswade Men from those

Diver-

Diversions. Nor was all their Zeal and Caution any more than was necessary, the Danger was great, and so was the Temptation; the Fort was to be maintain'd not only against an Enemy without, but a strong Faction within; the Sences, Appetites, and Passions were already gain'd to the Enemy's Party, nothing remain'd but Religion and Reason, to make good the defence; those Generals therefore that wou'd hold out, when the Garrison was inclin'd to Surrender, must not only display their Courage and Conduct, but exert their Authority likewise to the utmost. This the Antient Fathers did, whose examples have been follow'd by divers in our Age, tho without the same Reason, Authority or Success.

Having thus open'd the Case, as it stood in the time of the Primitive Christians, we shall proceed to examine, Whether there be any manner of Analogy between the *Roman* Theatre (as to the particulars whereof they are arraign'd by the Fathers) and ours? Whether *the Satyr of the Fathers comes full upon the Modern Poets*? Whether *the Parity of the Case makes their Reasons* View p. 276.

take place , and their Authority revive upon us ?

p. 277. Thus backt, as he ſuppoſes by *the Worthies of Chriſtendom, the flower of Human Nature, and the Top of their Species*, Mr *Collier* bids defiance to all the Stage Poets in general: He de-
p. 1. clares 'em to be *gone over into another*
p: 124. *Intereſt*, Deſerters to the Devil, *that aim to deſtroy Religion*, and whoſe buſineſs
Præf. is an ana of *Lewdneſs and Atheiſm*. For
p. 257. he has a huge mind to try his ſtrength with 'em, but he dares not enter the Theatres, they are the *Devils own Ground* ; but he challenges 'em to a tryal of skill at the laudable exerciſes of the Chriſtian Olympicks of *Moorfields* ; which, if they be ſo hardy as to accept, he'll call a Ring, and for a broken Head, or Limb, he and his Fathers defy both North and Weſt.

Diſingenuity of Mr. Collier. But hold, Mr *Vinegar* ! have you any commiſſion from the Fathers to give this Challenge in their Names ? Does it appear, that they have any ground, or reaſon of quarrel to the preſent Stage ? I believe not ; but as things may be packt together, and tranſlated, an able Interpreter may make 'em ſpeak

as

as he pleaſes. If they don't ſpeak to his mind he knows how to correct 'em, 'tis but *throwing in a word or two* (as he phraſes it) *to clear the ſenſe, to preſerve the Spirit of the Original, and keep the English upon its Legs.* 'Tis well he has the knack of Scowring the Fathers, otherwiſe their Teſtimonies wou'd look but ruſtily upon the preſent occaſion. But he can waſh as well as ſcowr, and underprop a failing Evidence upon occaſion. 'Tis pity Mr *Collier* was not bred to the Bar, this extraordinary quality had been of admirable ſervice there, to help a bad Memory, and prompt a baſhful Witneſs. The Fathers, good men, cou'd ſay but little to the Cauſe, but Dexterity and Management may do much, and an able Sollicitor (like Mr *Collier*) will make out notable proofs from very ſlender Evidence.

Præf.

The Fathers, as they had reaſon, prohibited Chriſtians all reſort to the *Roman* Games in general, and without diſtinction upon the account of the Idolatry there practiſed: But what's that to our Theatres, which have no ſuch ſtain upon 'em? If the Heathen Gods

Idolatry the main Objections of the Fathers to the Ancient Drama.

Gods appear upon our Stage, 'tis neither for their own, nor their Worſhipers honour. Idolatry is as much abhorr'd, and more expos'd there, than any where elſe. Why then is the Satyr reviv'd upon it? Is there any danger that the Spectators ſhould turn Idolaters, from our Repreſentations? That which ſcandaliz'd the Fathers moſt in the Dramatick Repreſentations of Antiquity was, that their Gods were repreſented lewd, and unjuſt, Adulterers, Pimps, *&c.*

* St *Auguſtine* abſolves their Comedies and Tragedies from any fault in the expreſſion, and accuſes only the ſubject matter. The ſame Indictment he prefers againſt *Homer*, (*viz.*) that he corrupted Mens Morals by drawing ſuch vicious Pictures of his Deities. **Terence* falls under his diſpleaſure likewiſe, for introducing his young Libertine animating himſelf to, and vindicating himſelf after a Rape, by the example of *Jupiter*, whoſe Intrigue with *Danae*, repreſented in a Picture, afforded him both matter of Encouragement and Excuſe. Notwithſtanding which objections, this Fa-

* Et hæc ſunt ſcenicorum tolerabiliora ludorum Comœdiæ ſcilicet & Tragœdiæ hoc eſt fabulæ Poetarum agendæ in ſpectaculis, multa rer. turpitudine ſed nulla, ſaltem, ſicut alia multa verborum obſcœnitate compoſitæ quas etiam inter ſtudia quæ honeſta, & liberalia vocantur, pueri, legere diſcereq; a ſenibus coguntur. De Civit. Dei lib. 2.

*Aug.Conf. lib. 1. cap. 16.

*Father confeſſes himſelf to have profited by the reading of 'em, tho he thinks the ſame uſe might have been made of more pious Books, which are fitter for the uſe of Children. Thus by the acknowledgment of this Father the Plays were not ſo bad, as Mr *Collier* wou'd infer from him. The quarrel of the reſt of the Fathers to the Drama, was upon the ſame account, tho Mr Surveyor has given a wrong proſpect of it. I hope there's no reaſon to apprehend, that *Jupiter* or *Mercury* ſhou'd be drawn into precedent at this time of day, or that any perſon of Quality ſhou'd turn Whore-maſter, or Pimp out of emulation.

* Didici in eis multa verba utilia, ſed et in rebus non vanis diſci poſſunt & via tuta eſt, in qua Pueri ambularent. lib. I Confeſs. cap. xv.

'Tis true, the Fathers frequently exclaim againſt the lewdneſs of the *Roman* Theatres, which Mr *Collier* all along endeavours, both by the turn and application, to diſcharge upon the Dramatick Repreſentations, in which I admire his dexterity more than his ingenuity. For I can't ſuppoſe Mr *Collier* to be ignorant, that there were divers ſorts of *Ludi Scenici*, which were all perform'd at the Theatre, of which ſeveral were ſcandalouſly lewd; but

Mimick Shews among the Romans ſcandalouſly lewd, the Drama not at all.

these he knows were no part of the Dramatick Entertainment.

Clemen's Alexandrius *cited against the Drama.*

But he finds Comedy and Tragedy ſometimes condemn'd for company among the other Shows of the Theatre, and therefore he is reſolved, out of his ſingular regard to Juſtice and Ingenuity, that whatſoever is pronounc'd againſt the Theatres in general, ſhall light upon the Drama in particular, which by the unanimous confeſſion of 'em all was the leaſt offenſive, and conſequently the leaſt deſerv'd it. To what purpoſe elſe is *Clemens Alexandrinus* cited? He *affirms, that the Circus and Theatre may not improperly be call'd the Chair of Peſtilence.* Whence does it appear, that the Dramatick Exerciſes are here aim'd at? Were the *Mimi*, *Pantomimi*, and *Archimimi*, leſs concern'd with the Stage, or more reſerv'd and modeſt in their practices upon it? Were dancing naked, and expreſſing lewd Poſtures leſs criminal, or offenſive to modeſty? No, *he won't ſay that*; altho the compariſon were made with the *Engliſh* Stage, which is, (according to him) much more licentious than the *Roman*, yet that by his own confeſſion has nothing ſo bad.

View p. 260 Nec inconcine ſtadia & Theatra Peſtilentiæ Cathædram quis vocaverit. Pædag. lib. 3. cap. ii.

View p. 277.

But

But ſuppoſing the Father to take his aim from Mr *Collier*'s direction, and prophetically to have levell'd at our times, what is the wondrous guilt, that provokes this ſevere Judgment ? *Noſcitur ex ſocio*, why 'tis e'en as bad as Horſe-racing ; a very lewd diverſion truly. Woe be to you Inhabitants of *New Market*, that live in the very Seat of Infection.

The Fathers ſometimes over rigorous

But the Fathers were men, meer men, as well as Mr *Collier*, and ſubject as well as he to be miſled by paſſion, and overacted by zeal, in the tranſports of which they were apt ſometimes to extend their rigour too far, and would upon any terms have (as a certain Learned Recorder has it) *enough for a decent* Execution. Thus *Tertullian*, none of the leaſt conſiderable among the Fathers, either for his Learning or Zeal, in this caſe eſpecially, tho he had already convinc'd the Ancient Tragedy of Idolatry, a Crime ſufficient in a Chriſtian Court of Judicature to be capital, yet muſt needs *ex abundanti* bring a freſh Indictment of Blaſphemy. *The Devil*, ſays he, *mounted the Tragedians upon Buskins, becauſe he would make our Saviour a Liar, who ſays,*

Sic & Tragædos Cothurnis extulit Diabolus, quia nemo poteſt adjicere cubitum unum ad ſtaturam ſuam, mendacem facere vult Chriſtum. Tert. de Spectac. cap. 23.

ſays, that no man can add a Cubit to his Stature. Look to it all ye Tiptoe Beau's.

Here the Devil ſhew'd himſelf an Engineer, to lay a Trap ſo long before hand, to contrive and invent theſe Buskins only to falſify in appearance, what was ſaid a thouſand years after; and the Father himſelf was a very *Matchiavel* to detect, and counterplot him at laſt. I have read of a famous *Scotch* Divine, that ſignaliz'd himſelf once upon occaſion, by much ſuch another diſcovery, when he found out, that at the diſmiſſion of all Creatures out of *Noah*'s Ark, the reaſon why the Hawks were ſo merciful to the Doves, as to let 'em eſcape unhurt was, that the Propheſie of *Iſaiah*, the *Lamb ſhould lye down with the Lyon*, might be fulfilled. This is the neareſt parallel that occurs to me from all my reading, in which the *Scotch* Father comes pretty near t'other for a ſtrange reach of apprehenſion, tho 'tis his misfortune to fall ſhort in the importance of the diſcovery.

But to wave all further inſtances of this kind from the Fathers, which are to be found in great plenty among 'em,

I

I leave 'em to be gather'd by thoſe that take more delight in ſuch Flowers ; and ſhall confine my ſelf to thoſe which Mr. *Collier* has pickt out for a Noſegay for himſelf.

To begin therefore with *Theophilus Antiochenus* ; He tells us, *that the Chriſtians durſt not ſee the Prizes of the* Gladiators, *for fear of becoming acceſſary to the Murthers there committed, nor their other Shows, upon the account of their Indency and Prophaneneſs.* View. p252:

Here Mr *Collier*, as an earneſt of his future fair dealing uſes the word *Shows*, and becauſe perhaps 'tis the only inſtance to be met with through all his Quotations, he is reſolv'd not to loſe the benefit of it, and therefore for fear it ſhould ſlip by unheeded, he gives it in a different character, and an aſteriſm along with it, and claps in the Margin *Spectacula.* By this ſample of his Fidelity to his Author, he thinks his performance warranted to his Readers, of whom he knows the greateſt part can't nor the reſt he hopes won't, be at the trouble to confront his Tranſlation with the Text ; and therefore before the end of this very Paragraph, he throws

off

off all obligation to Truth and Justice and falls to managing and instructing his Evidence.

* Ibid. Nec fas est nobis audire adulteria Deorum Hominumq; quæ suavi verborum modulantur mercede. Ad Autolyc. lib. 3.

* *The Stage Adulteries of the Gods and Heroes are unwarrantable Entertainments. And so much the worse, because the Mercenary Players set off 'em with all the charms and advantages of speaking.*

The Translator very well knew, that the Shews here aim'd at, were not the Tragedies and Commedies of Antiquity, but the Shews of the *Mimi*, wherein the Amours of the Gods or Heroes were not related only, but sung to Musick in luscious fulsome Verse, mimickt in lewd dances with obscene Gestures and naked Postures, and even the very Adulteries and Rapes themselves express'd by scandalous actions, for which purpose the very Stews were rak'd for Publick Prostitutes for the Service.

These were the Shews, that provok'd the just resentments of the Fathers, which had nothing in Common with the Dramatick Representations, but the Place, and the end of their Representation, which were the Publick Theatres, and Worship. But of all the Publick Diversions of the Heathens, the

the Drama only remaining to us, to keep the Authority upon its Legs, it was necessary to give it a new directi-on, and turn in the version, and there-fore the word *Players* was thrust in, to fix the Scandal in the wrong place.

That these were the Indecencies, and Lewdness of the Theatre, so bit-terly inveigh'd against by these Pious men, I cou'd bring testimonies innu-merable; but to avoid being tedious in a plain case, I shall single out St *Cyprian*, who being one of the *Worthies of Christen-dome*, and the *Top of his Species*, I hope Mr *Collier* will not except against his Evidence. * *The Theatres* (says he) *are yet more Lewd. There they strip them-selves of their Modesty, as well as Clothes, and the honour as well as screen of their Bodies is laid aside, and Virginity expos'd to the affronts both of View, and Touch.* Which Mr *Collier* knows was not pra-ctis'd in the Drama.

* Theatra sunt fædiora, quo convenis verundia illic omnis exuitur simul cum amictu, vestis honor corporis, & pudor ponitur, denotanda ac contrectanda virginitas revelatur. De Habit Virg.

But our *Histrio-Mastix* was aware, that there was nothing to be got by square play, therefore he has recourse to slight of hand, and palms false Dice upon us. In the very next Paragraph we find him prompting *Tertullian* to

rail

rail at the *Play-house*, and the *Bear-Garden* *. Which latter, I suppose, was brought in for the grace and dignity of the Conjunction. Here the *Play-house*, by his old way of Legerdemain, is substituted for the *Theatre*; and the most innocent of the *Roman* Diversions charg'd with the Guilt and Pollutions of all the rest, with which, by his own Confession, it was not so much as soil'd. But the shifting of Names levell'd the Scandal right for his purpose, and the unlearned Reader might perhaps be induc'd to believe, that the Father's quarrel lay against *Lincolns-Inn-Fields*, and *Covent-Garden*; and therefore he was resolv'd not to lose the benefit of so advantageous a Cheat, for so small a condescension as falsifying a Text.

* Nihil nobis &c. cum insania Circi cum impudicitia Theatri cum xysti vanitate. Apolog. adv. Gent. cap. 38.

With the same honest view and intention, he forces *Tertullian* to call *Pompey*'s Theatre *, a *Dramatick* Bawdy-house. Here, to conceal the Fathers Age, he shaves off his Beard, and dresses him after his own fashion, in a Steenkirk and a long Wig, that he may look like an acqnaintance of our Stage, and keep his Evidence in Countenance. A just

* Itaque Pompeius magnus solo Theatro minor, cum illam arcem omnium turpitudinum extruxisset, veritus quandoque memoriæ suæ Censoriam Animadversionem, Veneris ædem superposuit, &c.

just Translation wou'd not answer his purpose, and therefore he has taken the usual liberty of adding or altering, and has clapt in the *Dramatick Bawdy-house*, to clear, that is, pervert the sense. It is no justification, to say that he has not chang'd the Scene, that the Place is the same, tho he has made bold to change the Terms; in changing the Terms he has chang'd the state of the case, and made the Author accuse the *Drama* of those enormities, which were peculiar to theShews of the *Mimi*, and inveigh'd against only by him. Thus he uses his Father like an *Irish* Evidence, and makes him depose with as much latitude, as in a Court of Record, wou'd even in these corrupt times, cost a man his Ears.

To trace him through all his Quotations from the Fathers, were a task much more tedious, than difficult. It may suffice to take notice, that he keeps to his Principle, and never quotes any thing right, which he thinks may be made more serviceable by being perverted. To prevent this Artifice from being seen through, he endeavours, like a Fish in the Water, to conceal

the

the bottom by muddying the Stream.

St. *Cyprian*, *Lactantius*, *Chrysostome* and *Augustine* are all manag'd at the same rate; Mr *Collier*, like a stanch Beagle, makes the hits, whilst his Fathers, that like Whelps newly enter'd, are running Riot, have much better Mouths than Noses, and make up a great part of the Cry, but are of no service in the Chase. Those that have a mind to tumble and sift over Mr *Collier*'s Rubbish of Antiquity, may find all his Quotations in *Prynne*'s *Histrio-Mastix*, honestly transcrib'd, and more faithfully translated. To which, or to the Fathers themselves, I refer 'em. His Translations are all of a stamp, to repeat more of 'em wou'd be tautology; how different soever the Originals might be, the Copies have all the same Features and Complexions; both Draught and Colouring agree so well, that a very indifferent Judge might infallibly discover 'em all to be Copies by one Hand, by the Harmony of the Faults.

But to dismiss the Fathers, who have been oblig'd to an unnecessary attendance, thro the disingenuity of their Tran-

Tranſlator, I ſhall once for all obſerve, firſt, that the Authority of the Fathers ought to affect us no farther than their Reaſonings will come up to our caſe: Secondly, That their Arguments drawn from the Idolatry, lewd Repreſentations, and Cruelty practis'd upon the *Roman* Stage, and at their Shows, do not reach our Stage, where thoſe practices are had in abhorrence. Thirdly, That as they are cited by Mr *Collier*, both their Authority and Arguments are ſubverted by the corrupt Verſion. If theſe three things be fairly made out, as (I hope) they already are, we need not be any longer alarm'd at this unſeaſonable clamour from the Fathers.

The Authority of the Fathers ſhort of the Caſe.

But tho the main ſtrength of this *Attila* of the Stage lies in theſe *Worthies* of *Chriſtendom*, yet, like a cautious Commander, leſt they ſhou'd be ſurpriz'd, or unable to ſuſtain the ſhock of the Stage Militia alone, he has provided an Auxiliary Body of Heathen Philoſophers, Hiſtorians, Orators and Poets, to guard the Paſſes, and check the fury of the firſt Onſet. Here again he ſhews his care by his choice, he liſts

Caution of Mr C--ll--r

none but men of the firſt Magnitude, he's ſo ſevere that a Volunteer under ſix foot can't paſs Muſter. But after all, the Service of theſe Gigantick Men does not anſwer the terror of their Bulk and Figure; they are preſt men, that enter the Service againſt their Wills, and are plac'd in the Front, like a *Swiſs* painted upon a Door, for ſhew, not action. 'Tis true, they are forc'd to appear with their Fire-locks, and give one charge, but 'tis, like a *Moorfields* Volley, without Ball, or Bloodſhed.

Plato's Authority conſider'd.

The Leaders of theſe are a Triumvirate of Antient *Greek* Philoſophers, *Plato*, *Xenophon*, and *Ariſtotle*. The firſt of theſe appears not in perſon, nor has his proxy much to ſay for him, that I can find. Yet as little as 'tis, he ought to have produc'd his Credentials, or his Voice may fairly be proteſted againſt. For a hear-ſay Evidence ought at leaſt to be as well atteſted, as a Nuncupative Will to make it authentick. But, after all, what is it that he ſays, or rather that *Euſebius* ſays for him? Why, *that Plays raiſe the paſſions, and pervert the uſe of 'em, and by conſequence are dangerous to morality*. But ſince he has not thought

fit

fit to ſpecify either the nature or meaſure of the danger, thus conſequentially portended to morality, we need not amuſe our ſelves any longer about it.

Much ſuch another doughty Authority is that of *Xenophon*. * The *Perſians* (he ſays) won't ſuffer their youth to hear any thing, that's amorous or bawdy. They were afraid want of Ballaſt might make 'em miſcarry, and that it was dangerous to add weight to the Byaſs of nature. This quotation is ſtrangely drawn in; it does not ſo much as ſquint towards his purpoſe. Here's no mention of any thing relating to the Drama. Bawdry indeed was forbidden to be talk'd to thoſe, whoſe Reaſon was not yet grown ſturdy enough to curb the looſeneſs of their Appetites in thoſe Countries, where the heat of the Climate, and the warmth of their Conſtitutions inclin'd 'em very early, and hurried 'em very precipitouſly to irregularities of that nature. But if this paſſage wou'd not ſerve his Cauſe, it wou'd his vanity and oſtentatation of reading, and therefore was not to be ſlighted.

Xenophon.

* Ita de venereis etiam rebus advalde juvenes verba non facimus, ne accidente ad vehementem in eis libid. levitate, immodice huic libidini ſuæ indulgeant Cyropæd. lib.. p. 34.

Ariſtotle. Of as great ſervice is the Authority of *Ariſtotle*, one ſingle doubtful expreſſion of whoſe, he would wreſt to the overthrow of one of the moſt elaborate and judicious of all that great Philoſophers works ; I mean his Art of Poetry; in which he has taken the pains to preſcribe Rules for the more eaſie and regular compoſition of Dramatick Poems; which certainly had been in him as well a ſcandalous, as a ridiculous labour, if he had not thought the practice of 'em allowable. But he's ſo far from any ſuch indifference, that he frequently, both in that piece, and other parts of his Works, commends the writing of Dramatick Poetry, as the nobleſt exerciſe of the mind. Nor do we find any where in the works of that Philoſopher, *who* (by this Author's own confeſſion) *had look'd as far into humane Nature as any man*, a greater profuſion of Rhetorick than in the praiſe of of Tragedy, which he takes to be the higheſt exaltation of humane Wit.

Plays forbidden to young People upon the ſcore of the temptations from the Company.

As for this paſſage, which Mr *Collier* has pickt out, and levell'd at the Comedy of our Age, it amounts to no more than

than a general * caution against trust-ing youth into promiscuons Company, such as resorted to publick places, till they were sufficiently fortify'd against the danger of Corruption, to which they might thereby be expos'd. *Drunk-enness* was the Vice, which the *Philo-sopher* particularly instanc'd in, by which he plainly shews himself appre hensive of the Company, not of the Play; and therefore he would not have young people trusted with the liberty, and opportunity of contracting an ac quaintance, before they were arriv'd at some tolerable maturity of Judgment. But Mr *Collier* with a dexterity peculiar to himself, palms the general term of *Debauchery*, for the particular one of *Drunkenness* upon us, that the suspi-cion might thereby be shifted from the Audience to the Peformance.

To back this, and cover the convey-ance, he brings another Authority as little to the purpose, concerning the force and power of Musick, from whence he concludes, that *where the Representation is foul, the thoughts of the Audience must suffer.* What must they suffer? Wou'd the Musick, (as power-

* Adolescentulos autem & Iamborum & Comædiarum Spectatores esse lex prohibeat, prius quam ætatem attigerint, in qua & cum cæteris accubare jam licuerit, & ab omnibus, vel ebrietatis, vel aliarum inde nascentium rerum incommodis disciplina liberos efficiat. Pol. lib 7. c. 17.

View page 234.

ful as he ſuppoſes it) make the Audience drunk, or in love with Drunkenneſs? No, that was no Vice of the Stage, whatever it might be of the Spectators, yet even by them the Scene was not laid at the Theatres, tho the Plot might, and the Company perhaps be pickt up there. I ſuppoſe this Informer, as inveterate as his malice is againſt Play-houſes, will ſcarce charge 'em as Schools of intemperance of that kind, 'tis not the practice of the Stage, not ſo much as behind the Scenes; and I believe he will acquit Pit, Box, and Gallery of it. For whatever ſome may bring in their Heads, he will find but few with Bottles in their Hands there. This made him wave inſtancing in the particular of *Ariſtotle*; the retail ſcandal wou'd not fit our Theatres, and therefore he lumps it among 'em by the general name of Debauchery, and tacks this Citation concerning Muſick to it, which he hopes will give the Reader an Idea more ſerviceable to his Cauſe, than *Ariſtotle* intended, and make a ſuitable impreſſion upon him.

This Philosopher forbad the resort to Comedies, only to those whose virtues he durst not trust; not to hinder their diversion from the Stage, but to prevent their corruption from the Pit, as King *Charles* the 2d suppress'd Conventicles, for the sake of those, whose principles he suspected; not to disturb the Devotion of a few mistaken well-meaning Men, but to prevent the practices of many crafty ill designing ones.

'*Tully* cries out upon licentious *Plays* 'and *Poems*, as the bane of Sobriety, 'and wise thinking: That Comedy 'subsists upon Lewdness, and that plea-'sure is the root of all evil. *View p. 235.*

No one, I suppose, will defend Plays, that are really licentious, or if they seem to patronize any, wherein some warm-headed Enthusiastick Zealots pretend to find or make some passages exceptionable, they are willing to leave those Passages, if really guilty, to the mercy of Mr *Collier*'s Inquisition, and yet not deny their Countenance, and Encouragement to the prevailing merit of the main part of the performance. *Licentiousness not defended.*

But here I must needs take notice, that either Mr *Collier* or *Tully*, are extremely mistaken, or, which is all one to our purpose, that this quotation does not speak the sense of *Tully*. *Plautus* and *Terence* are the only Comedians of his acquaintance, whose works have been preserv'd to our times; and consequently are the only Standards, by which we can form any Judgment, or take any measure of the *Roman* Comedy before, or about *Cicero's* time. These Mr *Collier* assures us are modest to a scruple, especially *Terence*, *who has but one faulty bordering expression*. 'Plautus, 'who is of all antiquity the most exceptionable, rarely gives any smutty liberties to women, and when he does, 'tis to Vulgar and prostituted persons. 'The men who talk intemperately are 'generally Slaves. The Slaves and Pandars seldom run over, and play their 'Gambols before women. *Plautus* does 'not dilate upon the progress successes, 'and disappointments of Love in the 'modern way. This is nice ground, 'and therefore he either stands off, or 'walks gravely over it. He has some regard to the retirements of modesty, 'and

Mr Coll. *Character of* Terence *&* Plautus. *View* p. 20.

Ib. p. 15, 16, *&c.*

'and the dignity of humane Nature, 'and does not ſeem to make lewdneſs 'his Buſineſs.

This is a very fair character from an adverſary, a friend could ſcarce have given a more ample recommendation upon this head. Here ſeems to be a run of Candour and Ingenuity, for at leaſt a dozen pages together; the ancient Dramatick Writers are treated with ſo much civility, 'tis all ſuch Halcyon Weather, ſo fair a Sky, and ſo ſmooth a Sea, would tempt the cautiouſeſt Pilot from his Anchor; he would have no apprehenſions of a Storm, while all was ſo ſerene above, and ſo quiet and calm beneath him. But this is all *out of Character*, the Author forces his temper to ſerve his deſign, and careſſes the Ancients in pure ſpight to the Moderns, as cunning Stateſmen ſometimes court and cajole a Party they hate, only to make 'em their tools againſt another they fear, and ſo make 'em ruine each other, and ſave themſelves both the trouble, and the *odium*. This honeſt Policy Mr *Collier* has made uſe of; for, having routed (in his own vain conceit) by the help of theſe Ancients,

This Character Inſidious.

the

the preſent *Stage Poets*, he makes head upon his Confederates, and thoſe, that in the entrance of his Book deſerv d no cenſure, in the concluſion of it are allow'd no quarter. The more plauſibly and ſecurely to put this Srratagem in execution, he takes care to deſtroy his own Authority in their favour, by that of much better men againſt 'em, or that are (as he manages the matter) at leaſt in appearance againſt 'em.

The A's. citation' patch'd up of incoherent fragments.

This Author is a ſort of a *Long-lane* Writer, a Piece-Broker in Learning, one that tacks ends and ſcraps of Authors together to patch up a ſlight Authority, that hangs ſo weakly together, that it won't bear the fitting. Thus he has linkt together two or three ill ſorted ſentences out of *Tully*, that make as little to his purpoſe, as if he had quoted ſo many Propoſitions out of *Euclid*; the truth of which, tho every body might acknowledge, yet no body can find the uſe of in this place. But he found the name of Comedy joyn'd with an invective, and therefore he was reſolv'd, if he did not find it ſo, to make it of his Party, before he took his

his leave of it. * *Tully* complains, *that the Poets gave Love, the author of ſo many follies and diſorders, a place among the Deities, the irregularities of which were the conſtant ſubject matter of the Comedies of his time.*

* O præclaram emendatricem vitæ Poeticam, quæ Amorem flagitii, & levitatis auctorem in Concilio Deorum collocandum putet! De Comædiâ loquor quæ ſi hæc flagitia non probaremus, nulla eſſet omninò. Quæſt. Tuſc. lib. 4.

The Invention of the Roman *Comick Poets barren.*

The ſeverities of a harſh old Father, the amours of the Rake his Son, and the intrigues of the Knave his Servant, or the wiles of a mercenary *Proſtitute*, generally made up the buſineſs of thoſe *Comedies*. *Hereupon* Cicero *cries out, that if 'twere not for theſe Love extravagances, the* Comick Poets *would be deſtitute of a Plot.* In which he ſeems rather to tax 'em with barrenneſs of *Invention*, than *Immorality*. 'Tis true, the *Moral* of ſuch deſigns cou'd not be very extraordinary, nor cou'd any very edifying doctrine of application be rais'd from the uſual *Cataſtrophe* of theſe *Plays*. For the *Poet* generally took care, after he had embroil'd matters beyond all ſeeming poſſibility of a reconciliation, to diſentangle all by ſome

Pro-

Providential (if Mr *Collier* won't quarrel at the expression) *Incident*, and crown the young *Libertine* with his wishes, reconciling the Father to the Son, and the Master to the Servant. By this means Poetical Justice was eluded, and that which shou'd have been the ground and occasion of *moral Instruction* lost. The Antient *Comedy* was not therefore so innocent as his Character, nor so lewd and impure as his corrupted Quotations wou'd make it.

Poetick Justice neglected by them.

His next Authority is from *Livy*, whose Evidence, even tho it were faithfully reported by Mr *Collier*, comes not near our case. For *Livy* speaks here of the *Stage* Representations in general; but the *Drama*, properly so call'd, was not known amongst the *Romans* at the time of the Pestilence, when the *Ludi Scenici* were invented. But this is not all, he is not contented to make a false Witness only of this Historian, but he must add Forgery to Subornation, and put his hand to what was not his act and deed.

Livie's *Authority abus'd.*

The Motives are sometimes good, when the means are stark naught: That the Remedy in this case was worse than the Disease,

P. 255.

ease, and the Attonement more infectious than the Plague.

These words *Livy* utterly disowns; * he says, that the *Ludi Scenici* introduc'd upon this occasion, consisted of certain dances, or decent movements to Musick, perform'd by Artists fetch'd out of *Tuscany*, after the manner of their Country.

*Sine carmine ullo sine imitandorum carminum actu, Ludiones ex Hetruria acciti, ad Tibicinis modos Saltantes, haud indecoros motus more Thusco dabant. Dec. 1. l. 7.

Where lay the force of the Contagion in this? What danger of Infection from a modest Dance? After this *Livy* proceeds to shew what were the first steps that were made towards the improvement of these *Ludi Scenici*, and concludes his short account of their earliest Gradations with this Reflection. * *Amongst other things that have risen from small beginnings, I thought fit to take notice of Plays, that I might shew from how sober an Original this excessive Extravagance, which scarce the wealthiest Nations can bear, is deriv'd.* This Mr *Collier* translates, *The motives are sometimes good, when the means are stark naught.* 'Tis pretty plain, that 'tis not the

*Inter aliarum parva principia rerum ludorum quoque prima origo ponenda visa est, ut appareret, quam ab sano initio res in hanc vix opulentis regnis tolerabilem insaniam venerit. Ibid.

The Luxury and Expensiveness of these Shews, not their Immorality, condemn'd by Livy.

the Immorality, but the excess of *Luxury* and *Profusion* at these Shews, that *Livy* condemns, by his adding that *'twas greater than the wealthiest Nations cou'd well bear.* For 'tis to be suppos'd, that wealthy people have as much need of *Morality* as the poor, tho they are not oblig'd to the same measures of Thrift, and good Husbandry. Whether Mr *Collier*'s construction and application of this passage be the effect of his Malice or Ignorance, I leave the World to judge.

The following is yet a more perverse misconstruction, to which both Malice and Ignorance have clubb'd their utmost, even to emulation, so that 'tis hard to distinguish which has the better title to it. *Livy* tells us *, *that the* Romans *were so solicitous about methods of appeasing the Gods, that the anxiety of it was a greater affliction to their Minds, than the disease to their Bodies.* This our *Remarker*, who out of his superabundant understanding, knew better than the Author himself what ought to have been said, thinks fit to render thus, *The Remedy in this case is worse than the Dis-*

* Itaque Cn. Genutio, L. Æmylio mamerco secundum Coss. cum piaculorum magis conquisitio animos quam corpora morbi afficerent, &c. Ibid.

Diſeaſe, and the Atonement more infectious than the Plague.

Of the ſame ſtamp is the Citation from *Valerius Maximus*, whom he has quoted, whither with leſs Faith or Uuderſtanding, is matter of doubt, for he has given great cauſe to ſuſpect both. This Author, ſpeaking of the Prizes of their *Gladiators*, expreſſes his reſentments of that barbarouscuſtom,(in which Citizens of *Rome* were often butcher'd) after this manner. **Theſe things which were at firſt invented for the Worſhip of the Gods, and delight of Men, were converted totheir deſtruction, ſtaining both their Religion and Diverſions, with the Blood of Citizens, to the Scandal of Peace.* 'Tis plain, that by the *Animoſæ Acies* this Author meant nothing but the Nurſeries of *Cæſtiarii*, and *Gladiators*, and that by the *Civilis Sanguis* he intended no more of it, than was ſpilt in *arena* at thoſe Prizes in quality of *Gladiators* or *Cæſtiarii*, in which the Spectators had no concern further than in the barbarity of countenancing, and encouraging ſo cruel a practice.

Valerius Maximus *miſquoted*,

* Proximus militaribus inſtitutis ad urbana Caſtra, id eſt Theatra gradus faciendus eſt, quoniam hæc quoq; ſæpenumero animoſas acies inſtruxerunt excogitataq; cultus Deorum,& hominum delectationis cauſa, non ſine aliquo pacis ,rubore voluptatem, & religionem civili ſanguine, ſenicorum portentorum gratia, macularunt. Lib. 2. Cap. 4.

This,

Falseness and absurdity of Mr C——r's Paraphrase This, tho bloody and abominable enough to give an abhorrence to honest considerate Heathens, won't suffice Mr *Collier*, he despises single Sacrifices, and calls for *Hecatombs*; he's for breathing the Veins of the State, and slucing the Vitals of the whole Commonwealth at once. *They were the occasion of Civil Distractions; and that the State first blush'd, then bled for the Entertainment.*

P. 235.

This is rare Paraphrasing, Mr. *Collier* allows himself a very Christian latitude in his interpretations. But less wou'd not serve his turn, the *Drama* and *Arena* lay at some distance in Old *Rome*, and therefore this Gentleman was resolv'd to correct the Map, and bring 'em together. But what occasion for bloodshed at a *Comedy*? Why Mr. *Paraphraser* wou'd insinuate, that the Spectators and the Actors, like *Don Quixot* and the *Puppets*, fell together by the Ears, and so embroiling the State, engaged the whole Commonwealth in a Civil War. If I could be perswaded of this, I should allow thi Divrsion to be altogether as Antichristian, as Bear-baitings or Ridings, and could be content, that Mr *Collier*, like

Hu-

Hudibrass shou'd reduce both Actors and Spectators by force of Arms; the Prowess of the Champions seems so so exactly equal, that I see no cause to doubt, their Atchievements and Success proving parallel.

He concludes (says our Paraphraser) *the consequence of Plays intolerable; and that the* Massilienses *did well in clearing the Country of 'em.* Ibid. *This conclusion not to be found in* Valerius.

Where he finds this conclusion I can't tell, I am sure not in either of the Chapters cited by him, nor I doubt through the whole Book. But he's a Discoverer, and has good eyes, that will shew him at a vast distance what others can't see with the help of the best Telescopes. What he says of the *Massilienses* (as he calls 'em) is no more to his purpose, than the former Evidence against the Gladiatorial Shews. *Valerius Maximus* in his sixth Chapter says *, *That the* Marseillians *were a very severe People, that wou'd not suffer the* Mimicks *to appear upon their Stage, whose business generally it was to present the acti-*

* Eadem Civitas (viz. *Massilia*) severitatis custos acerrima est: nullum aditum in Scenam Mimis dando, quorum argumenta majore ex parte stuprorum continent actus, ne talia spectandi consuetudo etiam imitandi licentiam sumat. Cap. 6.

E *on*

on of Rapes to publick view, lest the sight of such licentious Practices, shou'd debauch the Spectators to the Imitation of 'em.

'Twere needless to insist long upon this passage, having already shewn the vast difference between the *Mimick* and *Dramatick* Representations. I shall only observe, that this Author, by saying that the people of *Marseilles* deny'd the *Mimi* the liberty of their Stage, intimates that they allow'd the Stage there, tho under severer restrictions than at *Rome*. Now if they permitted it amongst 'em at all, there is no doubt but *Tragedy* and *Comedy* (which by the unanimous confession even of their Adversaries, were the most innocent, and instructive of all the *Ludi Scenici*) took their turns upon it.

Stage allow'd at Marseilles.

Seneca, who is next produc'd, has but little to say to the matter: He is a little angry that the *Romans* were so fond of their diversion, as to bestow their whole time upon it, and neglect the study of Philosophy, and the improvement of their Reason. Nor was his complaint unreasonable; for the *Romans*, who were never much addicted to *Philosophy*, or any kind of

Seneca's *Authority nothing to the purpose.*

Spe-

Speculative Learning, were yet more averſe to 'em than ever under the Reign of *Nero*, when all ſorts of Arts and Literature, thoſe excepted which contributed to the Prince's pleaſures, lay under publick diſcouragement; on the other hand, the Stage, and all thoſe Arts that gratify'd and indulg'd the Sences, had not only the Countenance, but the Practice and Example of the Emperor himſelf to encourage 'em, and to excel in any of 'em was the high road to his Favour, and to Preferment. It is not therefore to be wonder'd, if the *Roman* Youth under that general corruption ſlighted thoſe Studies, the ſeverity of which made 'em as well unpalatable as unregarded. Nor are we to be ſurpriz'd, if *Seneca* declaim'd againſt theſe Entertainments, which drew away, and alienated the minds of the People from thoſe Studies, upon the merit of which he peculiarly picqu'd himſelf.

The ſumm of this *Philoſopher*'s Evidence amounts to no more than * that

* Nihil vero tam damnoſum bonis moribus, quam in aliquo ſpectaculo deſidere; tunc enim per voluptatem vitia facilius ſurrepunt. Epiſt. 7.

he thought Idleneſs a great corrupter of Manners, and that the Shows in uſe among the *Romans*, contributed to the making the people Idle, and tainting 'em with Luxury, and thereby rendring 'em more diſpos'd to Vice. His charge againſt the Shows is in this place general, and reſpects indifferently any of 'em, many of which were in their own Natures innocent, and void of offence, yet were equally ſubmitted to cenſure in this paſſage with the moſt ſcandalous. *Seneca* was not ſo mean a Judge of Men, or Things, as to think all their Shows equally reprehenſible, but he found all liable to the ſame abuſe, that is, detaining the people from their buſineſs, and giving them too great an itch after Diverſions. But this had not been worth our notice, were't not to ſhew, that our modern *Reformer*, tho he has been us'd to greater Stakes, can play at ſmall Game rather than ſtand out. For in the latter part of this ſhort Citation he has made a ſhift to ſteal in two falſifications

Yet perverted.

For there Vice makes an inſenſible approach, and ſteals upon us the diſguiſe of pleaſure.

* Tunc enim per voluptatem, &c. p. 236.

Here

Here he wou'd insinuate that the Vice, of which the *Philosopher* seems so apprehensive, was of the growth of the place, to which purpose he translates the words, *Tunc enim*, *For there*, by which he endeavours to make the infection local, and renders the words, *Per voluptatem*, *In the disguise of Pleasure*, that it may seem to come artificially, and industriously recommended. Whereas, all that he says imports no more, than that, when men's Minds, by the flattery of those Diversions, were disarm'd of that severity, that the *Stoicks* (of which Sect he was) think requisite to the guard of Virtue, they were more easily prevail'd upon, and led away by vitious inclinations.

There are yet behind in the Train, *Tacitus*, *Plutarch*, *Ovid*, and Mr. *Wycherley*, whom (whether to shew his Judgment or his Manners I know not) he has rankt amongst, and under the head of *Pagan* Authorities; and truly I think he may as well make a *Pagan* of him, as an Evidence in this case. But that ingenious Gentleman ought not to take it amiss; for since all those great Men of Antiquity, nay, even the *Fa-*

thers themſelves, the *Worthies of Chriſtendom*, *the Flower of Human Nature*, *and the top of their Species*, are obliged every one of 'em to wear a Fool's Coat, he has the leſs reaſon to repine at the Livery.

Tacitus, *&c.* impertinently cited.

Theſe are all ſummon'd to make up the Parade of Learning, and have no more buſineſs than an Ambaſſador's Coach of State at his publick Entry. *Tacitus* tells us, that *Nero did ill to make the neceſſities of decay'd Gentlemen pimp to the betraying of their honour and dignity. And that the* Germans *did well to keep their Wives out of harms way.* The complaint of *Tacitus* is nothing to us; his Caution indeed may be of ſervice, as matter of inſtruction to Mr *Collier*, and his Proſelytes, if he has any, who I hope will reap the benefit of the *German* Example.

Plutarch thinks, that Licentious Poets ought to be checkt: Ay, and licentious Criticks too, and corrected into the bargain: tho *Sancha Pancha* and *His Critick* were both ſubmitted to the laſh, till one learnt Wit, and t'other Manners, and both Modeſty. For ſawcy *Reformers*,

Reformers, as well as lewd *Poets*, require abundance of Discipline to keep 'em within bounds.

Ovid, and Mr *Wycherley*, as Poets, and Men of Wit, may be joyn'd, tho not as Heathens; and their Evidence, being exactly of a piece, is the more properly consider'd together. This amounts to a proof, that at the Theatres, as well as at all other places, where there is a promiscuous resort of company of both Sexes, the business of Intrigue will go forward. It were much to be wish'd, that no body came to the *Playhouse* for a less innocent diversion, than that of the *Stage*; to *Churches* and *Conventicles* with a less pious intention, than that of *Devotion*; to the *Park* for a less wholesome refreshment than that of *Air*, *&c.* But 'tis as much to be fear'd, that this universal Reformation will never be brought about, till the accomplishment of the Prophesie (if I may call it so, without offending Mr *Collier*) of one of our Poets

Ovid *and Mr* Wycherly *say nothing against the Stage, but the Audience.*

Till Women cease to Charm, and Youth to Love.

Too great severity of no service to Morality. So long as there are appetites, there will be means found to gratify em. I won't deny, but that the promiſcuous conflux of people of all Ages, Sexes, and Conditions, facilitates enterprizes of this nature. But I queſtion whether an abſolute reſtraint wou'd not more inflame the deſire, than it cou'd prevent the practice; and whither the Morals of the Public wou'd not ſuffer more by vitiating the Imaginations of the People in general this way, than they cou'd gain by the ſevereſt methods of prohibition the other. *Spain* and *Italy* are Countries as jealous and vigilant in this point, as any in the world, and yet the people ſo generally laſcivious, that there is no place where Virtue has leſs intereſt in the Chaſtity of either Sex. Whereas on the contrary, in many places under the *Line*, where the People go conſtantly naked, the familiarity of the Objects takes away all wantonneſs of Imagination, which the artificial difficulties of ſome Countries promote.

But *Ovid*, it ſeems, does in ſome meaſure plead guilty, and owns, that not

not only the opportunity *, but the business of the place sometimes promotes lewdness. Nor is it to be wonder'd at, since some of the representations there were so scandalously lewd, as to give offence to the loosest of their Poets. *Martial* tells us *, that he saw the Story of *Pasiphae* acted upon their Stage. But these were the Representations of their *Mimi*, the scandal of which reflects no way upon the *Drama*, either Antient or Modern, and will therefore give us no occasion to dilate upon 'em here.

* Ludi quoq; fœmina præbent Nequitiæ. De Trist. lib 2.

* Junctam Pasiphaen Dictæo credite Tauro, Vidimus, accepit Fabula prisca fidem. Mart.

Mr C——'s licentious Method of misquoting unsufferable.

I have at length run thro all his private Authorities against the Stage, wherein I can't find so much as one, which is not either impertinently, or falsely cited, as I doubt not, but will upon collation appear. For which reason I have all along put the words of the Original, or of the most approv'd Version in the Margin, that they might without trouble be collated, and my charge justified. He owns, that he *has taken the liberty of throwing in a word or two,* (in translating the Fathers) *to clear the Sense, to preserve the Spirit of the Original, and keep the* English *upon its Legs.*

Legs. I hope by this it appears, that he has *confounded* the *Senſe*, *corrupted* the *Spirit*, and ſet the *Engliſh* upon *Stilts*. His Modeſty's too plain a counterfeit, to cheat thoſe that are not wilfully blind, 'tis ſo ſlightly waſh'd over, that the Braſs appears at firſt view; ſo that whatever denomination he may give it, like an *Iriſh* Half-Crown, 'twill ſoon fall to its intrinſick value. After all, his pains in citations are as unluckily beſtow'd, as the Malefactors Fee, who, after he has brib'd the Ordinary, is call'd to read over again to the Court, and ſuffers at laſt for his ignorance.

To cloſe all, and crown his Victory, Mr *Collier* gives us ſome *State Cenſures* (as he calls 'em) to ſhew how much the Stage ſtands diſcourag'd by the Laws of other Countries, and our own.

P 240. *To begin with the* Athenians. *This People, tho none of the worſt Friends to the Play-houſe, thought a* Comedy *ſo unreputable a Performance, that they made a Law that no Judge of the* Areopagus *ſhou'd make one.*

The Athenians, *the greateſt friends in the world to the Stage.*

'Tis ſomething ſurprizing to find the Authority of the *Athenian* State produc'd againſt the *Drama*, of which they

they of all the people of the world were the greateſt Encouragers. And this very Law, which is urg'd againſt *Comedy* in particular, is an argument of the general Eſteem it was at that time poſſeſt of. For, had the Writing of *Comedy* been ſo unreputable a performance, as Mr *Collier* from this paſſage of *Plutarch* wou'd inſinuate, there had been no reaſon to ſuſpect, that any of the Judges of the *Areopagus* wou'd have been ſo madly indiſcreet, as to have forfeited his Character and Reputation, by ſo open and publick a Scandal; and conſequently a proviſion by Law againſt a folly of that nature, muſt have been as ſenſeleſs a Caution there, as an Act here wou'd be, to forbid any of the twelve Judges dancing upon the Ropes, or tumbling thro a Hoop in publick.

But this Law makes directly againſt the purpoſe it was quoted for, and ſeems plainly to argue, that *Comedy* was in ſo great reputation amongſt 'em, that perſons of the higheſt condition ſought the applauſe of, and made their court to the people by performances of that nature. For which reaſon they found it neceſſary to reſtrain their Judges by

This Law a direct Argument againſt Mr Collier.

a

a Law, from running into thoſe popular amuſements.

That theſe Performances were not in fact diſhonourable amongſt the *Athenians*, might be made appear from a million of inſtances, were it neceſſary. But the credit that *Ariſtophanes* had among the *Athenians*, which was powerful enough to ruine *Socrates*, is ſingly ſure ſufficient to deſtroy an aſſertion ſo weakly founded. So far were they from having *Comedy* in diſgrace, that they encourag'd, and maintain'd it at vaſt expence to the Publick, and thought it ſo proper an inſtrument of Reformation *, that they gave it free liberty of Speech, and priviledg'd it to ſay any thing, and of any body by name; and this not by connivance, but by Law; there lay no Action of Scandal either againſt Poet or Actors.

* Apud Græcos fuit Lege conceſſum ut quod vellet Comædia nominatim, & de quo vellet diceret. Cic. de Rep. apud S. Auguſt. de Civit dei, cap. 9.

The old Comedy of the Greeks *exceeding licentious.*

This probably gave occaſion to the exceſſive liberties of the old *Comedy*, which at length grew ſo offenſive, as to make way for a Reformation, and the introduction of the new *Comedy* upon the *Athenian* Stage. And here the reaſon why the *Areopagites* were not allow'd to meddle or engage in *Comedy*, appears pretty plain;

plain; for the Liberties, allow'd to the old *Comedy*, naturally engag'd 'em in Parties, Factions, and personal Quarrels, which a Judge ought, to the utmost of his power, to keep himself clear of. Beside, the ancient *Dramatick* Writers were generally Actors in their own Plays, which by no means befitted the gravity of a Judge.

These reasons (since *Plutarch* is silent) may suffice to shew, that the *Athenians* might have a very great honour for their Comick Writers, and yet forbid their Judges to be of the number. The Avocation from their proper Studies, the Laws of the Republic, the quarrels, and consequently the partialities they were by the exercise of that sort of Poetry liable to be engag'd in, and the Indignity to their Office, are sufficient to justify such a prohibition, even amongst a people, that had the highest respect for all other persons that excell'd in this kind.

Comedy, why no proper exercise for a Judge.

Nor was their kindness extended only to the *Drama*; for the *Bacchanalian* Games, even after the abdication of Tragedy and Comedy, tho they held not an equal rank with the other, yet had some share of their Favour; and *Æschines*, who, according to the

testi-

testimony of * *Demosthenes*, and † *Plutarch*, was but a third rate Actor *, yet was so well consider'd by the State, as to be sent on several Embassies, and particularly to conclude a Peace with *Philip* of *Macedon*, than which the State cou'd not have given him a more honourable Employment.

* Locata Opera tua illis Histrionibus, qui suspiriosi cognominantur, tertias partes actitabas. Demosth. Orat. de Coron: *And in the same Oration he calls him* Tertianum Histrionem.

† Æschines tertias partes in Bacchanalibus apud Aristodemum actitavit. Plut. Æschine.

* Æschines legationes obiit, & multas alias, & ad Philippum de pace. Ibid.

This, I suppose, may almost amount to a demonstration, that the *Athenians* had no such scandalous opinion of the Stage, as Mr *Collier* wou'd insinuate, making even *Plutarch* himself Judge in the case. It wou'd be impertinent after this to insist upon the great Employments, with which *Sophocles*, and some other of their Poets were honour'd; since the already mention'd honours and privileges are a sufficient evidence of the Publick Esteem.

Opinion of the Spartans.

His next State Opinion is that of the *Lacedemonians*; and here after a flourish of his own, he appeals to *Plutarch* again.

P. 240. *The* Lacedemonians, *who were remarka-*

ble

ble for the Wiſdom of their Laws, and Sobriety of their Manners, and their breeding of brave Men: This Government wou'd not endure the Stage in any Form, nor under any Regulation.

I find, if this Author can but make his reading appear, 'tis no matter whether his ſenſe does or not. Here is a Period of five lines and a half, without any principal Verb. But the Author is got into his Rhetorical ſtrain, and 'tis no matter for Grammar. For when his Fury's up, *Priſcian* had beſt ſtand out of his way; or take a broken Head quietly, or woe be to his bones.

But who told him, that the *Lacedemonians* were ſo remarkable for the Wiſdom of their Laws? They were indeed notorious for the unreaſonable ſeverity and ſingularity of 'em. But I beg Mr *Collier*'s pardon, if ill Nature and Singularity ben't arguments of Wiſdom, a certain ſowre, ſingular *Remarker* may have written a Book to call his own underſtanding in queſtion.

Theft tolerated at Lacedemon.

The Gentleman, I ſuppoſe, had heard of a famous Law-giver call'd *Lycurgus*, who was a *Lacedemonian*, and left his

Country

Country ſeveral wholeſome Laws, the juſt commendation of which particular Ordinances he was reſolv'd to transfer to the whole Body, or Syſtem of their Laws, in which Violence, Rapine, and Theft were not only tolerated, but recommended to practice and imitation; but all ingenious Arts, lay together with the Stage, under diſcouragement.

Character of the Spartans.

The *Spartans* were a people ſomething of Mr *Collier*'s Kidney, Cynicks in their Temper, Moroſe, Proud, and ill Natur'd, that hated mortally, as well the Improvements, as the Perſons of their polite Neighbours the *Athenians*, were fond of their primitive Ruſt, and Barbarity, had an averſion to Elegance, or Neatneſs of any kind; their principal Virtues were a ſenſeleſs inflexible obſtinacy, whether in the right or wrong, and a ſullen ſufferance under Adverſity. They were in ſhort incorrigible Humoriſts, a people that would neither lead nor drive, men that were as hard to be perſwaded to reform an old abuſe, as the *Iriſh* formerly to leave off drawing by their Horſes Tails, or a *Spaniard* would be to part with his Muſtachio's, or Mr *Collier* to re-

tract

tract an Error. This Frame and Constitution of mind, might perhaps recommend and endear 'em, as it seems to ally 'em to a person of the Authors complexion.

But why did this *Scourge* of the *Stage* suppress the reason of this Aversion of the *Spartans* to the *Drama*? Was it not for his purpose? Well, if he's resolv'd not to to tell us, *Plutarch* is better natur'd, and will. He says, * that the *Lacedemonians* allow'd neither *Tragedy* nor *Comedy*, that they might not hear any thing contradictory to their Laws.

* Comædias, & Tragædias non admittebant Lacones, ut neq; joco, neq; serio, eos qui legibus contradicerent audirent. Instit. Lacon.

This Authority falsified likewise.

Here was an Authority in appearance as serviceable to his purpose, as the old broad Money was to the Clippers, but he, like some of those unconscionable Artists, that when they had clipt a Six pence, woud clap a Nine-penny stamp upon it, cou'd not be contented with the advantage of diminution, but he by covetously endeavouring to raise the value, spoiled the currency of his Authority.

This Government (says he) wou'd not endure the Stage in any form, nor under any Regulation.

Politeneſs, the Objection of the Spartans to the Drama.

What warrant has he from *Plutarch* for this Aſſertion? *Plutarch* tells us, that they did not admit *Comedy* nor *Tragedy*, but he ſays not a ſyllable of Forms or Regulations. The *Lacedemonians* were a rough unpoliſh'd people, that were afraid, if the ſtudy of Politeneſs (the inſeparable companion of the *Drama*) were introduc'd, their Laws, which were as Clowniſh, and unlickt as themſelves, ſhou'd be affronted, and therefore kept *Tragedy* and *Comedy*, like Enemies, at a diſtance.

All ſorts of Plays not prohibited at Lacedemon.

But what does he mean here by the Stage? Wou'd he inſinuate, that all ſorts of *Shews* and *Games* were prohibited? If ſo, his Poſition is abſolutely falſe; for all the rough *Bear Garden* Play (if I may call it ſo) was not only tolerated, but very much encouraged by the State. Their Women too had their Religious Plays, a memorable ſtory of which *Pauſanias* * tells. And 'tis probable, that the Plays in uſe over all the reſt of *Greece*, were permitted there too in their Primitive Rudeneſs and Simplicity, conformable to the humour of the people, and the drift of their Policy.

* Lib. 4.

In

In the exclusion of the *Drama*, they aim'd only to preserve that Martial Spirit, which by the whole course and method of their Education and Exercises, they endeavour'd to infuse into, and nurse up in their youth, which they were afraid the Delicacy and Luxury of the *Drama*, as 'twas practic'd at *Athens*, might soften, and that the Elegancy and Pleasure of those diversions wou'd breed a niceness, which wou'd insensibly create a disgust in their youth to the Manners and Customs of their Country, and consequently make 'em think their Laws harsh and unpolish'd.

It was not therefore the Virtue of the *Spartans*, nor their care of Morality, that made 'em reject the *Drama*, but an austerity of temper, which render'd 'em ambitious only of Military Glory. In which, notwithstanding their Neighbours and Rivals the *Athenians*, with all their Delicacy and Luxury, were their equals, if not superiours. What infection of Manners from the Stage, cou'd that State fear, which tolerated Theft and Adultery? 'Tis plain, their fear was, lest the natural asperity of their humours, which they industriously

Morality, not the reason of rejecting the Stage.

ously cultivated, should be softned, and their minds enervated. For the same reason all sorts of Learning lay under neglect and discouragement.

Whatever were the reasons that induc'd 'em to banish the *Drama*, if Virtue was not, 'tis nothing to Mr *Collier's* purpose. As for their *breeding brave Men*, I believe they may be match'd from the opposite State of *Athens*, both for number and quality. But if the *Athenians* rivall'd 'em in Military Glory, they infinitely excell'd 'em in all other valuable Qualities, and had as much more Manners, as they had Wit or Wealth. So that if Mr *Collier* will needs have them for his Champions, I must oppose their old Antagonists to 'em, and leave them to decide the Fate of *Greece*. For I think the opposition as unequal, as that of *Ovid*,

Mulieber in Trojam, pro Trojâ stabat Apollo.

The next step he takes is into *Italy*, and there indeed he endeavours to draw a mighty Republick into a League Offensive and Defensive. And here, by by the means of St *Austin*, he draws *Tully* in ; but since *Tully* does not appear in *propriâ personâ* we shall not spend Time and Ammunition upon him, but pass on to *Livy :* Who, making his personal appearance, is more formidable.

Livy's Authority consider'd.

P. 241.

We read in Livy, *that the young people in* Rome *kept the* Fabulæ Atellanæ *to themselves. They wou'd not suffer this diversion to be blemish'd by the Stage. For this reason, as the Historian observes, the Actors of the* Fabulæ Atellanæ *were neither expell'd their Tribe, nor refus'd to serve in Arms. Both which Penalties, it appears, the common* Players *lay under.*

Postquam lege hac fabularum ab risu, ac soluto joco res avocabatur, & ludus in artem paulatim verterat, Juventus histrionibus fabellarum actu relicto, ipsa inter se more antiquo ridicula intexta versibus jactitare cæpit, quæ inde exodia postea appellata, consertaq; Fabellis potissimum Atellanis sunt, quod genus ludorum ab Oscis acceptum tenuit juventus : nec ab histrionibus pollui passa est. Eo institutum manet, ut Actores Atellanarum nec tribu moveantur, & stipendia tanquam expertes artis Ludicræ faciant. Dec. 1. l. 7.

Here Mr *Collier* has us'd a piece of Ingenuity uncommon with him, and put the words, *Ab Histrionibus pollui* in the Margin to justifie his Translation. This is a strain of fair play, that he has not been persuaded to come up to, since his first quotation from *Theophilus* *Anti-*

Antiochenus. Not but that he was satisfy'd of the reaſonableneſs of the conduct, (as appears by his uſing it, when 'tis for his turn) but becauſe he had cauſe to fear the ſervice of it.

In this Tranſlation is another of his elegancies of Speech: *Were neither expell'd their Tribe, nor* refuſed *to ſerve in Arms.* He means, I ſuppoſe, prohibited, or denied the liberty of ſerving in Arms: for *refus'd to ſerve in Arms* is not *Engliſh.*

Ancient Romans *an unrefined People.*

To underſtand this paſſage of *Livy* rightly, we muſt conſider that the *Romans* in the Infancy of their State were a ſevere ſort of people, not much unlike in that particular to the *Lacedemonians,* ambitious only of Empire, and ſollicitous for nothing ſo much as the glory of their Arms: This humour laſted ſome Ages, and grew and encreas'd with their acquiſitions; every augmentation of their State animated 'em to new Conqueſts, and their 'Ambition riſing with their hopes, ſucceſs made 'em fierce and haughty. 'Twas the univerſality of this Spirit, (which wou'd be dangerous to any other than a Popular Government) that laid the Foundation,

dation, and was the Inſtrument of their future greatneſs. To ſupport, and keep up this Spirit, all manner of Arts here, as at *Lacedemon*, lay under neglect and contempt, except ſuch as contributed to the forming of their Youth to hardineſs, and military virtue *. So that when there ſeem'd to be a neceſſity of inſtituting expiatory Plays, the *Romans* were ſuch abſolute ſtrangers to things of that nature, that they were forc'd to fetch Artiſts out of *Tuſcany*.

* Virtus ſuperſtitione animis Ludi quoque Scenici nova res bellicoſo populo, inſtituti dicuntur. Et ea ipſa peregrina res fuit. Ludiones ex Hetruria acciti. Ibid.

It is no wonder if the *Romans*, who were a people very proud, and conceited of their own performances, treated all thoſe Arts, and Artiſts, which were not adapted to their proper Genius with contempt, eſpecially after they had receiv'd thoſe Improvements, which render'd 'em more artificial, and conſequently more difficult. By which means the *Roman* Youth, who at firſt began to imitate the *Tuſcan* Players, were forc'd to throw up thoſe refin'd diverſions to their † *Slaves*, and ſtick themſelves to the old, rude, ſimple way of mixing indigeſted Verſes, and crude extempore raillery. Thus the

* Imitari deinde eos juventus, ſimul inconditis inter ſe jocularia fundentes verſibus, cepere. Ib.

Acting of Plays firſt left off by the Roman *youth, becauſe of the difficulty.*

† Vernaculis Artificibus. Ib.

Hiſtriones, *who ſo called.*

the *Ludi Scenici* being refin'd, fell wholly into the hands of *Mercenary Players*, who were upon this occasion distinguish'd by the name of* *Histriones*, the *Roman* Youth retaining to themselves only the *Fabulæ Atellanæ*, which, because of their rudeness and simplicity, requir'd no great skill or application, as the other did; which, for that reason, perhaps they were either too Saturnine, or too proud to learn of those, whom they esteem'd as Vassals, or Slaves.

That this was the reason of their giving over the acting their other Plays, and not any turpitude, or dishonesty in the things themselves, *Livy* himself declares, by saying *, that after the introduction of the Fable, they became too artificial for the practice of their youth, and therefore reserving to themselves the *Atellanæ* only, they left the rest of the Shews to those that made it their sole business.

'Tis observable, that the Historian in this account of Plays includes not the *Drama* at all; for he speaks here only of the Fables, which, after the *Satyræ*, were introduc'd by one *Livius*, and

* Vernaculis Artificibus, quia Hister Tusco verbo Ludio vocabatur, Histrionibus nomen inditum. Ibid.

* Postquam lege

and were repeated in Verſe with action and geſtures to Muſick. *Tragedy* and *Comedy* were not known to the *Romans* till ſome ages after, the progreſs of their Arms had not made them acquainted with the Learning of *Greece*, and the Wealth and Luxury of *Aſia*.

This mark therefore of Infamy, which was ſet upon the *Hiſtriones* (from which (as Mr *Collier* obſerves) the Actors of the *Fabulæ Atellanæ* were exempt, can't properly ſtick upon the Actors of *Tragedy*, and *Comedy* as ſuch, that Law having been made long before the *Drama* was brought to *Rome* from *Greece*.

Conjectural Reaſon why Players were noted with Infamy.

But it was the misfortune of the *Drama* to make its Publick Entry into *Rome*, not only long after this voluntary, and unanimous ſeceſſion, or ſeparation of the Youth of *Rome* from the *Mercenary Players*, but even after the Law had branded theſe latter with Infamy and Diſgrace, by excluding 'em from their Tribes, and denying 'em the liberty of bearing Arms. Whether, becauſe making a buſineſs, and profeſſion of diverſion only, the *Roman* State, which encourag'd thoſe exerciſes only

that

that tended towards hard'ning their Youth, for labour and military action, as partly thro inclination, so also out of necessity and State interest, being in its infamy surrounded by Neighbours more potent than themselves, and oblig'd to subsist almost altogether upon the purchase of their Swords, thought fit, by a publick discouragement, to deter their Youth from giving themselves up to an Employment, that so little suited the posture, and condition of their Affairs at first, and the vastness of their Ambition afterwards. Or, that after the first separation, occasion'd (as *Livy* hints) rather by the incapacity and unfitness of the *Romans* for Elegancy, and polite Exercise, the practice of the Stage, fell wholly into the hands of Slaves, and Mercenary Foreigners, to joyn with whom, the Magistrates and People, who were extremely proud, and jealous of the honour, and dignity of their Citizens as such, thought it so great an indignity and debasement that they made provision by this Law against it. Or, lastly, that their *Mimes* & *Pantomimes* were already, before the making of this Law, arriv'd at that lewd heighth of impudence, that we have already taken

taken notice of, which obliged the Government to take this method to fright their Citizens from mixing in the practice of ſuch impurities.

Of theſe Reaſons the two firſt ſeem joyntly to have contributed to the production of this Law: and *Livy*, tho he does not formally aſſign any reaſon for this ſevere uſage of the Players, yet ſeems implicitely to intimate 'em to us in the notice that he has taken of 'em, tho not as cauſes, yet as circumſtances conſiderable at that time. The ſilence of *Livy* concerning any ſuch licentiouſneſs in their Shews at that time, is a ſufficient argument againſt the laſt cauſe. For that Hiſtorian, who upon all occaſions ſhews abundance of zeal for the honour of his Country, would not have fail'd to have done 'em juſtice upon this occaſion, had this rigour been the product of their Morals, and regard to Virtue. It is apparent therefore, that this diſcouragement of the Shews, or rather this reſtraint of the Action to Servants and Strangers, was the reſult of their Policy, not Manners, and is therefore an impertinent inſtance to Mr *Collier*'s purpoſe,

Two firſt moſt probable.

who

who I ſuppoſe writes for the Reformation of Men's Morals, not Politicks.

Drama at first neceſſitated to uſe the Actors of the Ludi Scenici.

'Tis probable, that when *Tragedy* and *Comedy* came upon the *Roman* Stage, being deſtitute of able Actors of a higher Character, they were neceſſitated to make uſe of the Actors of the *Scenic Shews*, who, tho us'd to Repreſentations differing very much both in their manner and end, yet by their practice and pronunciation and geſtures, had both Voice and Motion under great command; which made the exerciſe of the *Tragick* or *Comick* Stage, tho new and unknown to 'em before, not difficult.

The Actors of Tragedy and Comedy, therefore only call'd Hiſtriones.

By this means the Actors of *Tragedy* and *Comedy*, who cou'd not be aim'd at by a Law made long before any ſuch were in being, might yet be brought under the cenſure of it in quality of *Hiſtriones*, or Scene Players before noted. Thus theſe different Characters meeting conſtantly in the perſons of the ſame men amongſt the undiſtinguiſhing Crowd, the Infamy of one might affect the other.

But

But granting the meaning and intention of that Law to reach the *Dramatick* Actors, and that uſing a craft, which ſubmits 'em to thoſe compliances, for which the other are cenſur'd; they alſo are offenders againſt the deſign of it, and conſequently are comprehended within the intent of it, and liable to the penalty. Yet even thus this inſtance, giving it all the ſcope that may be in the utmoſtlatitude of conſtruction, is no way ſerviceable to this Reformer's purpoſe. This would have appear'd very plain, had the Law itſelf, inſtead of the inſtance from *Livy*, been produc'd.

* † The Pretorian Edict runs thus, *Whoever appears upon the Stage to ſpeak, or act, is declar'd infamous. Which* Labeo *expounds thus. The Stage is any place fitted up for the uſe of Plays, where any one is to appear, and by his motion make himſelf a publick Spectacle.*

* Prætorian Edict.
† Infamia notatur qui Artis ludicæ, pronunciandive cauſa in Scenam prodierit.

Scena eſt, ut Labeo definit quæ ludorum faciendorum cauſa quolibet loco, ubi quis conſiſtat, moveaturq; ſpectaculum ſui præbiturus, poſita eſt. *L. 1. & 2. F. de iis qui notantur infamia.*

This Law being conceiv'd in general terms againſt all that ſpeak or act, upon the Stage for the diverſion of the

the People, seems indeed naturally to include *Comedians*, and *Tragedians*, who do both speak, and act upon the Stage, and make a shew of themselves to the People too. Yet it does not serve our Adversaries cause at all, who must shew, that their Profession was branded for the Immorality of it, or he talks nothing to the purpose.

Labeo's *position shews the intent of that Edict*

This Exposition of *Labeo's* upon this Law, like the Preamble to one of our *Acts* of *Parliament*, may let us into the meaning of the Letter, and the motives that induc'd 'em to make it. What this Learned *Roman* Lawyer here observes as matter of offence, is only, that they did, *Spectaculum sui præbere, make a shew of themselves* for hire; which the Pride of the *Romans* might very naturally make 'em think to be a Prostitution of the Dignity and Character of a Citizen of *Rome*, which deserv'd to be punish'd with the privation of that which they had dishonour'd.

Mr Colliers *disingenuity in this point.*

To secure this point, the words, *ab Histrionibus pollui*, which he renders *to be blemish'd by the Stage*, are (as has already

already been obſerv'd) put into the Margin, by which he hopes to caſt that blemiſh upon the Morality of the performanee, which in ſtrictneſs regarded only the Perſons, and Dignity of the Actors, and that not upon any Moral, but a Political Conſideration. By theſe Inſtances it may appear, what violence of Conſtruction is uſed to rack and torture theſe antient Authors to confeſs, and depoſe againſt their Conſciences. Stretching the Text is nothing with him, to ſerve his purpoſe it muſt be diſmember'd, that he may have the cementing the fragments as he pleaſes; by which means he has ſhewn 'em in more unnatural figures, than even *Poſture Clark* knew; Heads and Tails are ſo promiſcuouſly jumbled together, that the moſt familiar poſture you find 'em in, is that of a Dog couchant, with their Noſes in their A——s.

The Roman Cenſure extended only to the Mercenary Actors as ſuch.

But if after all, this Cenſure ſhou'd reach the *Mercenary* or Hireling Actors only, and meerly upon that account, I think 'twill be pretty evident, that 'twas not the exerciſe of their Myſtery that made 'em ſcandalous, but the Motives

tives that induc'd 'em to it. To clear this point, let us look a little forward, and to the former Law, we shall find the following subjoyn'd.

* *Those that enter the Lists for the sake of Gain, or appear upon the Stage for Reward, are infamous, says* Pegasus, *and* Nerva *the Son.*

* Eos enim qui quæstus causa in certamina descendunt, & omnes propter præmium in Scenam prodeuntes, famosos esse Pegasus, & Nerva filius responderunt. *L. 2. de iis qui notantur infamia.*

Here 'tis plain that 'twas not the nature of their Profession that drew the censure upon 'em, but the condition of their exercising it, which was for hire, whereby they became *Mercenaries.* This disgrace, affecting only the *Mercenary* Actors, reflects no way upon the *Poets* of the *Drama*, and their Performances. For had they been scandalous, 'tis not to be imagin'd, that so many of the greatest men that ever *Rome* bred, and the tenderest of their honour, wou'd have amus'd themselves about Works, in which they must have employ'd abundance of Time, Learning, and Judgment, to forfeit their Reputation and Dignity.

Scipio *and* Lælius *Writers to the Stage, or assisting to it.*

Scipio Africanus and *Lælius* were publickly suspected to have assisted *Terence* in the composition of his Plays; and the Poet, when tax'd with it, is so far

far from vindicating his great Patrons, (which had it been matter of reproach and diminution of honour to those noble Persons, he certainly would have done) that he does in a manner confess the charge to be true, and with a dexterity, in which he was singularly happy, converts what was intended as an imputation, to a complement upon himself, and values himself more upon the condescension, and friendship of men of their high Character and Station, than upon the merit of his performance; which, this objection was rais'd to lessen, by dividing the honour.

Julius and *Augustus Cæsar*, are both said to have busied themselves at vacant hours in Tragedy; and even *Seneca* the Philosopher. However, Mr *Collier* has lately seduc'd him over to his Party, and made a Malecontent of him, was once very well contented, and easy at a Play, and that too, not a sober *Tragedy* or *Comedy*, * but one of their *Noonday Drolls*, a kind of their *Ludi Senici*, more wretched and contemptible, than our *Smithfield Farces*, and less modest. Yet his Gravity was it seems refresh'd by it, tho he's grown

Julius *and* Augustus Cæsar, *and* Seneca, *&c.*

* In meridianum Spectaculum incidi lusus Spectans, & sales, & aliquid Laxamenti Epist. 7.

so

ſo very ſqueamiſh, ſince his acquaintance with Mr *Collier*, that it would be a hard matter to reconcile him to a grave *Tragedy*, tho of his own Writing (before his rigid new friend, Mr *Collier*) ſome of which are ſuppos'd to be yet extant amongſt his Nameſake's Collection of *Tragedies*.

Brutus, who left behind him (notwithſtanding his fatal engagement in the aſſaſſination of *Cæſar*,) as high an Idea of his Virtue, and as a perfect character of an excellent moral man, as even *Cato* himſelf, was as great an admirer and encourager of the *Drama*, as any *Roman* of 'em all. And *Tully* himſelf, who had as much Vanity and Pride as any man breathing, thought it no diminution of his dignity and character, to contract an intimate friendſhip with *Roſcius* an Actor, and publickly to eſpouſe his Intereſt, and defend his Cauſe, which a man of his vanity and caution would not have done, had the Cenſure of that Law upon his Profeſſion, any way affected in the publick eſteem the reputation of thoſe among 'em, that had any perſonal merit, as *Roſcius*, *Æſopus*, and ſome others.

But

But tho theſe, and many others of the moſt eminent among the *Romans*, were avow'd Patrons, and the ſuppos'd at leaſt, if not the real Author of many of their Dramatick Pieces, yet our *Remarker* finds, that in the time of *Theodoſius* all ſorts of Players did not come up to the Reputation of thoſe Great Men, and make the top figures of their time, and therefore he claws 'em away with another ſwinging Authority.

Law of the Theodoſian Code *conſidered.*

In the Theodoſian Code, *Players are call'd* Perſonæ inhoneſtæ, *that is, to tranſlate it ſoftly, perſons maim'd and blemiſh'd in their Reputations. Their* Pictures *might be ſeen at the Playhouſe, but were not permitted to hang in any creditable * place of the Town.*

P. 241:

* In loco honeſto.

So ſays Mr *Collier*, but the Emperors *Theodoſius*, *Arcadius*, and *Honorius*, by the Authority of whom this Law was enacted and continued in force, were ſomewhat leſs ſevere, and ſomething more particular, and this Gentleman's Verſion of that Law, however ſoft he may pretend it to be, is no very fair one. Faithfully render'd it runs thus.

* *If, in the publick Porches, or other Places of the City where Statues use to be dedicated to us the Picture of any mean habited Pantomime and Charioteer with his ruffled Garment, or base Droll Actor be put up, let it be immediately pull'd down: nor shall it be lawful for the future to represent persons of such despicable Characters in places of honour. But in the entrance of the* Circus, *or before the Stage of the Theatres they may be allow'd.*

* Siqua in publicis Porticibus, vel in his Civitatum locis, in quibus nostræ solent Imagines consecrari pictura Pantomimum veste humili, & rugosis sinubus Agitatorem, aut vilem efferat Histrionem, illico revellatur: neq; unquam post hac liceat in loco honesto personas inhonestas adnotare. In aditu vero Circi, vel in Theatri proscenis ut collocentur, non vetamus. *L. Siqua. Cod. de Spectac.*

Meaning of the Theodosian *Law.*

This, when produc'd faithfully, and at length, is a worshipful Authority for Mr *Collier's* purpose, and the *Strowlers* all over the Kingdom must needs be extreamly mortified, when they reflect upon this Article, and find, that they are not yet so proper Companions for the King, as to be *hail fellow, well met* with him at a Publick Entry, or Audience. These Emperours, , it seems, thought it a sort of Indignity to have every Scoundrel *Hackney Coachman*, *Antick Tumbler*, or *Droll Actor* set up in in Effigie by their own Statues, which in the times of Paganiſm were the objects of Solemn Worſhip, and afterwards of the higheſt veneration imagi nable below it. They thought it a derogation to Majeſty (as well they might) to have objects of ridiculous mirth and ſcorn plac'd ſo near 'em, and that the tickling to laughter, which theſe produc'd in the people, wou'd leſſen the awful Reſpect and Reverence expected to be paid to the other.

But not to carry matters ſo high ; If any one ſhou'd take a fancy to ſet *Tom Dogget*'s Effigies in his Sailors dreſs, familiarly cheek by jole in the ſame, or the next Niche to the King upon the *Exchange* (tho that ben't ſo ſolemn a place of honour to our Kings, as the *Roman Porticus* to their Emperors) I ſuppoſe it wou'd be reſented as an affront, and be by order pull'd down. But if any man ſhould take a fancy to the ſign of the *King's Head*, and his next Neighbour to Mr *Betterton*'s, I hardly think there would come any order from *Whitehall* to demoliſh or Lamb black the Sign. And tho perhaps *Parallel inſtances.*

haps the two firſt may actually be found at *Murray*s or ſome other eminent Limners in the ſame Room, yet I fancy the Painter will hardly incur the penalty of *Crimen læſæ Majeſtatis*, tho he ſhould happen to have drawn 'em both with the ſame Pencil too. Princes, tho very zealous and tender of their honour, (as they have reaſon to be) yet are not half ſo nice and ſcrupulous as Mr *Collier*. Theſe inſtances are exactly parallel to, and ſhew the difference between the drift of the *Theodoſian Code*, and of his extravagant Paraphraſe, which having already given the words of, I leave the Reader to judge of the Intention.

His inſtances from our *Engliſh* Statutes and the Petition of his Godly Citizens, I ſhall take no notice of, both becauſe I find it ſufficiently done already to my hands, and becauſe I think 'em nothing to his purpoſe, as I think indeed of the greateſt part of what I have already examined; but hitherto they ſeem'd to carry a face of Learning and Authority, which might miſlead the unlearn'd, or ſurprize the unwary, if they were not warn'd in

time

time of his disingenuity in Quotation.

His Authorities drawn from the several *Canons* of some *Councils*, are liable to the same reprehension with the rest of his Citations. But I am willing to compound with my Reader for my past prolixity, and to dismiss 'em without any further trouble, or examination; especially since the formal Reasons of 'em are contain'd in the Objections from the *Fathers*, and already answer'd there. Since therefore the Idolatry, Lewdness, and Cruelty of the *Roman* Shews, (which provok'd the indignation of the Fathers, and the censure of those Councils) are banisht our Stage, I see no reason, why the Batteries, that were rais'd only to demolish them, shou'd be continu'd against it. But Mr *Collier*, and the Bishop of *Arras* are gotten into Confederacy, and are resolv'd, that tho the Theatres have long since perform'd their Articles on their parts, not to allow 'em the benefit of the Capitulation, and surprizing 'em, lull'd into security by a long cessation of Arms, to raze 'em utterly to the ground.

Authorities from the Councils already answered.

Quarrel to the Stage unjust.

Delenda est Carthago was the word, the ruin of the Stage was agreed upon between em, but they wanted a fair pretence of quarrel ; and therefore General *Collier* publishes a tedious *Manifesto*, fill'd with specious pretexts, to give a colour to his proceedings and at the same time makes his Invasion. His quarrel to the Stage is like that of the Wolf to the Lamb, when the Prey was ready, the varnish of Justice was but a formality, that serv'd like a Hypocrite's Grace, to make his Meal the more decent ; when the personal accusation proves too light, the Family differences are thrown into the Scale, and he runs 1500 years backward to make weight. Thus he makes a true *Italian* grudge of it, no change of Air, or Soil can can make it degenerate, but it remains entail'd upon the Posterity, aud successors of those, between whom it first began, tho the true reason why it ever began, were long since ceas'd, and perhaps forgotten.

But after he has, like a hot mettled Cur, with a bad Nose, over-run the Scent, and cry'd it false thro all the Fields of Antiquity, he begins to be afraid

afraid of being whipt home, and therefore begins to draw towards it of himſelf. He's ſenſible, that the compariſon betwixt the *Roman* and *Engliſh* Stages will not hold water, and to anſwer the leaks, he begins to ply the Pump, in order to keep it afloat, but it works as hard, and refunds as little as a Uſurers Conſcience.

But it may be objected, is the Reſemblance exact between old Rome *and* London? *will the Parallel hold out, and has the* Engliſh Stage *any thing ſo bad as the* Dancing *of the Pantomimi? I don't ſay that. The* Modern Geſtures, *tho bold, and lewd too ſometimes, are not altogether ſo ſcandalous as the* Roman. *Here then we can make em ſome little abatement.* P. 277.

Ay! is that your Conſcience? can you make but little abatemant? I find you've a Stomach like a Horſe, nothing riſes upon it, let it be never ſo provoking either, for quantity or quality. Dancing naked with Geſtures, expreſſive of Lewdneſs between both Sexes at a time and publick and open proſtitutions in the repreſentations of the Rapes and Adulteries of their Gods, were frequently the diverſions of the

Ancient Stage infinitely more ſcandalous, and lewd than the Modern.

Roman

Roman Theatres. All theſe provoke no Qualms in him; he can ſcarce make any abatement. What wou'd a queaſie Stomach'd Atheiſt give for his digeſtion.

Stage dancing as now practiced inoffenſive to Modeſty.

But where's the Boldneſs, and Lewdneſs of the Modern Geſtures; which Mr *Collier* makes bold to charge 'em with? I dare anſwer for the Audience, that cou'd they find any ſuch thing in our Dancing, they wou'd be ſo much more reaſonable than he, that they wou'd part with all that part of the Entertainment. But perhaps he ſuſpects ſome intentional Lewdneſs, which is not expreſſed any way, and thinks that Monſieur *L'Abbe* is fallen into Sir *Fopling Flutter*'s ſtratagem, and is ſparing of his Vigour in private, only to be laviſh of it in publick, and thinks no one Woman worth the loſs of a Cut in a Caper, which is deſigned to make his Court to the whole Sex. This indeed is a dangerous deſign, and the diſcovery is worth Mr *Collier*'s time and pains, 'tis a Plot upon the Virtue of the whole Sex; therefore if he has any ſuch thing in the Wind, e'en let him follow his noſe, and cry it away as loud as he pleaſes.

Well,

Well, but he begins to relent again already, these wamblings are a certain sign of Breeding, he's in a longing condition, that's plain. Come t'other strain Sir, and up with't. So now it's out.

And to go as far in their Excuse *as we can, 'tis probable their* Musick *may not be altogether so exceptionable as that of the* Antients. P. 277.

Really Sir this is very kind, and con descending. But do you truly, and from your heart think, that our Theatre Musick is not altogether so pernicious, as the Musick of the Antients? Now were I as cross, and captious as a Stage Reformer, and as full of Mr. *Collier*'s own Devil of Opposition, as himself, I cou'd raise his, and divert the Spleen of other People. But Foolery apart, I desire to know wherein consists this imaginary Force of Musick, that *Charms, and Transports, Ruffles, and Becalms, and Governs, with* such *an arbitrary Authority*, that can make *drunken Fellows, as sober, and shamefaced, as one wou'd wish*, If he can tell me this, *erit mihi magnus Apoll*, or, what's but one remove from him, first *Knight*

Mr Coll.'s *Notion of the extravagant Power of Musick ridiculous.*

Collier's *Moral Essay Vol. 2d P. 21.*
Ib. P. 22.

Knight of his own order of the *Welch Harp.* Our Fiddlers find to their coſt ſometimes the want of this coercive power, but perhaps they can't play a *Dorion*, and for that piece of Ignorance deſerve the Fate they ſometimes meet with, when they unluckily fall into the Company of theſe *Drunken Fellows*, and get their heads broke with their own Fiddles, in return for their Muſick. Yet to do the Gentleman all the Juſtice, ay and the Favour too, that we can, in return for his late Civility, I muſt own, that I have ſeen at a Country Wake, or ſo, one of theſe Harmonious Knights of the Scrubbado, or a Melodious *Rubber* of *Hair* and *Catgut*, lug a whole Pariſh of as arrant Logs, as thoſe that danced after *Orpheus*, by the Ears after him, to the next empty Barn, frisking, and curvetting at ſuch a frolickſom rate, that they could ſcarce keep their Legs together; nay, ſuch was the power of the Melody, that even the ſolitary deſerted Gingerbread Stalls wagged after; and all this without the help of one illegal ſtring, and but four very untunable ones. What cou'd *Timotheus*, or even *Orpheus* himſelf do more. How-

However I wou'd not have the Gentleman ſwell too much in the Pride of his Victory, I wou'd not have him inſult too ſoon. For, tho poſſibly theſe *Knights* of the *Harp* and *Catgut might know, how to arm a ſound, and put force and Conqueſts in it*, yet had there not been a Favourable Conjuncture of Circumſtances, the Harmony, as charming as it was, had not ſucceeced ſo miraculouſly, nor produc'd ſuch extatick Raptures. For example, had this *Deſcendant* from *Orpheus* ſurpriz'd 'em at a time, when the *Holyday* Clothes were laid up in *Lavender*, when the Hay, or Harveſt was abroad, or the Snow upon the Ground, and the Cattle wanted Foddering, when the Calf was to be ſuckled, and the Cheeſe to be ſet, he might have thrummed his Harp out, and cou'd no more have ſtirred thoſe very Clods, that leapt as mechanically before at the firſt twang, as if they had been meer Machines (Inſtruments ſtrung, and tuned to an Uniſone) then he cou'd have raiſed the Turf, they trod upon, by vertue of *Ela*, and *F-ffaut*. The Critical Juncture miſt, *Roger* had not jogged a foot out of his way, nor

Moral Eſſay vol. 2 P. 21.

Madge

Madge out of her Dairy, they had been as regardleſs of his Harmony, as a *London* Milk Maid, after the firſt week in *May*; an antient *Britton* might as eaſily have been charmed from his ſcrubbing Poſt.

Power of Muſick owing to contingent circumſtances.

There are indeed certain opportunities to be found by thoſe that skilfully watch 'em, wherein Mens Souls are to be taken by ſurprize, wherein they give themſelves up wholly to the direction of their Senſes, when Reaſon tired with perpetual mounting the Guard, quits her Poſt, and leaves 'em to be drawn away by every delightful Object, every pleaſing Amuſement. At theſe times Sound, Colour, Taſte, and Smell have all an unuſual Influence; a Face, a Voice, or any thing elſe, that gives us pleaſure for the time, Commands us, and we are hurried, like Men in Dreams, we know not how, nor whither. Yet this is eaſily accounted for, without recourſe to natural Magick, or any ſuitable Power in thoſe Agents, that work upon us. Our Souls are at theſe times, like Veſſels adrift, at the mercy of Waves and Winds, from what corner ſoever they blow;

blow; our Senſes are the Compaſs they ſail by, from whence thoſe Blaſts of Paſſion come, that drive us ſo uncertainly about, but 'tis without any peculiar inherent force of Direction more in one point than another.

Influence of ſounds indeterminate.

Thus far Muſick, as well as other things that gives us delight, and flatter the Senſes, may influence us. It may when we are under a lazy diſpoſition of mind, produce a degree of ſatisfaction ſomething above Indolence, but the motions of it are languid and indeterminate, that incline us only to an unactive eaſineſs of mind, a barren Pleaſure, that dies without Iſſue, with the Sounds that begat it; ſo little danger is there that *it ſhou'd be in the power of a few mercenary Hands, to play the People out of their Sences, to run away with their underſtanding, and wind their Paſſions about their Fingers, as they liſt.* I ſuppoſe few will take it upon this Gentlemans word, that *Muſick is almoſt as dangerous, as Gunpowder; and requires no leſs looking after, than the Preſs or the Mint.* P. 279.

This Gentleman ſure has a Noiſe of Muſick in his head, that has put the Stumm in his Brain into a Ferment, and cauſed

caused it to work over into all this windy fancy and froth. He has been a Tale-gathering among the Antients, and wou'd put his Romantick Rhapsody upon us for Authentick. But what is yet more unreasonable is, that without offering one Argument to prove either the reasonableness of his Opinion, or the reality of his Instances, he dogmatically asserts things monstrously, exceeding the stretch of the most capacious faith, and yet expects that, which alone is sufficient to destroy the credit of things infinitely more probable, the vast distance of time shou'd warrant the truth of them. As if he believed all Mankind to be proselyted to the Paradox of a certain Father *certum est quia impossibile*.

But if the Power of the Antient Music was so great, as he would perswade us, certainly *Timotheus* was a Fool for suffering
P. 280. *his harp to be seized for having one string*
P. 179. *above publick Allowance.* For if *altering the notes, were the way to have the Laws repealed, and to unsettle the Constitution*, he might with a twang, instead of taking a string from his Harp, have put one about the Magistrates Neck, and

for

for a Song have ſet himſelf at the head of Commonwealth. But this Author, who is all along a *Platoniſt* in his Philoſophy, is in this point an arrant Bigot. The whole ſcheme and ſtrain of the Platonick Philoſophy, is very romantick and whimſical, and like our Author's works, ſavours in every particular more ſtrongly of Fancy than Judgment, yet in nothing more, than in the imaginary power of Harmony, to which he aſcrib'd the Regulation, and Government of the Univerſe, and other Powers more fantaſtical and extravagant, than that of the *Pythagorean* numbers.

The Author a Platoniſt.

Now were I in as croſs a mood, and as much at leiſure to be impertinent as this Admirer of the Antient Muſick, who has ventur'd to affirm it as *certain, that our Improvements of this kind, are little better than Ale-houſe Crowds, with reſpect to theirs.* I cou'd with a certainty of Evidence, next to Demonſtration, maintain juſt the Reverſe of his Aſſertion, and prove that the Muſick of the Antients fell infinitely ſhort of the Modern in point of perfection, as well in Theory as Practice, and that,

Moral Eſſay, Vol. 2. P. 23.

H waving

waving the fabulous accounts, (which none but an Enthusiastick Bigot can seriously insist upon) all our Memoirs from Antiquity will scarce make the Harps of *Orpheus* and *Arion*, *&c.* to triumph over a Jew's Harp, or Rival a *Scotch* Bagpipe.

Not acquainted with the Subject he treats of.

But after all, it seems that he has been raving all this while in Pedantick Bombast, at he knows not what. He confesses that he is not acquainted with the *Play-House Musick*, and that he is no competent Judge. *I don't say this part of the Entertainment is directly vitious, because I am not willing to censure at Uncertainties.* How long, I wonder, has he been thus modest? had he been thus tender all along, he had suppress'd his whole Book, and the truth had suffer'd nothing by the loss of it. But in earnest, is he deaf? or does he wax up his ears when he goes to a Play, as (he says) *Ulysses* did, when he sail'd by the *Syrens*? No, neither; but, if we may believe him, he never comes there. *Those that frequent the Play-house are the most competent Judges.* Why that's honestly said, they are so; keep but to this, and there's some hope of

P. 278.

P. 278.

an

an accommodation. But alas! tho his zeal is a little Aguiſh now, the hot Fit comes on apace, and then right or wrong, *He muſt ſay, that the performances of this kind are much too fine for the place.* Ibid.

Tho he has never heard of one, nor ſeen t'other, yet he cries hang ſcruples, the Muſick muſt be bawdy, Atheiſtical Muſick, and the dancing *bold and lewd too ſometimes*. Now whether he means that the *Fiddler* himſelf is an Infidel of a *Fiddler*, or that he has an unbelieving *Crowd*, he is deſir'd to explain; for they are both left to be catechiz'd by him. But as for the ſounds produc'd betwixt them, care has been already taken to clear 'em, not only from guilt, but from all manner of meaning whatſoever. As for the dancing, which he calls bold, it may in one ſenſe be allow'd him; for it muſt be granted, that he that ventures his neck to dance upon the top of a Ladder, is a very bold Fellow. If this conceſſion be of any uſe to him, 'tis at his ſervice, whether the fraternity of Rope-dancers take it well at my hands or not. But for the Lewdneſs, I muſt remind him of his *His charge raſh.*

appeal to *those who frequent the Play-houses*, (whom he allows to be) *the most competent Judges*. But as their Judgment in these matters appears to be indisputable, so the modesty of the better part of 'em at least, (I mean the Ladies) who are the particular favourers of this part of the entertainment, is unquestionable. Their countenance therefore in so plain a matter, which being a question of fact, admits of no other decision, ought to be lookt upon as a definitive Judgment against him, and a sufficient vindication of our *Stage-dancing*.

Comparative Morality of the Vocal Musick of the Antient and Modern Stages.

I should here dismiss this point without further debate, if I did not find him closing it on his side with a notorious false assertion concerning the comparative Morality of the vocal Musick of the Ancient and Modern Stages, which, not designing to resume this branch of the Controversie any more, I am bound here to take notice of, and rectifie.

P. 280. *If the* English *Stage is more reserv'd than the* Roman *in the case above-mentioned. If they have any advantage in their* Instrumental *Musick, they lose it in their* Vocal. *Their Songs are often rampantly*

pantly lewd, and irreligious to a flaming excess. Here you have the Spirit, *and* Essence *of Vice drawn off strong scented, and thrown into a little compass. Now the* Antients, *as we have seen already, were inoffensive in this respect.*

Here again I am at a loss to know whether this is a fault of ignorance or design. But be it whether he pleases, the falseness of his assertion is unpardonably scandalous; for whether he has ventur'd to affirm beyond, or contrary to his knowledge, tis manifest he did it with an intention to impose upon his Readers, by asserting that which he could not know to be true, if he did not certainly know it to be false.

The Vocal Musick of the Antient Stage was of two sorts, one whereof was interspers'd among their Dramatick Writings, and consisted of Hymns, and Praises of their Gods, which were sung and danced by the Chorus to certain grave Aires and Measures. Here indeed the Poets must have been more impertinently and perversely lewd, than Mr *Collier*'s own corrupt imagination can positively make the Moderns to be, *Antient Vocal Musick.*

if they cou'd have found room for any thing very indecent; tho an ill natur'd Critick, with much less Gall or Straining, than Mr *Collier* has made use of, might shew, that they were not so absolutely inoffensive, as he affirms. The Chorus represented the Spectators, and their business was to make occasional reflections upon the several incidents and turn of the Fable, which was the artificial Instrument, the Antient Poets us'd to convey the Moral into the Audience, and teach 'em what to think upon such occasions, and how to behave themselves in reference to their Gods and Religion, and were therefore suppos'd to speak the sense of the Poet, or what at least he desir'd should be taken for such. Now I dare answer for the meanest of those Poets, upon whom this Author has made his reflections, that taking our Estimate of their understandings by his own diminutive survey of 'em, there is not amongst 'em one so arrant a Blockhead, as under the circumstances of the Antients to have taken more liberty, than they did.

Chorus, its office.

But

But if their Chorus was modeſt and harmleſs enough; the other part of their Stage Vocal Muſick will make ample amends, and make the lewdneſs of our Poets appear, as demure as a Quaker at a ſilent meeting. The Antients had luſtier Appetites, and ſtronger Digeſtions, than the Moderns, and their Poets cookt their Meſſes accordingly, they did not ſtand to make minc'd Meat, or artificially to ſteal in their Ribaldry, and diſguiſe it in nice Ragou's after the modern way; they were for whole Services, ſubſtantial Treats of Bawdy. Nor do I find, that it recoil'd upon the Stomachs of the generality of their Gueſts for many Ages together. The Reader I ſuppoſe will immediately gueſs that I mean the *Ludi Scenici*, which made the Amours of their Gods, and Heroes their ſubject, in which the lewdeſt actions were repreſented in the lewdeſt manner, and ſung in the moſt fulſome luſcious Verſe. Upon our Stage no ſuch Practices are allow'd, if a light wanton thought happens to creep into a Song, 'tis not ſuffer'd to ſhew its face bare, but is preſently maskt, and cloathed decently in Metaphor,

Their Mimi.

that many wou'd not ſuſpect the modeſty of it, and even the moſt ſqueamiſh can't take offence without offering violence; for it comes into your Company like a baſhful young ſinner, ſhe's civil company amongſt ſober people.

The Antients, 'tis plain, were not by abundance ſo ſcrupulous; if they had, thoſe lewd Drolls had never been compos'd, much leſs repreſented. But they were for all naked, without the vail of Figure or Dreſs, they requir'd Nudities in Speech, as well as Action, the Audience went away with ſatisfaction, and the Poet with applauſe.

By this we may ſee, that our *Stage* upon the compariſon is not ſo *rampantly lewd*, as Mr. *Collier* repreſents it, nor the ancient ſo inoffenſive. To dilate upon this head, would be both improper and impertinent; but theſe few hints, which, all that are acquainted with the practice of the *Roman* Stage, know to be true, whether Mr *Collier* does or not, may ſuffice to ſhew what an unfair Adverſary the Stage has met with; and to prove that he is not an upright, or not a competent Judge of theſe matters, in which he unauthoriz'd

undertakes

undertakes to determine, and arrogantly obtrudes his falſe Judgment upon us.

Another of his objections to the Stage in general, *is their dilating ſo much upon the Argument of Love.* P. 281.

His Objections from the Topick of Love, a Declamatory Rant.

Upon this article he is very laviſh of his Rhetorick, and lays about him in Tropes and Figures, he is got into his old road of declamation, and poſts Whip and Spur thro his Common place upon the ſubject. His fancy, like a Runaway-horſe, has got the Bit between her Teeth, and ramps over Hedge and Ditch, to the great danger of his Judgment; no bars or fences of ſenſe or reaſon can ſtop her Cariere, till jaded and out of Wind ſhe flags of her ſelf. Here then, let us come up with him.

I don't ſay the Stage fells all before 'em, and diſables the whole Audience: 'Tis a hard Battle, where none eſcape However, their Triumphs and their Trophies are unſpeakable. Neither need we much wonder at the matter. They are dangerouſly prepar'd for Conqueſt and Empire. There's Nature, and Paſſion, and Life in all the circumſtances of their Action. Their Declamation, P. 282.

clamation, their Mein, their Geſtures, and their Equipage, are very moving and ſignificant. Now when the Subject is agreeable, a lively repreſentation, and a paſſionate way of expreſſion, make wild work, and have a ſtrange force upon the Blood and Temper.

Meer Frenzy. What means all this unſeaſonable Cry *Fire, Fire*, where there is not ſo much as a ſpark? If the Audience were meer Tinder, they were out of danger. Sure the Author had Wildfire in his Brains, that the thoughts of the Players could put him into ſuch an uproar. 'Tis granted the Actreſſes may appear to advantage upon the Stage, and yet their *Triumphs* and *Trophies* not be ſo unutterable neither. For as *dangerouſly* as *they are prepar'd for Conqueſt and Empire*, the higheſt of their acqueſts, that I could ever hear of, was a good keeping, which has fallen to the ſhare of but a few of 'em; when multitudes of their Sex have arriv'd at greater matters without any ſuch formidable preparations. However, here's *Mein*, and *Equipage*, and the Author ſeems afraid, leſt the raw Squires of the Pit ſhould take 'em for *Quality*

Quality in earneſt, and be dazled with the luſtre of the ineſtimable Treaſure of Glaſs, and Tinſel, and ſo catch the real Itch of Love from their counterfeit Scrubbado. And truly there's as much reaſon to fear, they ſhou'd be purſu'd for their Fortunes, as their Love off the Stage.

To anſwer this Rant of Whimſie and Extravagance ſeriouſly, were as ridiculous an undertaking as *Hudibras*'s diſpute with the Managers of his Weſt Country Ovation, and by the ſample we have of our Antagoniſt, the iſſue wou'd probably be as cleanly. But if any one thinks an anſwer to this charge neceſſary, he may ſee as much as it will bear, and more than it deſerves, in a late Piece entitled, *A Review of Mr* Collier'*s View*, &c.

He has yet another charge upon the Stage left, and that is their encouraging of Revenge. *What is more common than Duels and Quarrelling, in their Characters of Figure? Thoſe Practices, which are infamous in Reaſon, Capital in Law, and Damnable in Religion, are the* Credit *of the Stage. Thus Rage and Reſentment, Blood and Barbarity are almoſt deified; Pride* P. 283.

Pride goes for Greatneſs, and Fiends and Heroes are made of the ſame metal. And thus the notion of Honour is miſ-ſtated, the Maxims of Chriſtianity deſpiſed, and the Peace of the World diſturb'd.

One would think he had found out another paſſage in *Valerius Maximus*, and that the *Civilis Sanguis* was abroach again. But *Rome* contented him then, now nothing leſs than the Peace of the whole World muſt be diſturb'd about a Bawble. Sure he thinks all the World of the *Country-Wife*'s opinion, that *the Player Men are the fineſt folks in it.*

Revenge not encouraged by the Stage.

But ſo far is Revenge from being encourag'd, or countenanc'd by the *Stage*, that to deſire and proſecute it, is almoſt always the mark of a *Tyrant*, or a *Villain*, in *Tragedy*, and *Poetick Juſtice* is done upon 'em for it ; it is generally turn'd upon their own heads, becomes the ſnare in which they are taken, and the immediate Inſtrument of their miſerable *Cataſtrophe*. Thus in the *Mourning Bride*, *Don Manuel*, to glut his luſt of Revenge, puts himſelf into the Place and Habit of his unhappy Priſoner, in order to ſurprize, betray, and inſult his own pious, afflicted Daugh-

Inſtance in the mourning Bride.

Daughter, over the ſuppos'd Body of her Murther'd Husband. In this poſture Poetick Juſtice overtakes him, and he is himſelf ſurpriz'd, miſtaken for him whom he repreſented, and ſtabb'd by a Creature of his own, the villanous Miniſter of his Tyranny, and his chief Favourite. Nothing is more common than this ſort of Juſtice in *Tragedy*, than which nothing can be more diametrically oppoſite, or a greater diſcouragement to ſuch barbarous Practices.

Paſſion not proper in Comedy.

Comedy indeed does not afford us many inſtances of this kind; *Rage* and *Barbarity* are Crimes not cognizable by her; they are of too deep a Dye, and the Indictment againſt 'em muſt be preferr'd at another Bar. If ſhe admits of any thoughts of Revenge, they muſt be ſuch as ſpring from the loweſt Claſs of Reſentments; that flow rather from a weakneſs of Judgment, or a perverſeneſs of Temper in the Parties that conceive 'em, than from the Juſtice of the Cauſe, or the greatneſs of the Provocation. Accordingly they ought to have no great malignity in 'em, they ought to ſpend themſelves in little Machinachinations, that aim no farther than the crossing of an Intrigue, the breaking of a Match, *&c.* and never to break out into open violence, or ravage in Mischief. The Passions have little to do in Comedy, every one there according to his capacity acts by design, or carelessly gives himself up to his humour, and indulges his pleasure and inclinations. This equality of temper of Mind, with the diversity of Humours, is what makes the business of Comedy. For while this general calm lasts, all busily pursue their several inclinations, and by various ways practise upon one another. And the Man of Pleasure follows his design upon the rich Knave's Wife, or Daughter, while the other is working into his Estate. The Cully is the Sharper's Exchequer, and the Fop the Parasite's, or Jilt's, *&c.* which, were the Passions too much agitated, and the Storm rais'd high, wou'd become impracticable; the Commerce wou'd be broken off, and the Plot wholly frustrated. Besides that both the Thoughts and Actions of Men, very much disorder'd by Passion, or fill'd with too deep Resentments, are naturally

rally violent and outrageous, and absolutely repugnant to the Genius, and destructive of the End of Comedy.

I grant that some Passions, such as *Love*, *Jealousie*, *Anger*, are frequently, and sometimes justly employ'd in Comedy; but then they are to be kept under, and must not be suffer'd to get the Ascendant, and domineer over Reason; if they do, they are no longer Comick Passions. Love must not carry 'em beyond Gallantry, and Gaiety of Spirit in the Pride of Success, nor further than a light disquiet, such as may excite their Industry, and whet their Invention under disappointments. Jealousie must not hurry 'em beyond their Cunning, or make their Impatience betray their Plot. Nor must their Anger break out into Flames, and push 'em upon rash unadvis'd Actions. Such Revenges therefore, as are the result of Passions so moderated, and circumstantiated, are allowable in Comedy; which can never produce any such terrible effects, as to deserve all these furious Claps of Thunder, which Mr *Collier* has discharg'd upon 'em.

Love, Jealousie, &c. how to be used in Comedy.

Horace

Horace indeed tells us, that Comedy will raiſe its voice ſometimes, and ſcold, and ſwagger violently.

Hor. Art. Poet.

Interdum tamen & Vocem Comœdia tollit,
Iratuſque Chremes tumido delitigat ore.

Expoſition of Horace's *Obſervation.*

But this very Inſtance ſhews, that the Paſſion of Comedy ſhou'd proceed no farther than Scolding, or Menaces. Nor do theſe fit every one's mouth, a Father, a Husband, or a Maſter, when they conceive their Authorities to be outrag'd, may be allow'd to vent their Indignation, to unload their Stomachs, and in the diſcharge of their Choler to break out into expreſſions of Threatning, or Reproach. But this is not to be allow'd upon ſlight Provocations, or to every Perſon in Comedy, who by their Place and Character can pretend to no ſuch Power, or Authority. Theſe Rants of Paſſion are not to be indulg'd amongſt Equals in Comedy, much leſs to Inferiours; becauſe ſuch provocations naturally produce effects too great, and too like Tragedy.

Chremes, in the *Heautontimorumenos* of *Terence*, who is produc'd by *Horace* as as an example of the heighth of Comick Passion, was a Husband, a Father, and a Master, injur'd (at least in his own Opinion) and abus'd in all these capacities by his Wife, his Son, and his Slave; his Authority slighted, and what was worse, his Understanding, (of which he was not a little conceited) affronted, and He practic'd upon, and made a Cully of by his Son, and his Slave, even in the exaltation of his Wit, and Cunning, by his own Plot and Management. These were provocations as high as Comedy could well admit, and consequently the rage, which they must naturally produce in a man of his Temper, and Opinion of his own Prudence, must be in proportion. Yet, what follows? *Chremes* does not lose his Reason in his Anger, * *His Son* (he tells you) *shall be reduc'd by Words to Reason: But as for* Syrus, *that Rogue, that had made him his Sport and his Laughing-stock, he would take such care of him, and put him in such a Trim, he should not dare*

Instance from Terence ex.

* Hic, ita ut liberos est æquum, dictis confutabitur. Sed Syrum—— Si vivo adeo exornatum dabo, adeo depexum, ut dum vivat meminerit semper mei: Qui sibi me pro ridiculo, ac delectamento putat. Non (ita me Dio ament) auderet facere hæc Viduæ mulieri, Quæ in me fecit.

to put his tricks upon a Widow hereafter, as he had done upon him. What is there in all this, that Mr *Collier* with all his Scruples about him can quarrel with? 'Tis true, a Scéne or two after he falls upon his Son, in very opprobrious terms, and calls him Drunkard, Blockhead, Spendthrift, Rake-hell, *&c.* But his Fury ſpends itſelf in a few words, and he comes immediately to compoſition with his Son, and is eaſily wrought to forgive even *Syrus* too, ſo that all his fury is ſpent, not to revenge the affront receiv'd,. but to reclaim his Son.

P. 283. *Tragedy in the Judgment of Ariſtotle.*

But Mr *Collier*'s Reſentments are of another Nature; *Rage, Bloud* and *Barbarity* are the Ingredients of 'em, and conſequently they're no compoſition for the Ingredients of *Comedy*; and *Tragedy*, as we have already ſhewn, is no encourager of 'em, but juſt the contrary. I can't ſee how he can make 'em to be of the proper growth of the Stage. For *Tragedy*, by giving 'em ſo odious a Dreſs and Air, and ſo calamitous a Cataſtrophe, as it always does, takes the moſt effectual courſe abſolutely to eradicate 'em, and to purge the minds of the Audience of thoſe turbulent Gueſts. Upon this

this Prospect it was, that *Aristotle* pronounc'd so largely in favour of Tragedy, *That it made Terror and Compassion the instruments, by which it purified and refined those very Passions in us, and all of the like nature.*

Arist. Poet. lib. cap. 6. δι' ἐλέου καὶ φόβου περαίνουσα τὴν τῶν παθημάτων κάθαρσιν. P. 283.

Duelling and Rencounters against the Nature and Laws of Comedy.

But, if *Tragedy* be no Encourager of such Disorders, much less can *Comedy*, which meddles not at all with 'em, be with any colour of Justice accus'd. *Comedy* has nothing to do with either *Fiends*, or *Heroes*, whatever Stuff, or *Metal* they may be made of. 'Tis indeed a Fault to bring Duels and Rencounters upon the Comick Stage, from which some of our Poets can't excuse themselves. But 'tis a Fault rather against the rules of Poetry, and true Dramatick Writing, than those of Morality. For, in Poetry as well as Painting, we are oblig'd to draw after the life, and consequently to copy as well the Blemishes as the Beauties of the Original; otherwise the finest colours we can bestow, are no better than gay dawbing. The fault therefore of the Poet lies not in shewing the imperfections of any of his Persons, but in shewing them improperly, and in the wrong place, which is an Error of his Judgment, not his Morals, and wou'd be as great if he ſhou'd untowardly produce in *Comedy* the higheſt Examples of Heroick Virtue and Fortitude.

Duel in Love in a Tub, againſt the rules of omedy.

An Inſtance of this kind we have in *the Comical Revenge, or Love in a Tub,* of Sir *George Etherege,* in which the Duel, and the Action of *Bruce* after it are of a ſtrain above *Comedy.* Thoſe niceties of Honour, and extravagancies of Jealouſie and Deſpair are unnatural on the *Comick* Stage; and the Reſcue from the Ruffians, for which *Bruce* in the ſame Scene is oblig'd to his Rival, however brave and generous an action it may appear, conſider'd ſimply in it ſelf, is a treſpaſs againſt Juſtice and Propriety of Manners in that place. Indeed that whole Walk of the Play, and the ſet of Characters peculiarly belonging to it, are more nearly related to the *Buskin,* than the *Sock,* and render the Play one of thoſe which we improperly call *Tragicomedies.* The other Walk, as 'tis one of the moſt diverting, ſo 'tis one of the moſt natural, and beſt contriv'd that ever came upon the *Stage.*

This

This may ſuffice to ſhew that a *Comick* Poet can't treſpaſs againſt the Laws of Morality in this nature, without offending against the Laws of his own Art; and conſequently that ſuch a fault ought rather to be lookt upon as an Error of his Judgment than of his Will, which may deſerve the correction of a *Critick*, but not of a *Moraliſt*.

But ſuppoſing that a Writer of *Comedy* ſhou'd (as many of 'em have done) either thro want of Skill or Caution in the conduct and management of his Plot, ſo embroil his Gentleman as to reduce him to the hard choice either of accepting or refuſing a challenge, the queſtion is, whether the Poet ought to allow him to accept, or anſwer it, like (what the World calls) a Man of Honour, or to introduce him and his Friend playing the Caſuiſts like *Philotimus* and *Philalethes*, and argue him out of his reſentments. In this caſe the Poets buſineſs is to draw his Picture, not to inform his Conſcience; which wou'd be as ridiculous in him, as for Sir *Godfrey Kneller* to ſet up for taking Confeſſions, and enquire into the Principles of any man, in order to take a

Comick Poet oblig'd to draw according to nature.

Collier's *Moral Eſſay about Duelling.*

I 3 true

true draught of his Face. The Poet, as well as the Painter is to follow, not to pretend to lead Nature: and if cuſtom and common practice have already determin'd the Point, whether, according to Equity, or not, the Poet exceeds his Commiſſion, if he preſumes to run counter to 'em. So that if a Comick Poet be ſo far overſeen, as to bring his Gentlemen into the Field, or but ſo far towards it as a Challenge, there is no taking up the matter without action, or (which is all one to Mr *Collier*'s objection) ſhewing a readineſs, and diſpoſition for it on both ſides. And the Poet ſtands in need of all his Skill, and Addreſs to ſave their Honour, and reconcile 'em without engagement.

No breach of Morality without offending againſt the Laws of the Stage.

Since therefore both by the nature of his ſubject, and the rules of his art, a *Dramatick* Poet is limited, and oblig'd, he can't reaſonably be charg'd with any thing, as a treſpaſs againſt Morality, in which he does not offend likewiſe againſt them. For *Dramatick* Poetry, like a Glaſs, ought neither to flatter, nor to abuſe in the Image which it reflects, but to give them their true colour and proportion, and is only valuable

able for being exact. If therefore any man diſlikes the Figures, which he ſees in it, he finds fault with Nature, not the Poet, if thoſe Pictures be drawn according to the life; and he might as juſtly ſnarl at the wiſe Providence which governs the world, becauſe he meets more ugly Faces than handſome ones, more Knaves and Fools than Honeſt and Wiſe men in it, and thoſe too, generally more proſperous and fortunate.

But becauſe ſome of thoſe Gentlemen, that have taken pains to proclaim War againſt the preſent Stage, and have publiſh'd their cenſures of it, ſeem to have no true Idea of the buſineſs of a *Dramatick* Poet, and have arraign'd ſome of the preſent Writers for the Stage, either through malice or miſ-underſtanding, of high crimes and miſ-demeanours, in many particulars for doing thoſe things which the duty of a Poet oblig'd 'em to; it may not be amiſs, for the information of Mr *Collier* more eſpecially, and thoſe whom his furious miſgrounded invectives may have miſ-led, to enquire into the nature and Laws of *Stage* Poetry, and the Practice of it, both among the Antients and Moderns, as far as concerns Morality, and the depending Controversie only, and no farther.

P. 1. Mr Collier in his end of Stage Poetry.

And here we may joyn issue with Mr *Collier*, and allow, that *The business of Plays is to recommend Virtue, and discountenance Vice; To shew the Uncertainty of Humane Greatness, the sudden turns of Fate, and the unhappy Conclusions of Violence and Injustice. 'Tis to expose the Singularities of Pride and Fancy, to make Folly and Falshood contemptible, and to bring every thing that is Ill under Infamy and Neglect.*

Mistaken in his method of prosecuting that end.

Thus we set out together, and are agreed upon the end of our Journey, but we differ about the road to it. Here therefore we part, and whether we shall meet again is the question. Mr *Collier*, by the tenour of his discourse thro the whole Book, seems to think, that there is no other way of encouraging Virtue, and suppressing Vice, open to the Poets, but declaiming for or against 'em, and wou'd therefore have *Plays* to be nothing but meer *Moral Dialogues*, wherein five or six persons shou'd meet, and with abundance of Zeal and Rhetorick preach up Virtue, and decry Vice. Hereupon

upon he falls upon the Poets with all the Rage and Fury imaginable, for introducing in their Plays vicious Characters, ſuch as in *Tragedy*, *Tyrants*, *Treacherous Stateſmen*, *Crafty Prieſts*, *Rebellious Subjects*, *&c.* In *Comedy*, *Libertines*, *Whores*, *Sharpers*, *Cullies*, *Fops*, *Pimps*, *Paraſites*, and the like.

Now, whether this conduct of the Poets, or his Cenſure of it be more juſtifiable, is the ſubject of our Enquiry. To facilitate which, it will be proper to eſtabliſh ſome certain Standard, by which we may meaſure the Morality or Immorality of a Dramatick Poem, and try thereby ſome of the moſt celebrated Pieces, as well of the Antients as Moderns; that their Beauties and Deformities of this kind, either abſolute or reſpective, may appear either ſeverally, or upon collation, and the Poet be accordingly juſtified or condemn'd.

Morals of a Play wherin ſhewn.

The Parts therefore of a Play, in which the Morals of the Play appear, are the *Fable*, the *Characters*, and the *Diſcourſe*. Of theſe the *Fable* (in Tragedy eſpecially) is the moſt conſiderable, being (according to *Ariſtotle*) the *Primum Mobile* by which all the other parts

Poet. c. 6. Ἀρχὴ μὲν ἐν καὶ οἷον ψυχὴ ὁ μῦθος τῆς τραγῳδίας.

parts are acted and govern'd; and the principal Instrument by which the Passions are weeded and purg'd, by laying before the Eyes of the Spectators examples of the miserable Catastrophe of Tyranny, Usurpation, Pride, Cruelty, and Ambition, *&c.* and to crown suffering Virtue with Success and Reward, or to punish the unjust Oppressors of it with Ruine and Destruction.

Folly and Knavery, the Subjects of Comedy.

In *Comedy*, as it acts in a lower Sphere, so the Persons are less considerable. *Knaves*, *Misers*, *Sots*, *Coquets*, *Fops*, *Jilts* and *Cullies*, all which *Comedy* corrects by rendring 'em unsuccessful, and submitting them in her Fable; to the Practices and Stratagems of others, after such a manner, as to expose both Knavery, Vanity, and Affectation, in the conclusion, or winding up, to the Scorn and Derision of the Spectators. And thus by making Folly and Knavery ridiculous to the View, Comedy gains her end, stops the contagion, and prevents the imitation more effectually than even Philosophy herself, who deals only in Precept can do, as *Horace*, and before him *Aristotle* have observ'd, by presenting that lively to the Sight, which

which the other can only inculcate in words.

Segnius irritant animos demissa per aures, De Art.
Quam quæ sunt oculis subjecta fidelibus. Poet.

Thus while in the large Forest of Humane Affections, *Tragedy* labours to fell those sturdy overgrown Plants the Passions, *Comedy* employs itself in grubbing up the underwood of Vice, Folly and Affectation ; and if its Operations are of less importance than those of the former, they make ample amends by their more extended, and almost universal Influence.

But this it seems is not the design of Præf.Pag. the Modern *Stage* Poets ; *Virtue* and *Re-* 1, 2. *gularity* are their *Great Enemies* ; and to promote *Lewdness* and *Atheism*, and to *destroy Principles is their business*, if we may believe Mr *Collier*, who has taken abundance of malicious Pains to incense the World against 'em ; and like an experienc'd Incendiary, not only gives the Fire, and blows the Coals, but furnishes Fuel of his own too, to encrease the Flame.

To

Mr Col-lier's *Character of the Ancient Poets invidious.*

To inflame the Reckoning of the Modern Poets, especially the *English*, by the comparison, he enlarges very much upon the great Modesty and Regard which the *Antients* had to Vertue, and *Decorum*, fallly insinuating thereby as great Neglect and Violation of 'em among the *Moderns*. What he has said in Commendation of the Antients, simply and abstractedly taken, without any Application of comparison,or relation to those that have exercis'd themselves the same way in this Age,and in our Country, may be allow'd as their due; And Mr *Collier*'s deference to the just merits of those great Genius's of Antiquity wou'd turn to his own Praise, if it were paid only as a debt to Justice. But proceeding from a disingenuous design, invidiously to depreciate the worth, and blacken the reputation of others, the Justice is sunk in the Malice of it, and the venom couch'd under it gives an ill Complexion to the fairest Part of his Productions. That this was the motive that induc'd Mr *Collier* to speak honourably of the Stage Poets, is apparent from his perpetual grumbling, and snarling at 'em, even in the midst of his most favoura-

ble

ble account of 'em. For tho upon many occasions he declares very largely in their favour, yet 'tis only to balance and ſway the competition betwixt them and the Moderns on their ſide, and by raiſing the value of their Characters, to depreſs the others in the eſteem of the World. This partiality will plainly appear upon the examination of ſome of thoſe Pieces of Antiquity, which Mr *Collier* ſo juſtly commends, with ſome of thoſe of later production, which he ſo unjnſtly decries.

Fable the principal part of a Play.

Mr *Collier* is not content to charge the *Engliſh* Poets with Faults of Negligence, or even of licentious wantonneſs; but he treats 'em with the utmoſt deſpight, and brands 'em with the Infamy of a profeſs'd Hatred to Virtue, a ſtudied Lewdneſs, aud of ſubverting the end and uſe of their Art. If this were really their Aim, unqueſtionably the Fable, which is the Principal Part, and of greateſt Influence and Operation, is contriv'd and modell'd ſo as to be ſerviceable to their grand deſign. That this may more certainly appear, we ſhall take the Pains to analize ſome of thoſe Plays, at which Mr *Collier* takes greateſt offence,

offence, together with ſome of the moſt celebrated of Antiquity.

The *Oedipus Tyrannus* of *Sophocles* has by the univerſal conſent of the learned of all Ages, the greateſt reputation of the *Dramatick* Performances of Antiquity, I ſhall therefore begin with that, and ſhew that the Fable of that deſervedly admir'd Piece is by no means ſo noble, inſtructive, and ſerviceable to Virtue, by its main or general Moral, as many of thoſe Plays, againſt which and their Authors Mr *Collier* inveighs with ſo much Bitterneſs.

Fable of the Oedipus *of* Sophocles..

The Fable of the *Oedipus* is this; *Laius*, the Father of *Oedipus*, and King of *Thebes*, was inform'd by an Oracle, that it was his fate to be ſlain by his own Son, who ſhould be born of his Wife *Jocaſta*. To elude the threats of the Oracle, *Laius*, as ſoon as the Child was born, delivers him to one of his Servants to be murder'd. This man, mov'd to compaſſion by the innocence of the Babe, inſtead of taking away his life, perforating both his Feet, and paſſing a Bend thro 'em, hang'd him up by the Heels, and left him to the diſpoſal of Providence. In this poſture he was found

found by a Domeſtick of *Polybus* King of *Corinth*, who, taking him down, carried him to his Maſter, who being childleſs, receiv'd, educated, and own'd him as his own. *Oedipus* being at length grown up, and being in a conteſt of words with a *Corinthian*, he reproach'd with his unknown Birth, and being a Foundling, of which till that moment he had by the expreſs order of *Polybus*, been kept in ignorance, reſolves to conſult the Oracle at *Delphi* about his Parentage, and is order'd by the Oracle to ſeek no further, for that it was his deſtiny to kill his Father, and beget Children upon his Mother. Upon this anſwer, he reſolves for ever to abandon *Corinth*, his ſuppos'd Country, and in order thereto, takes his way towards *Thebes*, and on the Road meets *Laius*, and a quarrel ariſing between 'em, he kills him, and all his followers, one excepted, to whom upon his ſupplication he gives quarter. Arriving at *Thebes*, he finds that City in great confuſion, both for the loſs of their King, whom he knew not to be the perſon ſlain by him upon the Road, and for the prodigious ravage and waſte committed by the Monſter *Sphinx*, who di-

diſtreſs'd 'em ſo, that they durſt ſcarce ſtir out of their Walls. To rid themſelves of the terrour of this Monſter, the *Thebans* offer their Queen and Crown to any man that could reſolve the Riddle propounded by the *Sphinx*, upon the reſolution of which only they were to be quit of her. This *Oedipus*, notwithſtanding the miſcarriage of divers before him, who failing in their attempt were deſtroy'd by her, undertakes, and ſucceeding in it, the Monſter breaks her own Neck, and he in reward, receives the Crown, and Queen to Wife. For ſome time *Oedipus* governs with great prudence, and has ſeveral Children by *Jocaſta.* At length a furious Plague ariſing, and making great Havock in the City, *Oedipus* deputes *Creon* to the Oracle, to conſult about the Cauſes of, and Means to be deliver'd from the Peſtilence.

Thus far the Hiſtory of *Oedipus* proceeds before the Action of the Play commences; and tho the whole action of the Play naturally ariſes from this antecedent part, yet *Sophocles* has very artificially reſerv'd it to be deliver'd by way of Narration at the unravelling of the

the Plot, which is the moſt natural and beautiful of all Antiquity. But what is only conſiderable to our purpoſe is, that hitherto *Oedipus* bears the character of a Juſt and a Wiſe man; and if he be involv'd in any thing that bears an appearance of Guilt, invincible Ignorance (which the Schoolmen hold to be a good Plea) is his excuſe.

But if he is hitherto innocent of any intentional Guilt, he is thro the whole courſe of the Action exemplarily pious. At his firſt appearance upon the Stage, he ſhews an extraordinary concern for the calamities of his Country, and an anxious ſolicitude for a Remedy. *Jupiter's Prieſt* addreſſes to him, as if he were their tutelar Deity, and tells him, that 'twas this miſerable experiment of his being unable to relieve 'em, that had convinc'd him, and thoſe with him, *that he was not equal to the Gods, and had made 'em have recourſe to their Altars.*

Piety of Oedipus.

Θεοῖσι μὲν νυν οὐκ ἰσούμενόν σ' ἐγὼ,
οὐδ' οἵδε παῖδες, ἑζόμεσθ' ἐφέστιοι.

Sophocl. Oedip. Tyrann.

This was a bold complement from a *Prieſt*, and the *Prieſt* of *Jupiter* too, the

Soveraign of the Gods. But not to insist too much upon this Passage, *Creon* enters, and breaks off the Parley betwixt 'em; He brings word from the Oracle, that the Murtherer of *Laius* must be expell'd the Territories of *Thebes*. Who was this Murtherer was yet a Secret, the Oracle not making that discovery. *Oedipus* hereupon summons a meeting of the People, and makes Proclamation, that if any one privy to the Fact wou'd come in, and make a discovery, he shou'd, if concern'd therein, be indemnified in his Person, and be oblig'd only to leave *Thebes*. But that if he cou'd inform of any other Person therein concern'd, he shou'd be liberally rewarded, and purchase his Favour by such Discovery. And if any one, conscious of this matter, did out of fear for himself or his Friend, obstinately refuse to break silence, he requir'd all his Subjects not to give him harbour or sustenance, or to hold any manner of Commerce or Correspondence with him. After this he proceeds to imprecate the Actor or Actors of this Regicide, and extends the curse to his own House, if with his privity he was protected there.

Oedipus' *Proclamation.*

But

But this method failing to produce the desir'd effect, he consults *Tiresias* the Prophet, by whom *Oedipus* himself is accus'd of killing his Father, and committing Incest with his Mother; which Accusation being afterwards confirm'd by the concurring report of the old Servant of *Laius*, by whom he was expos'd in his Infancy, and of the Domestick of *Polybus*, despairing in the horrour of these involuntary crimes, he tears out his own Eyes; and *Jocasta*, who equally ignorant was involv'd in the guilt of Incest, hangs herself.

This Plot, however noble and beautiful to admiration, for the Structure and Contrivance of it, is yet very deficient in the Moral, which has nothing great or serviceable to Virtue in it. It may indeed serve to put us in mind of the Lubricity of Fortune, and the Instability of human Greatness. And this use *Sophocles* himself makes of it; for the *Chorus* closes the Tragedy with this remark, by way of advice to the Audience, *that they should not rashly measure any man's Felicity by his present Fortune, but wait his extremest Moments, to make a true estimate of his Happiness.*

Moral of the Fable defective.

Χο. Ω πάτρας Θήβης ἔνοικοι λεύσσετ', Οἰδίπους ὅδε,
Ὃς τὰ κλείν' αἰνίγματ' ᾔδει, καὶ κράτιστος ἦν ἀνήρ,
Ὅς τις οὐ ζήλῳ πολιτῶν καὶ τύχαις ἐπιβλέπων,
Εἰς ὅσον κλύδωνα δεινῆς συμφορᾶς ἐλήλυθεν;
Ὧν θνητὸν ὄντ' ἐκείνην τὴν τελευταίαν ἰδεῖν
Ἡμέραν ἐπισκοποῦντα, μηδὲν ὀλβίζειν, πρὶν ἂν
Τέρμα τοῦ βίου περάσῃ, μηδὲν ἀλγεινὸν παθών.

Moral of the English Oedipus *the same.*

Mr *Dryden*, who has borrow'd this Story from *Sophocles*, has ſumm'd up his Moral in the two concluding lines of his Play, in which not only the application ſeems to be the ſame, but the Lines themſelves are a contracted Paraphraſe of *Sophocles* own concluſion.

Let none, tho ne're ſo virtuous, great, and high,
Be judg'd entirely bleſt before they dye.

Meerly ſpeculative.

This Moral, as it carries nothing in it but a lazy, unactive ſpeculation, can be no great Incentive to Virtue ; ſo on the other hand, as it lays before us the Miſeries and Calamitous Exit of a perſon of ſo Heroick Virtue, it ſeems to carry matter of diſcouragement along with

with it; ſince the moſt conſummate Virtue meets with ſo diſproportionate a return.

But with Reverence to the Aſhes of *Sophocles*, and ſubmiſſion to the better Judgment of Mr *Dryden*, this does not ſeem to be the true and genuine Moral of this Fable. For according to this Moral, the misfortune of *Oedipus* ought to have been the reſult of a kind of negligent Oſcitation in the Gods, and a looſe adminiſtration of Providence. Whereas on the contrary it appears, that all the Actions of *Oedipus*, as well thoſe that were Pious, Wiſe, and Brave, as thoſe that were Criminal, or rather Unfortunate, were the neceſſary and unavoidable Conſequences of a fixt decree of Fate, backt by ſeveral Oracles, carried on, and brought about by variety of Miraculous or Providential Incidents. This *Tireſias* ſeems to hint plainly to *Oedipus*, when he tells him. *Not very natural.*

Αὕτη γε μέντοι σ' ἡ τύχη διώλεσεν.
Fortune herſelf, (or Fate) deſtroys thee;

And *Oedipus* himself, finding by the relation of *Jocasta*, that the circumstances of the death of *Laius*, agreed with those of the persons slain by him on the Road, and beginning to be convinc'd of his own guilt, ushers in his account of that action, with the fatal necessity that oblig'd him to leave his own Country; and relates his Piety, as 'twere by way of alleviation for what follows. He pleads, that being inform'd by the Oracle, that he should kill his Father, and commit Incest with his Mother, he had quitted the expectation of a Crown, and made himself a voluntary, and perpetual Exile from *Corinth*, to avoid the Crimes he was threatned with.

Κἀγὼ πακούσας ταῦτα, τὴν Κορινθίαν
Ἄστροις τὸ λοιπὸν ἐκμετρούμενος χθόνα,
Ἔφευγον ἔνθα μήποτ' ὀψοίμην κακῶν
Χρησμῶν ὀνείδη τῶν εμῶν τελούμενα.

The *English Oedipus* is more plain, and expresses himself more clearly in defence of his Innocence, ev'n while he suspects himself to have been an Actor in the Tragedy of *Laius*.

To

To you good Gods, I make my last appeal, Oed p. 39.
Or clear my Virtues, or my Crime reveal:
If wandring in the Maze of Fate I run,
And backward trod the paths I thought to shun,
Impute my Errours to your own decree;
My Hands are guilty, but my Heart is free.

Here *Oedipus* ſeems to ſuſpect the truth of the matter, and alledges his own Ignorance, and the decree of the Gods in his Juſtification; but the Ghoſt of *Laius* clears the point of Fatality, and makes a better Apology for *Oedipus*, than 'twas poſſible for him to do for himſelf.

But he who holds my Crown, Oh must I speak? Oed. p. 33.
Was doom'd to do what Nature most abhors;
The Gods foresaw it, and forbad his being,

 Before

Before he yet was born. I broke their Laws.
And cloath'd with flesh, the pre-existing Soul.
Some kinder Power, too weak for destiny,
Took pity, and indu'd his new form'd Mass
With Temperance, Justice, Prudence, Fortitude,
And every kingly Virtue; but in vain.
For Fate, that sent him hoodwinkt to the world,
Perform'd its work by his mistaken hands.

These instances consider'd, together with the Order, Contrivance and Nature of the Fable, as well of the *Greek*, as the *English* Poem, will readily point out to us a greater Moral, and more naturally arising from the subject, than that which the two Poets have assign'd. For it seems plainly to hold forth to us, *the irresistable Power of Fate, and the Vanity of human Wisdom, when oppos'd to the immutable decrees of Providence, which converts to its own purposes, all our endeavours*

Proper Moral.

deavours to defeat 'em, and makes our very Opposition subservient to its own designs.

Seneca, who has taken this Fable from *Sophocles*, with very little alteration, has however given this turn to the Application, in conformity to the Doctrine of the *Stoicks*, who were the Predestinarians of Antiquity, and held as Ours do, a Fatality, that directed and controul'd all human Actions, that all things came to pass by pre-ordination and invincible necessity, and that there was no such thing as a free Agent in the World.

Moral of Seneca

Some Learned Men are of opinion, that this Tragedy was written by *Seneca* the *Philosopher*, and this change of the *Sophoclean* Moral, in favour of his Principles, seems to be no despicable Argument on their side. But whether they be in the right or wrong, I can't but wonder that Mr *Dryden* should overlook this alteration, or rather amendment to *Sophocles*'s Moral, it being the principal part of the Play, and the mark at which all is levell'd. But perhaps Mr *Dryden* being justly prepossessed for the performance of *Sophocles* in preference to *Seneca*'s, his aim was not so much

Seneca *the Philosopher suppos'd the Author.*

His Morals neglected by the Authors of the English Oedipus.

much to enquire after any improvements, as additions to *Sophocles's* design, and by that means let slip this, which was not to his purpose, which was to fit it up to the *English* Stage; for the use of which it needed not correction, so much as enlargement; the simplicity of the Original Fable and the Chasms, which the omission of the *Chorus* must necessarily make, requiring to be fill'd up, and supply'd with an *Underplot* and proper *Episodes*. And indeed he seems to confess as much, when he says, that *Seneca* supply'd *'em with no new hint but only a relation, which he makes of his* Tyresias *raising the Ghost of* Laius.

Preface to Oedip.

But having declar'd for the *Moral* of *Seneca*, as more natural than that of *Sophocles*, considering the disproportion both of Reputation and Merit of these two Authors in the *Dramatick* way, I must expect the censure of those Criticks, that judge by wholesale, or hearsay, that will admit of no errour in any Author, that themselves, or those, in whom they have an implicit Faith, admire; nor allow any Graces to him, that has not the good fortune to be their Favourite. I shall therefore produce *Seneca's ca*'s application at large in his own words, as I have already done *Sophocles*'s, and then back my opinion with an Obſervation or two, drawn from the ſtate of the Fable, as it lies in theſe Authors, and leave 'em to the courteſie of the Reader.

The laſt Song of the *Chorus* in *Seneca*, which is what the Poet delivers by way of Inſtruction, or Application to the Audience, runs thus.

Cho. *Fatis agimur : cedite fatis.* Senec. Oedip. p. 107.
Non ſolicitæ poſſunt curæ
Mutare rati ſtamina fuſi.
Quicquid patimur mortale genus,
Quicquid facimus, venit ex alto :
Servatq; ſua decreta colus
Lacheſis, dura revoluta manu
Omnia certo tramite vadunt ;
Primuſq; dies dedit extremum,
Non illa deo vertiſſe licet,
Quæ nexa ſuis currunt cauſis.
It cuiq; ratus, prece non ulla
Mobilis, ordo. Multis ipſum
Timuiſſe nocet. *Multi ad fatum*
Venere ſuum, dum fata timent.

The

Summ of Seneca's *Moral.*

The summ of this is; *That there is* (according to the Doctrine of the Stoicks) *an over-ruling Providence, or Fate, that disposes and governs all things; That the Sources of mens Fortunes, and the Springs of their Actions are plac'd out of their reach, inaccessible to human Prudence, and inflexible to Entreaties; that they move in a constant course, inviolable even to the Gods themselves; that causes and their effects are inseparably linkt, the first day (of Life) determining the last; that the Caution of many has been destructive to 'em, and that in shunning their Fate, they have run upon it.*

That this is the most natural Application, the very contrivance of the Fable in all these three Plays, will sufficiently make out. *Seneca*, and the *English Authors* have, in imitation of *Sophocles*, made the *Parricide* and *Incest* of *Oedipus* the proper Act, and Deed of *Fate*, of which he was only the unhappy and unwilling Instrument. Both his Father and himself had been forewarn'd, and had us'd their utmost endeavours to evade the calamities that threatned 'em. But those very efforts, however seemingly prudent, became the Snare in which

which they were taken, and the means of verifying the Prediction of the Oracle. For the exposing *Oedipus* in his Infancy, was the occasion of his Ignorance of his true Parents, and that Ignorance of all his ensuing miseries. All these Authors give us a high Idea of his Virtue and Prudence; and *Seneca* as well as the aforecited Authors, makes him sacrifice his Expectations of a Crown, and become a voluntary Exile out of an Abhorrence of those Crimes, which were predicted of him.

Hic me Paternis expulit regnis Timor.
This fear has banish'd me my Fathers Realm.

Oedipus's Justification of himself.

And when he had been accus'd of the murder of *Laius*, upon the Information of the Gods, he appeals to his own Conscience for his Innocence.

Obiisse nostro Laium scelere autumant
Superi Inferiq; sed animus contra innocens.
Sibiq; melius quam Deis notus, negat.

The

The Gods accuſe me ; but my guiltleſs mind
The better Judge acquits me.

And in the next Scene upon the news of *Polybus*'s death, he cries out,

Genitor ſine ulla cæde defunctus jacet,
Teſtor, licet jam tollere ad cælum pie
Puras nec ulla ſcelere metuentes manus.
Extinct my Father by a Bloudleſs death!
Now I may ſtretch to Heaven my guiltleſs hands
Fearleſs of any ſtain.

Harmony of the Greek, Roman, *and* Engliſh *Authors.*

Thus they all agree to make him juſt and virtuous in his Intentions to an Heroick Pitch, yet they involve him in a Fatal Neceſſity even before his Birth, of acting thoſe things, to which in his Nature he had the greateſt abhorrence, and make his Piety and Averſion to Wickedneſs, the very means to entrap and entangle him in that Guilt, which he ſo induſtriouſly fled from, and which occa-

occasioned the Calamities, that afterwards befel both himself and Family.

The structure and disposition of this Fable, afford no occasion of complaint, or reflection upon the Levity of Fortune, or the Instability of Human Affairs. For nothing is more evident, than the steady and regular administration of Providence thro the whole course of the misfortunes of *Oedipus*, and his Family. Nothing befel them, which was not predicted long before hand, and of which they had not a terrible apprehension, as well as a certain Expectation. And when they bent their endeavours to defeat the decrees of Fate, such a manifest Series of Providential Incidents attends their management, as suffices not only to baffle their Cunning and Devices, but likewise to shew the Uncontrolableness and Superiority of that Power, which influenced their Counsels, and serv'd itself of their Presumption, as the immediate Instrument to accomplish, and effect its Purposes, and at the same time to demonstrate the Vanity of Humane opposition to the Will of Destiny.

Levity of Fortune not the occasion of the Fall of Oedipus.

Opposition of Providence.

Had

Preſumpti-on of Laius. Had *Laius* ſubmitted himſelf to the Pleaſure of Providence, and not preſum'd to have thwarted the Divine Appointment, and triumphed over his Deſtiny, his Son had not been ignorant of his true Parentage; and being a perſon of Inclinations ſo extraordinary Virtuous, 'tis morally impoſſible he ſhould willingly have incurr'd the guilt of two Crimes of ſo monſtrous a Size as *Parricide* and *Inceſt*. Or had *Oedipus* ſubmiſſively reſigned himſelf to the Conduct and Direction of Fate; whatever his Regret and Abhorrence of his predicted Fortune had been, he had return'd to *Corinth*, and his Patience, and Reſignation had avoided that Miſery, which his miſtaken Piety and Oppoſition brought afterwards upon his head.

Another Moral. This conſideration may ſupply us with another Moral to this Fable, different from any (that I know of) hitherto rais'd upon it by any Poet, either Antient or Modern. It may inſtruct us, *that the Will of Heaven is not to be diſputed by Mortals, how ſevere ſoever, even to Injuſtice, the Conditions of it may ſeem to us; and that whoever ſets up his own Wiſdom in oppoſition to it, ſhall in that Preſumption*

ſumption meet both his Crime and his Puniſhment.

Nothing, if we conſider it ſimply in itſelf, could be more heroically pious than the reſolution of *Oedipus* to abandon a Crown, his Parents and Country, rather than ſuffer thoſe Pollutions with which he was threatned. But if we conſider the Impiety of advancing his own Judgment in his conceit above that of his Gods, and thinking by his own Wiſdom, to reverſe the immutable decrees of deſtiny, his Vanity deſerv'd the heavieſt chaſtiſement. The ſame may be ſaid of his Father. It may be objected, that this irreſiſtible Predeſtination was not ſo univerſally receiv'd an Opinion among the Antient Heathens, but that many held the contrary; and that conſequently 'tis but ſuppoſing *Oedipus* one of the number, and my Moral falls to the ground. I grant it does ſo, if he were, but the contrary appears from the Story itſelf. For if *Oedipus* did not believe ſuch a Fatality, why did he upon the credit of an Oracle, which muſt ſignifie no more to him than one of *Partridge*, or *Gadbury*'s Aſtrological Banters, leave his Friends, and his

Preſumption of Oedipus.

Oedipus *in* Sophocles, *and the reſt of the Tragedians a Predeſtinarian.*

great Expectations? But this ſuppoſes him a rank Fool, to abdicate for a *tale of a Tub*, a Story that he did not believe. If he did believe, he ought not to eſcape the Cenſure and Puniſhment of a raſh preſumptuous man, for ſuffering his Vanity to triumph over his Faith, and daring upon an inſolent opinion of his own Ability to inſult his Religion, and hope to prevail againſt, and defeat the purpoſes of Fate.

French *Moral.*

Some French Criticks, that ſeem ſenſible of the defect of the Moral in *Sophocles*, have endeavoured to ſupply that want, by ſtarting an imaginary Guilt, and impute as a Crime to *Oedipus*, his curioſity to know his Fate. I call it an imaginary Guilt, becauſe I think it is urg'd againſt him without Foundation. For certainly it could never be a Sin in him, when his Parentage was become doubtful to him, to have recourſe to ſuch means, as his Religion allow'd, to clear up his doubts, and take off the Reproach that was thrown upon him. Divination was ſo far from being a Criminal Art among the Ancient Heathens, that it was practic'd with great Reputation in all

Necromancy and all ſorts of Divination allowed by the Religion of the Heathens.

its

its ſeveral kinds, and the Profeſſors of any part of it, were eſteemed as Prophets, and held in great veneration. It could not therefore be ſcandalous to conſult 'em upon any occaſion, much leſs the Oracle of *Apollo*; to repair to which, was thought an act of high Devotion, and was the conſtant Practice of all the Cities and States of *Greece*, upon all great and ſudden Emergencies. But their miſtake lies in raiſing a *Chriſtian* Moral upon a *Pagan* bottom; to fill up, they have grafted a Doctrine many ages younger upon the old Stock, and piec'd out a defect with an Abſurdity.

Conjecture at the Reaſons that induc'd the Authors of the English Oedipus *to prefer the* Greek *Moral to the* Latine.

I am apt to think upon conſideration, that the Authors of the *Engliſh Oedipus*, in adhering to the ſimple old *Greek* Moral, acted rather by Judgment and Choice, than Overſight. For the *Moral* of *Seneca*, tho more naturally deducible from the Story, is yet leſs ſerviceable, or (to ſpeak more properly) more deſtructive to Practical Morality, as preaching up the Doctrine of abſolute and univerſal Predeſtination, by which men are denied the liberty of ſo much as a thought, as free Agents, and are ſuppos'd to be acted, and workt like Machines by an in-

invisible, irresistible Agent, which winds 'em up like Watches, and orders their several Movements. This Doctrine, as it destroys all title to Merit from the best, so it takes off all fear of Guilt from the most villanous actions, and must necessarily (if heartily believ'd) discourage men from the severer and more troublesome Duties of Religion, and Morality at least, and dispose them to resign themselves loosely up to the government of their Appetites, and indulge their sensual Inclinations; to gratify which could be no sin, to oppose 'em no Virtue, and deserve neither blame nor thanks, according to this Principle.

Seneca's *Moral not proper for the* English *Stage.*

Besides the unserviceableness of this Moral to the general end of *Dramatick* Poetry, it was upon that Score disabled for the particular service of the *English Stage*, where it could not hope for a favourable Reception; and might therefore be by these Authors judiciously rejected. For tho this Musty Rag of Heathen *Stoicism* be still worn by a Party amongst us, that affect to distinguish themselves by Opposition, and Contradiction, tho to their own Principles,

ciples, and that pretend to act contrary to the natural result of their Opinion, and profess a severer Morality than their Neighbours; yet by the more Polite and Civilized Part of the Nation, who are the chief Frequenters, and Support of the *Dramatick* Performances, it has been long left off, as a Principle destructive to Humanity, Virtue, and all good Manners; and consequently would have been exploded upon the Stage, and hazarded the success of the whole Piece.

Greek *and* Roman *Moral unserviceable to virtue.*

But whether this Moral were neglected by 'em out of design or oversight, is not much to our purpose. 'Tis evident, that neither the *Greek* nor *Latin* Moral, have any tendency to the promotion of Virtue, and the Reformation of Manners, but rather to the contrary. So that if Mr *Collier* has any thing of this Nature to object against any of the present Stage Poets, they may defend, or at least excuse such a slip by this Precedent, which being the Master-piece not only of *Sophocles*, but of all Antiquity; for that reason, I hope Mr *Collier* (who has already declar'd, that this Author has *nothing but what is great and solemn throughout*) will not charge him

P. 28.

him with any ill deſign, or acting upon Malice prepenſe againſt Virtue. But if he ſhould, he has already taken his Tryal before *Ariſtotle*, a more competent and more upright Judge, and ſtands acquitted on Record, and muſt be allow'd to be *rectus in Curia.*

Oedipus, *why ſo minutely examined.*

I have been the more particular in examining the general Moral of this Play, and have conſider'd not only what has been made of it, but what might have been drawn from it, that I might for the remainder be excus'd from the trouble of deſcending to minute circumſtances, and for the future be allow'd to ſumm up what I have to ſay to any other Plays of Antiquity upon this general head of the Fable, and ſo proceed to our Poets, with whom alſo I ſhall be as brief as the matter will allow me.

The reſt of *Sophocles*'s Plays, being much leſs conſiderable for their Succeſs in the World, I ſhall diſpatch the conſideration of 'em in as few words as poſſible. His *Ajax Flagellifer* ſtands firſt in order, and affords us no great matter to reflect upon.

Fable of of Ajax Flagellifer.

Ajax, diſappointed and diſgrac'd in his ſuit for the Arms of *Achilles*, reſents extreamly

treamly the Iujury and Indignity , and reſolves to be reveng'd upon the whole *Grecian* Army. In order thereto he makes a Sally from his Quarter by night, in order to kill all the Principal Officers. *Minerva*, to divert the miſchief intended, infatuates him, and turns him looſe upon ſome herds of Cattle, amongſt whom, miſtaking 'em for *Greeks*, he makes moſt terrible havock; and returning to his Tent and Sences in the morning, he perceives his Errour, thro the confuſion , ſhame, and vexation of which, he grows deſperate, falls upon his Sword, and dies. This is the whole of the *Fable*. For the conteſt that follows between *Teucer*, *Menelaus*, and *Agamemnon*, is an Epiſode detach'd from, and has nothing to do with, and ſcarce any dependance upon the main Action.

Here we ſee a man of Impetuous, Ungovernable Paſſion, and of a Nice, Capricious Honour, that conceives himſelf injur'd in the moſt ſenſible part, his honour, and meditates a Revenge proportioned to the Fierceneſs of his Temper, and the imagin'd Greatneſs of the Affront. *Minerva* interpoſes, and turns his Rage, and Fury, firſt to his further diſgrace, and then to his deſtruction.

Moral ſomewhat obſcure. The *Moral* of this Play is not very obvious, and *Sophocles* himſelf does not hint it at or near the concluſion of the Play, but leaves it to be pickt out by the Audience, or Readers; which may be done two ways. Firſt, By conſidering the Quality of the Inſtrument or Engine of *Ajax*'s Ruine, which was a *Goddeſs*; and the manner of bringing it about, which was by making him ridiculous thro a *Deceptio Viſus*, or an Illuſion of the Sight; and then the *Moral* will be,

Moral. Quos Deus vult perdere, prius dementat.

When the Gods reſolve upon a mans ruin, they take away his Wits.

Or 2dly, We may conſider the Character of the Perſon, a man of Undaunted Boldneſs, and Turbulent Headſtrong Paſſions, and the Nature of his Attempt, which was to kill all the *Grecian* Chiefs; and then the Moral may be

——Qui

—Qui non moderabitur Iræ
Infectum volet esse Dolor quod suaserit.— 2d Moral.

He that suffers himself to be precipitated into action by his Rage, will have cause to rue the effects of it.

The first of these is the most genuine, and natural. For the misfortune of *Ajax* seems not to arise so much from a repentance of his Undertaking, as from indignation, and a bitter sense of the Scorn and Contempt he had drawn upon himself by so ridiculous a miscarriage, and the trick put upon him by *Minerva*. This is all that naturally arises from the Action; and the Author, who seems sensible of the barenness of his Plot, forages without his lines to subsist his Moral. By this means he has provided himself of a noble Moral, which he intimates in the close of the first Scene, betwixt *Minerva* and *Ulysses*, where the Goddess, after having inform'd *Ulysses* how she had besotted *Ajax*, *advises him to take warning, and not to be so far transported upon any good Fortune, or presume so far upon his own Prowess as to provoke the Gods by insolent*

Moral of the Author not arising naturally from the Action.

solent Language; *who lov'd Modesty, and hated Arrogance.* And about the middle of the Play, a Messenger relates to the *Chorus*, what pass'd between *Chalcas* and *Teucer* about the quarrel, and hatred of *Minerva* to *Ajax*, *Which was for presuming upon the sufficience of his own Strength and Courage, and refusing her Protection and Assistance, which she offer'd him against the* Trojans. But this is wholly without the Action (which cannot properly suggest any such thing) and is introduc'd by way of Narration, only to justifie the proceeding of *Minerva* against *Ajax*, and is no longer insisted on after the death of *Ajax*.

2d Moral not very natural.

The other Moral, as it does not seem to flow so naturally from the Fable, as the first, so it seems never to have been in *Sophocles*'s thoughts. For the last disgrace, and the Desperate Action that follow'd it, are the effect of a supernatural Agent, (*viz.*) *Minerva*, and produc'd by a sudden Infatuation after a supernatural manner; and therefore the Poet cou'd have no just occasion to reflect upon the natural ill consequences of Passion, how outrageous or ungovernable soever. For this reason I shall pursue

pursue the consideration of it no farther.

The next in order is the *Electra*, in which there is scarce the shadow of a Plot, nor much more of a Moral. *Orestes* (who after the murther of his Father *Agamemnon*, had by the care of his Sister *Electra* escap'd the fury of his Mother *Clytemnestra* and her Paramour *Ægisthus*,) comes to *Argos* with his Tutor, whom he sends to deceive his Mother with a Sham Story of his Death, and in the mean time discovers himself to his Sister, with whom he consults about means to revenge the Death of his Father; is introduc'd to his Mother as a stranger, kills her, and afterwards *Ægisthus*.

Fable of the Electra.

Thro the whole Play the Poet does not so much as squint toward a Moral, he lets nothing fall by which the Audience may so much as guess what he drives at. But by the contrivance of the Fable, wherein a Wife, that had embrued her hands in her Husbands blood, after having abus'd his Bed, is, together with her Adulterer and Fellow Murtherer, after a succession of some years of prosperous Villany, overtaken by by Vengeance from the hands of the Son, and slain; we may conclude with *Horace*,

Moral.

> *Raro antecedentem scelestum*
> *Deseruit pede pœna claudo.*

That Divine Vengeance seldom fails to overtake great Villanies.

This is all the *Moral* that I can find in this Play, nor do I perceive that *Sophocles* himself took care by any overt Expression to intimate it to the Audience.

Fable of the Antigone.

The *Antigone* is something better contriv'd. *Antigone*, contrary to *Creon*'s order, buries her Brother *Polynices*. *Creon* orders her to be shut up in a Cave alive, and commands, that no body shou'd relieve her. *Hæmon* his Son pleads for her, and unable to prevail, goes to the Cave, and finds that *Antigone* his Mistress had hang'd herself. In the interim *Tyresias* comes to *Creon*, and tells him, that he did amiss, and that he ought with all expedition to repair his Fault. *Creon* continues obstinate, and reviles the Prophet, who returns the complement, and threatens

Creon

Creon with the calamities that ſhou'd come immediately upon his Family for his Impiety and Obſtinacy, and ſo leaves him. *Creon* after his departure relents and makes haſte to ſave *Antigone*, but comes too late, and finds his Son raving for the loſs of his Miſtreſs, and hardly eſcapes being killed by him. *Hæmon* kills himſelf, and his Mother upon the News herſelf.

Here *Sophocles* ſpeaks out for himſelf Moral. and tell his Audience what Judgment they are to make of theſe ſurprizing Events, which had in a moment overturned a flouriſhing Family. The Chorus in the Concluſion ſays

Χο. Πολλῷ τὸ φρονεῖν εὐδαιμονίας
πρῶτον ὑπάρχει. χρὴ δὲ τά γ' εἰς θεοὺς
Μηδὲν ἀσεπτεῖν. ——

Wiſdom is the firſt ſtep to Happineſs. The Gods muſt not be irreverently treated. For the great Puniſhments, that attended the Profane liberties of ſpeech of Inſolent Men, were Leſſons of Humility at laſt.

The *Oedipus Coloneus* is a Play, that Oedipus Coloneus we are told was very much admir'd at *Athens*; and it is no great wonder. For it was written on purpoſe to Flatter, and

and do honour to the *Athenians*, and therefore cou'd ſcarce fail of a good reception. This Policy of *Sophocles* will furniſh us with both a Plot, and a Moral, which 'twill otherwiſe be hard to find in this Play. The Poet was now in his old age, and had long out-lived Mr *Dryden*'s *Fumbling Age of Poetry*, and perhaps began to be ſenſible of ſome decay, and therefore to ſupport the weight of that reputation, which he had acquired in the vigour of his Poetry, he pieces out the Lyons Skin with the Foxes Tail, and ſuſpecting his own power to move their Paſſions as formerly, makes uſe of their Vanity to ſcrue them up to the deſired pitch of Admiration and Satisfaction. This, if the Reader pleaſes, may ſerve inſtead of a Plot, and the ſucceſs of it may afford us this Moral; that *no people is ſo ſtrongly fortified againſt Flattery, but that, if their Vanity be skilfully tickled, it will be rous'd, and exert itſelf in favour of the Flatterer.*

This is, indeed, beſide the Action, and in probability was not the Moral, which *Sophocles* intended for the Publick; but 'tis plain, that 'twas the

ſecret

ſecret Motive upon which he acted, and the genuine Moral of his Conduct.

The Fable of *Oedipus Coloneus*, ſuch as it is in this. *Oedipus*, under the Conduct of his Daughter *Antigone*, arrives at a Grove near *Athens* conſecrated to the *Furies*, whither he had been directed by the *Oracle* to go. *Creon*, endeavours to fetch him away by force; *Theſeus* intervenes, and reſcues him. *Oedipus* dies at laſt in the place appointed by *Fate* and the *Oracle*.

Fable of Oedipus Coloneus

This is a plain ſtory, without either Turn or Conſequence, upon which there is no poſſibility of raiſing a *Moral*. *Sophocles* ſeems to have endeavoured at ſomething like one in the Concluſion. For when the Daughters of *Oedipus* lamented immoderately his death, the *Chorus* tells 'em, *That they ought not to bewail any longer one that was come to his deſir'd end.*

No Moral.

The *Trachiniæ* ſeems almoſt as little contriv'd for Edification as the foregoing. *Dejanira* being inform'd that *Hercules* grew amorous of his Captive *Jole*, to retrieve and enſure his Affection to her, ſends by *Lichas* an envenom'd Shirt, which ſhe ſuppos'd to have been dipt

Trachiniæ *its Fable.*

dipt in a Philtre. This unhappy Present being upon his Back, immediately corroded the Flesh in ſuch manner, that in a rage he daſh'd out *Lichas* the Bearers Brains. *Dejanira* hearing the Fatal Effects of her Errour, kills herſelf. *Hercules* having charged his Son *Hyllus* to marry his Concubine *Jole*, burns himſelf.

Moral of Sophocles.

The reflection that *Sophocles* makes upon all this, is, that, *'tis all* Jupiter*'s doing*. *Hyllus*, in the cloſe, *boldly accuſes the Gods of * Injuſtice, for deſerting their own Off-ſpring*. He adds,

* *ἀγνωμοσύνην, which ſignifies Folly or Injuſtice.*

Τὰ δὲ νῦν ἑςῶτ᾽, οἰκτρὰ μὲν ἡμῖν,
Αἰσχρὰ δ᾽ ἐκείνοις.

Theſe things are a heavy Affliction to us,
But a ſcandal to them.

The *Chorus* ſeconds his Complaint, and ſays, that *all their Calamities are of* Jupiter*'s ſending*.

κοὐδὲν τούτων ὅ,τι μὴ Ζεύς.

This

This Fable and Application afford very little matter of Moral Inſtruction; and the uſe that the Poet himſelf makes of it, is rather a diſcouragement to Virtue, ſince neither the Heroick Qualities, nor Actions of *Hercules*, nor the relation to *Jupiter*, could exempt himſelf or Family from ſuch lamentable diſaſters.

However, the misfortune of *Dejanira* may ſerve as a caution againſt Jealouſie and Adultery, which two failings in conjunction, occaſion'd her ruin. And *Hercules* himſelf may be an inſtance of the dangerous conſequenees of a licentious ungovern'd Flame, which at laſt was the deſtruction of him, who had withſtood, and baffled the utmoſt Malice and Invention of *Juno*.

The Fable of the *Philoctetes* is this. *Philoctetes* having an incurable Ulcer in his Foot, from the bite of a Serpent in his Voyage to *Troy*, was deſerted, and left by the *Greeks* alone upon the deſart Shore of *Lemnos*. But his Preſence being declar'd abſolutely neceſſary to the taking of *Troy*, *Ulyſſes* and *Pyrrhus* are ſent to fetch him. He refuſes obſtinately to go along with 'em, but *Hercules* ap-

Philoctetes, *the Fable.*

appearing, and perſwading him, he complies.

No Moral. This likewiſe is a barren Story, of which *Sophocles* himſelf has made no moral Uſe, and has ſcarce given occaſion for any one elſe to do it.

Philoctetes had been barbaronſly expos'd by his Confederates the *Greeks*, for which he was irreconcilably angry with 'em, eſpecially *Ulyſſes*, who had been the Executioner of their Reſolutions in relation to him. He therefore refuſes obſtinately to go with, or to thoſe that had ſerv'd him ſo baſely ; but *Hercules* appearing, and telling him, that upon thoſe terms, and no other, he muſt expect his cure, and proſperity , the man had ſo much Wit in his Anger, as to prefer Health and Fame before ſullen Revenge, which muſt be his own as well as their diſappointment.

Speech of Hercules *not pertinent to the Action.* P. 93, Mr *Collier* wou'd paſs the Speech of *Hercules* upon us for a Moral. But by his leave, how *remarkably Moral ſoever the Concluſion of this Play* may be, the morality of it no way depends upon the Action foregoing. *Hercules* prevails with *Philoctetes* to go with *Ulyſſes*, and *Pyrrhus* promiſes him Health, Honour, and

and Riches, and recommends the care of Religion to him.

εὐσεβεῖν τὰ πρὸς θεούς.

Which, ſays he, *Jupiter regards above all things.*

This was indeed good advice, and matter of Inſtruction to the Audience, as well as *Philoctetes*; but not ariſing any way from the main Action, it might as properly have been ſaid at any other time, and upon any other occaſion, as this; and if it muſt ſerve for a Moral, might as juſtly have been the Moral of any other Play.

Thus I have run through *Sophocles*, Ibid. *whoſe Plays* (by Mr *Collier*'s own confeſſion) *are form'd upon Models of Virtue, joyn Innocence with Pleaſure, and deſign the Improvement of the Audience.*

Upon this account, and the great Reputation of this Author, I have been more particular with him upon this head, than I deſign to be with any of the reſt of the Antient *Tragedians*. I have ſet before the Reader the ſeveral Models of all his remaining Plays, and have enquir'd into the Diſpoſition of the Fable in relation to the ſervice of *Morality*, that upon collation we may with more certainty meaſure the comparative Morality of his and the Modern Plays on this Article.

Art. Poet. Cap. xiii. *Euripides*, who came neareſt him both in Time and Reputation, is yet more defective in this point. *Ariſtotle* has tax'd him with want of Conduct in the *Oeconomy of his Fable*; but this Cenſure being levell'd rather at the want of Artifice, than of Moral in the Plays of *Euripides*, I ſhall make no further uſe of it here. The character of this Author's works wou'd make us naturally expect, that he ſhou'd be more careful of this Article, than either *Æſchylus*, or *Sophocles*, who aim'd more at the Pathetick.

Character of the Plays of Euripides *in general.* The Plays of *Euripides* betray all along an affected Oſtentation of Learning, and as great an Ambition to be thought a Philoſopher, as a Poet. For this reaſon he abounds more in Points, and Sentences of Morality, florid Harangues, and ſubtle Speculations, than *Sophocles*; but he does not touch the Paſſions, or raiſe the Concern of an Audience like him. And therefore whatever we may think of his Dialogues conſider'd ſeparately,

rately, and independant of one another, his Plays in the aggregate are far inferiour to those of *Sophocles*.

Euripides has yet remaining nineteen *Tragedies*, to examin all which, as we have done those of *Sophocles*, wou'd be an impertinent, as well as a tedious labour, both to the Reader and my self. I shall therefore content my self to instance in a few of 'em, and refer those that have the Curiosity and Patience, to proceed further to the Author himself.

The *Orestes* challenges the first place upon the score of its Reputation, and the great Success it had on the revival of it, five hundred years after the death of the Author.

Fable of the Orestes

This play commences, where the *Electra* of *Sophocles* and his own conclude. *Orestes*, by the help of his Sister *Electra*, having slain his Mother, is very much troubled in mind, and haunted by Furies, and desponds upon the account of his Guilt. *Tyndarus*, his Mother's Father, endeavours to revenge her death, and excites the People against him, who vote him to be ston'd to death with his Sister. *Menelaus*, with his Wife *Hele-*

na, and Daughter *Hermione*, arrives in the mean time and offers his aſſiſtance to his Nephew in this exigence, but is o-ver-aw'd by *Tyndarus*, and deſerts his Party. *Pylades* comes opportunely, and perſwades *Oreſtes* to appear, and make his defence in perſon, which he does, but without ſucceſs, yet upon his promiſe that his Siſter and himſelf ſhall be their own Executioners, he is let go by the Mob upon *Parole*. Being return'd to his Siſter, they conſult about means of *Safety*. *Electra* adviſes him and *Pylades* to ſeize upon *Helen* and *Hermione*, to kill *Helen*, and to Article with *Menelaus* for their own ſafety, with a Sword at *Hermione*'s Throat; and if her Father wou'd not comply with their demands, firſt to diſpatch her, then themſelves. This Project is put in execution, and the Ladies are ſurpriz'd, *Apollo* reſcues *Helen*, and appearing, reconciles *Menelaus* and *Oreſtes*, and makes a match betwixt him and *Hermione*, and betwixt *Pylades* and *Electra*, and promiſing happineſs to 'em all, tells 'em, that *Helen* is made a Goddeſs, and ſo concludes the Play.

In

In this Play most of the Characters are wicked, *Orestes* and *Electra* are *Parricides*; *Tyndarus* is (in his heart at least) the *Murtherer* of his Grand-children; *Menelaus*, the *Betrayer* of his Nephew, and Niece, whom he ought to have protected; *Helen*, an *infamous* Woman, and the accidental cause at least of the Miseries of a great part of *Asia* and *Europe*, yet clear of any intentional Guilt in this case; *Pylades* is engaged with his Friend in an unjust attempt to murther *Helen* and her Daughter; *Hermione*, who is next to a Mute in the Play, is the only unexceptionable Character. *Characters all vicious.*

This Play begins well, the Agonies of a guilty Conscience, the Despair, and the Horrors of *Orestes* promise a good Moral: But the hopes of that soon vanish; for the first word of comfort from *Menelaus* dispels all his Anxiety for his crime, and converts it to a solicitude for his Safety. In order to this, he enters upon a piece of Villany, more execrable than that for which he was then prosecuted, because 'twas without provocation: A Feint of that kind had been an allowable Stratagem to have *Not of a piece all through.*

brought *Menelaus* to Articles; but to project it in earnest was an unparallell'd piece of Barbarity. But what after all is more surprizing and unnatural is, that the *Catastrophe* is happy, and the Parricides rewarded, and all this seems to be the result of *Electra*'s latter contrivance, which however wicked was successful and prosperous.

Moral. The *Moral* (if I may call it so) of this Story is properly this, that there *is no dabbling in Villany, but that those that are once enter'd, must wade thro, if they will be safe, and justify one Crime by another.* But that which makes the winding up of this Play more notorious, is, that the Gods are made the Arbiters of all; *Apollo* appears in person, and justifies *Orestes*, and promises him his protection, and ensures the happiness of *Pylades* and *Electra*, who had been the sole Incendiary and Contriver of all this Mischief; which is adding Impiety to the want of Poetick Justice, and making Providence accessary to Parricide, and the Gods Abbetors of Violence and Injustice, not to take notice of the Deifying of *Helena*, who, tho *Jove*'s Daughter, is a Woman of a very

very infamous Character all through the Play.

I ſuppoſe the *Moral* of this Play will hardly riſe in Judgment againſt the Moderns. Nor has the *Electra* of of the ſame Author any more reaſon, it being liable to the ſame exceptions with the former, only in this the Murther is perpetrated, in that but deſigned; in ſhort, this Play is the ground work of the former, and the action of this gives the reaſon, and occaſion of all that happens in t'other. Here likewiſe the Gods are impertinently brought in to finiſh that, which wou'd of it ſelf have cloſed very naturally without 'em. For after the Death of *Ægiſthus* and *Clytemneſtra* there was nothing more to be done. But this Poet, who is very fond of Machines, tho unneceſſary, after all's over brings down *Caſtor* and *Pollux* to condemn the Fact, acquit the Murtherers of their Siſter, and transfer the Guilt to *Apollo*, whom they accuſe of* uttering a *fooliſh Oracle*.

* οὐκ ἔχρησέ σοι σοφά.

However the Fable of this Play being the ſame with that of the *Electra* of *Sophocles*, we may do it the ſame Grace, and allow it the benefit of any *Moral*

that

that may be raiſed out of it, tho not without ſome violence, as this Author has managed it. What that is I have al- ready obſerved in the foregoing Re- marks upon the *Electra* of *Sophocles*.

Media, &c. The *Medea*, *Hippolytus*, *Ion*, *Hercules diſtracted*, and ſeveral other are likewiſe built upon various Models. In theſe, as in moſt of *Euripides*'s Plays, the Gods are always at one end or t'other of the buſi- neſs, they are either the Promoters of the Crime, or the Protectors of the Criminals. All is acted by *Machine*, the *Action* is frequently forced, and the *Cata- ſtrophe* generally unnatural. Yet notwith- ſtanding this extraordinary licence, which this Poet aſſumes in almoſt all his Plays, but very few of 'em are ſo mo- dell'd as to be ſerviceable to Virtue upon that Score.

Medea, after a courſe of Murthers, ha- ving ſlain her own Brother, and Chil- dren with her own hands, and *Pelias*, *Creon*, and *Creuſa* by her charms, is taken particular care of by *Phœbus*, and pro- vided of a flying Chariot to make her eſcape from Juſtice in.

Fable of the Hippolitus. *Hippolitus* has the Character of a juſt, and a Pious Perſon, and his conduct all

all thro the Play, both in relation to his Mother in Law *Phædra*, and his Father, by whose curse he is devoted, and brought to ruine, justifies this Charactr, and he in the Agonies of Death expresses a greater concern for, and a more sensible impression of his Fathers misfortunes and afflictions, than his own. A Disposition so extraordinarily pious, one wou'd think, shou'd, if it might not exempt him from those disasters that attend the Infirmity of humane Nature, and the malignity of his Fellow Mortals, at least protect him from any supernatural calamities, and ensure the favour of Heaven to him. But he was a Votary to *Diana*, and his vow of Chastity gave such offence to *Venus*, who thought herself slighted, that she resolves his ruine, and declares her resolution, and the methods she intends to take to effect it, in the Prologue which she speaks. And she lays her Plot so, that by means of an antecedent Promise to *Theseus* she engages *Neptune* in the Destruction of an innocent Young Man, whose only crime is an obstinate, inviolate Chastity; and *Phædra*, who is her instrument, is involv'd in the guilt of a heinous, but

invo-

involuntary Crime. The conſideration of the ſeveral Fables of theſe Plays cou'd furniſh the Audience with no venerable Ideas of their Gods, who cou'd be the Promoters, or Protectors of ſuch horrid Actions; nor cou'd any encouragement to Juſtice and Morality be drawn from 'em, which afforded ſuch examples of Partiality, and prejudice among their Deities, that the blackeſt Crimes cou'd not forfeit their favour, nor the moſt exemplary Virtue enſure it.

Ion *a moral Tragedy.*

Remarques ſurle xix Chapitre de la poetique d' Ariſtote.

The *Ion* is reckoned by the Learned Monſieur *Dacier* among that kind of Tragedies, which *Ariſtotle* calls *Moral*, and which this judicious Commentator defines thus; *The Moral Tragedy is a ſort of Tragedy contriv'd purely for the formation of Mens manners, whoſe Cataſtrophe is always happy.* And in the Page immediately foregoing, *The Moral Tragedy* (ſays he) *treats neither of Death, Torments, nor Wounds, but of the happineſs of ſome Perſons recommendable for their Virtue.* Here therefore one might reaſonably expect a perfect Model of Virtue, and a exact Scheme of Manners; for which reaſon it may ſeem juſtly to challenge our conſideration.

Ion

Ion, a Slip of *Creusa* by *Apollo*, is privately born, and expos'd by his Mother, is taken up by *Mercury* and conveyed to *Delphi*, where he is found by the Priestess, and brought up in the Temple of his Father, of which he is at length made the Treasurer, or Keeper of the rich Moveables, in which Office he discharges his trust faithfully. Thus far the Prologue spoken by *Mercury* informs the Audience of the History of *Ion* before the Play commences.

Fable of Ion precedent to the Action.

Creusa his Mother, having no Issue by her Husband *Xuthus*, repairs with him to theOracle at *Delphi*,to petition for an Heir. The Husband puts up his request according to form,and is answered, that the first man he shou'd meet in his return from the Altar, was his Son; this happens to be *Ion*, who is upon the faith of the Oracle received by him as his Son. *Ion*, who being a Foundling, was ignorant of his Parentage, in return joyfully acknowledges him to be his Father, and is proved of so honourable an Extraction. This enrages *Creusa*, who not suspecting the relation of *Ion* to herself, supposes him to be some by-blow of her Husbands, as *Xuthus* him-

Fable commencing with the Action.

self

ſelf does, but begotten before his Marriage to *Creuſa.* In this rage ſhe reſolves and attempts to poyſon *Ion*, which is diſcovered, and *Ion* in revenge purſues her life. She takes refuge at the Altar, from whence while *Ion* is endeavouring to force him, the *Propheteſs* interpoſes, and produces the Swathing Bands, and other things in which *Ion* was wrapt when found. Theſe *Creuſa* knows, and diſcovers him to be her own Son by *Apollo*; *Minerva* appears, and confirms her Story, and adviſes 'em both to conceal this circumſtance from *Xuthus*, and concludes with a ſort of *Epilogue*, predicting the happineſs of *Ion*, and other Children, which *Creuſa* was to have by her Husband.

Main Condition of Moral Tragedy neglected in this.

If this was deſigned for a *Moral* Tragedy, as Monſieur *Dacier* thinks, and as the Contrivance of the Fable, as well as the Cataſtrophe ſeems to argue, it muſt be confeſſed that *Euripides* has forgot the main circumſtance. For the good Fortune of thoſe Perſons, whom he makes happy in the Concluſion is not owing to their Virtue or Prudence, but to the favour of *Phæbus*, who had too great a Perſonal Intereſt in 'em, to ſuffer 'em to miſcarry.

Creuſa's

Creüsa's Character is vitious all along, she was withChild by *Apollo*, and privately delivered, and to conceal her Shame, she exposes the Infant as a Prey to the Wild Beasts, as she herself confesses to her old Servant, and Confident, the Contriver and Instrument of her intended Villany afterwards. Creüsa's *a wicked Character.*

Καὶ τέθνηκεν, ὦ γεραιὲ, θηρσὶν ἐκτεθείς.
He died a Prey to the Wild Beasts.

Here she confesses herself guilty of a Crime, that is capital in our Law, and is so far from repenting, that she engages immediately in the design of another of a Dye something deeper, because Treachery and Violence enter the composition; in this she is active in the Murther, in the former she was only Passive. This Character can hold forth nothing of Instruction, except it teach Women, that have given up their Honours, to secure their Reputations by murthering their Bastards; and furious, jealous Wives to destroy their Husbands Children and Heirs by other Women.

The Character of *Ion* is indeed not so criminal; his highest commendation is, Ion's *Character indifferent.*

that

that he had not imbezzled the Stores of *Apollo* committed to his keeping. Now, tho Faithfulneſs be very commendable in a Servant, yet his was never exercis'd in ſo ſuperlative a way, or endur'd any ſuch ſevere tryal, as might upon that ſcore entitle him to the great Fortune and Preferment which befel him afterwards. His higheſt Merit was bare Honeſty, enough to have procur'd him a Certificate now adays upon change of Service; not to challenge any conſiderable Reward. He laid claim to no active virtues, his Innocence was his ſtrongeſt Plea, and that too ſeems to be a little ſullied at laſt by his too eager Proſecution of Revenge upon *Creuſa.* A generous Heathen (without reaching the Pitch of *Chriſtian* Morality) wou'd have forgiven, or ſlighted the Feeble Malice of a Woman, eſpecially at that Critical Juncture, when he ought to have ſhewn himſelf worthy of his ſudden exaltation by ſome extraordinary act of Generoſity. But his colluſion at laſt with his Mother to cheat *Xuthus* is a piece of Condeſcenſion ſo baſe, as forfeits all pretence to common merit or honeſty. For he that is content to hold

his

his good Forrune by Trick and Imposture, don't deserve it.

Thus we see in this *Moral* Play, of the two fortunate Persons, one is wicked, and ought not to be drawn into Precedent, much less to be propos'd for an Example; t'others Virtue is of so dwarfish a size, and so weakly a Constitution, that 'tis not very likely to propagate, and by no means a proper Standard to measure full grown Worth by. And therefore this Play (tho we shou'd, with Monsieur *Dacier*, allow it to be of the Moral kind) is like to do no great service to Morality by the Design and Management of its Fable.

Of no Service to Morality.

Because I have mention'd the *Hercules Furens*, I will not pass it absolutely over in Silence, tho it affords no great matter of reflection; having had occasion to take notice of the Character and Sufferings of *Hercules* in the *Trachiniæ* of *Sophocles*. There is indeed this considerable difference to the disadvantage of this Play, in regard to the *Moral*, Art, and Beauty of it, that here the misfortunes of *Hercules* are wrought altogether by Machine: *Juno*, *Iris*, and *Lyssa* or *Madness* (which is here supposed a *Dæmon*) are

Hercules Furens *compar'd with the* Trachiniæ *of* Sophocles.

N all,

all, and only concern'd in the contrivance; whereas in *Sophocles* things are naturally brought about, and made the result of Jealousie and Credulity. What therefore in that is but obliquely charg'd upon the Gods, is here directly laid upon 'em. So that, what from the last Speech of *Hyllus*, and the *Chorus* is there urg'd against the *Moral* of that Play, holds more strongly against this. Besides the atrocity of the Fact, which extending here to the Lives of his Wife and Children, aggravates the guilt of *Juno*, who cou'd not limit her malice to his Person, without comprehending those Innocents, who by no crime of their own cou'd have incurr'd her displeasure.

These few instances may suffice to give us a true estimate of the care of *Euripides*, in the formation of his Fables in general, in relation to the Grand or General *Moral*.

Character of Æschylus.

Æschylus shou'd follow, who, tho first in order of time, comes naturally last into consideration, as affording very little upon this Topick. This Author seems scarce to have design'd any *Moral* to his Fables, or at least to have regarded ed it very little. His aim was wholly at the Pathetick, and he deals almoſt altogether in Objects of Terror; accordingly his Flights are frequently lofty, but generally irregular, and his Verſe rumbles, and thunders almoſt perpetually, but it uſually ſpends itſelf, like a Wind-Gun, in Noiſe and Blaſt only. He ſets out glorioully, launches boldly, blown up with a Tympany of Windy *Hyperboles*, and Buckram *Metaphors*; but he carries more Sail than Ballaſt, and his courſe is accordingly uneven; he is ſometimes in the Clouds, and ſometimes upon the Sands. In ſhort, *Æſchylus*'s ſole Care and Ambition ſeems to have been (as Mr *Bays* has it) to *elevate* and *ſurprize*; in the eager purſuit of which, he has miſs'd many things, which are the laſting graces of his more temperate Succeſſors. The Groundwork of his Plays are plain ſimple Stories, without either Plot or Moral, told only in the moſt pompous formidable manner the Poet cou'd invent, to ſtrike a Pannick Terror into the Audience; and conſequently they afford no great matter of reflection here. I ſhall therefore diſmiſs this Poet without any formal examination to this Article, and only present the Reader with one Instance of his neglect of *Moral*, which stares me in the Face in the very first Page of his *Prometheus*.

Edit. Hen. Steph.

His Prometheus immoral.

Power and *Force*, two Poetical Persons, are sent by *Jupiter* to assist *Vulcan* in the chaining *Prometheus* to a Rock. They begin the Prologue, and declare his crime, which was *communicating the Celestial Fire to Mortals*; and the reason of his Punishment, which was *that he might learn to acquiesce in the administration of* Jove, *and shake off his tenderness for Mankind.*

Κρ. ϗ Β. Τὸ σὸν γὰρ ἄνθος παντέχνου πυρὸς σέλας
Θνητοῖσι κλέψας ὤπασεν. τοιᾶσδέ τοι
Ἁμαρτίας σφὲ δεῖ θεοῖς δοῦναι δίκην.
Ὡς ἂν διδαχθῇ τὴν Διὸς τυραννίδα
Στέργειν, φιλανθρώπου δὲ παύεσθαι τρόπου.

Jupiter *abus'd by the Poet under the Persons of* Power *and* Force.

This reason is pretty singular and extravagant, that a Brother Immortal shou'd be treated so inhumanely by *Jupiter*, and his Fellow Gods, only for his *Philanthropy*, or Love to Mankind; and must needs have a very serviceable effect upon Mortals. For no doubt but *Jupiter's* Altars must smoak very plentifully,

fully, when Men were inform'd, that ſo well he ſtood affected towards 'em, that 'twas Capital in any of his Under-Gods to bear 'em any good will. This muſt needs impreſs upon 'em a great veneration for his Perſon, and zeal for his Service ; their Gratitude muſt needs work over abundantly for ſo ſignal a Grace.

The abuſe back: by Vulcan.

That this was all *Prometheus*'s offence *Vulcan* aſſures us in his reply. *Vulcan* ſeems to have ſome Bowels of Commiſeration for this poor Devil of a God, and in a compaſſionate ſort of Remonſtrance tells him, *that this comes of his fondneſs of Mankind, and thereby provoking* Jupiter, *who was fierce, and implacable, as all new Governours are.*

> τοιαῦτ' ἀπηύρω τοῦ φιλανθρώπου τρόπου.
> — Διὸς γὰρ δυσπαραίτητοι φρένες.
> ἅπας δὲ τραχὺς ὅστις ἂν νέον κρατῇ.

This account of *Jupiter* ſeems to countenance a harſher Tranſlation, than I have given of the fore-going words Διὸς τυραννίδα, and to expound 'em in the ſcandalous ſenſe of Tyranny, rather than of a juſt and equal adminiſtration of Affairs.

After this Prologue I ſuppoſe no good Moral will be expected from this Fable; the reſt of *Æſchylus*'s Fables are manag'd after a manner little more ſerviceable, for which reaſon I ſhall not tire the Reader with the examination of 'em.

Deficiency of the Greek Tragedy.

After the deceaſe of this Triumvirate of Poets, the *Tragedy* of *Athens* diſappears. Not but they had many Tragedians after 'em, but neither did they riſe to a heighth of Reputation equal to theſe, nor did their works very long ſurvive 'em that I know of. Here therefore we loſe the view of the Ancient Tragedy, for above five hundred years together.

Tragedy at Rome.

The next ſight we have of it is at *Rome*, where we find in all but ten *Tragedies*, which are all collected under the name of *Seneca*'s, tho belonging (as many Learned men think) to ſeveral Authors. Of theſe nine are of *Greek* Extraction, all but one taken from Plays yet remaining to us. The *Medea*, *Hippolytus*, *Troas*, and *Hercules Furens* are taken from Plays all bearing the ſame names in *Euripides*, except the *Troas*, which, tho it bears the ſame name, yet is not upon the ſame argument with the

Borrow'd from the Greeks.

the *Troades* of *Euripides*, but is taken from the *Hecuba*, another Play of the ſame Poet. The *Oedipus*, and *Hercules Oetæus*, are deſcended immediately from the *Oedipus Tyrannus*, and *Trachiniæ* of *Sophocles*. And 'tis very probable the *Thyeſtes* is owing to the ſame Author, tho the *Greek* Original be now loſt. For 'tis not only certain that *Sophocles* wrote three Plays which bore that name, but the Model ſeems to bear more reſemblance to the manner of *Sophocles*, than either of the other Tragedians. The *Agamemnon* plainly belongs to *Æſchylus*, as does likewiſe the *Thebais*, in right of his Ἑπτὰ ἐπὶ Θήβαις, tho the *Thebais* of *Seneca* being imperfect, it does not ſo plainly appear whether he copy'd it immediately from thence, or at ſecond hand from the *Phæniſſæ* of *Euripides*. The *Octavia* only is of *Roman* Original, its Author is uncertain. For 'tis juſtly ſuſpected to belong to neither of the *Seneca*'s.

This Author, (for Mr *Collier* ſeems to take all theſe Plays to be the work of one man) is cenſur'd and ſtands in ſome meaſure condemn'd, by Mr *Collier*, and therefore I ſhould wave any other ſcrutiny into his conduct, if I did not find him in some measure justified, and in a manner absolv'd upon the comparison with the Moderns.

Seneca the Philosopher suppos'd the Author of 'em.

But, if we believe with those Prodigies of Letters, *Lipsius*, *Joseph Scaliger*, and *Heinsius*, and divers others very eminent for their Learning, *that we are beholding to the famous* Seneca *the Philosopher, for three at least of these Plays, the Medea, Hippolytus,* and *Troas*, to which *Farnaby* adds the *Oedipus*, we shall be oblig'd to pay more deference or respect to 'em, and not to pass a rash and unmannerly censure upon any of the remains of so illustrious an Author.

Seneca *udjustly aspers'd by Mr* Collier. *P. 94.*

But *Seneca* is not at present in Mr *Collier*'s favour, he is declar'd an *injudicious, licentious Poet, upon whose liberties the Modern Poets proceed*; and therefore he is not to be receiv'd into Grace, till he has had the Penning of a Recantation for him If Mr *Collier* did believe that *Seneca* the Philosopher was the Author of any of those Plays, he ought upon the merit of his other works, (by which he may at least pretend to vie with Mr *Collier* both zeal and service in the cause of Virtue)

Virtue) to have treated ſo excellent a Perſon with more reſpect and honour, than to have rank'd him with, and made him the Ringleader of thoſe, whom he reckons *Atheiſts* and *Buffoons*. If he did not, he cou'd in Juſtice have done no leſs than ſet him clear of the Imputation, which by ſo rude and indiſcreet a charge he has brought him under. For he cou'd not but know, that the learned Perſons before-mentioned, whoſe Authority is of great weight amongſt Men of Letters, had deliver'd their Opinions, that he was the Author of ſome of thoſe Plays, eſpecially the Judicious *Heinſius*, whom he cites, and I ſhou'd ſuppoſe he is well acquainted with, unleſs he does (which I ſuſpect) like ſome Perſons, that boaſt of their familiarity with great men, whom they have not the honour to know.

Had he known their Opinions in this matter, it had but been a becoming piece of Modeſty to have laid his reaſons for his diſſent from 'em before his Reader; and not haughtily to have ſlighted their Authorities as not worth his notice. Or at leaſt he ought not in good manners to have treated the Memory of that Philo-

ſopher

ſopher at ſo ſcoundrel a rate. I ſuppoſe he will hardly juſtifie this Indignity from the miſrepreſentations that have been given of him. For, not to enter improperly into a diſpute about the validity of thoſe Reports here, whatever his private infirmities might be, we are ſure from his works, that he bent his Studies and Endeavours to the ſervice of Morality as heartily and ſucceſsfully, as ſome Chriſtians who with greater helps and ſtronger invitations, ſeem to value their Services much higher, with leſs reaſon.

Seneca *careleſs of Poetick Juſtice.*

However *Seneca*, tho he cannot without extream injury be accus'd of Writing for the encouragement of Debauchery, has been very careleſs of Poetick Juſtice in winding up his Fables. *Phædra* in the *Hippolytus*, and *Lycus* in the *Hercules Furens* are only the Malefactors that are brought to condign Puniſhment. For, as for *Oedipus*, we have had occaſion already to clear him from the Aſperſion of Guilt, tho his Misfortunes are the moſt notorious, and his Calamities the moſt deplorable of any upon the Antient Stage. *Ajax Oileus*, whom Mr. *Collier* produces as the only inſtance of this

Ajax *and* Oileus.

this kind, is indeed none. For he is no Person of the *Drama*, nor has his Fate any influence upon the ſucceſs of the Action either way. He is only mention'd by *Eurybates*, in the relation which he makes of the Voyage of the *Greeks* from *Troy*, to encreaſe the horror of that Storm, of which he was then giving a deſcription; which is no more to the buſineſs of the Play, than 'twou'd have been, if Mr *Congreve* in his *Mourning Bride* ſhou'd have taken occaſion from the Wreck of his Hero on the ſame Seas, to have brought in the Storm that caſt away the *Turkey* Fleet, and deſcrib'd the manner of Sir *Francis Wheeler*'s Wreck.

An improper inſtance of it.

But if *Seneca* has been remiſs upon this Article he ſins at leaſt by Precedent, and may plead in his Juſtification, that he leaves the Story generally no worſe than he found it. He built, as we have already obſerv'd, upon other mens bottoms, and cou'd not make any great alterations in the Foundations they had laid, without endangering the ſuperſtructure. *Ariſtotle* obſerves, in favour of the Poets of, or near his time, that taking the Fables of their Plays from

Seneca limited by Precedent.

Sto-

Stories vulgarly known either from Hiſtory, or the works of ſome precedent Poet, they had not the liberty of receding ſo far from the receiv'd Tradition in the Contrivance, and diſpoſition of their Fables, as was frequently requir'd to the forming a juſt and truly artificial Model. This may be urg'd with more juſtice in defence of *Seneca*, who, taking his Models from Authors of great reputation, wou'd have been thought guilty of a high piece of Preſumption, if he had varied too much from Originals ſo well known and received. Beſides, had he chang'd the Fortune of his Principal Perſons he had effac'd the Images of 'em, which had been impreſs'd upon the Audience, who wou'd not have own'd, or acknowledg'd 'em for the perſons they pretended to repreſent, who were beſt, or pethaps only by thoſe marks to be diſtinguiſh'd.

Hippolytus *of* Seneca *examined.*

However, it muſt be granted, that in his *Hippolytus*, wherein he has ventur'd to deviate a little from the Original, he has done it very judiciouſly, and very much to the advantage of the *Moral*; the application of which he has thereby render'd not only more eaſie and natural,

tural, but it ſelf likewiſe more uſeful, and inſtructive. In *Euripides* the Gods do all. His Perſons move like Puppets by wires; *Venus* contrives and acts all. *Phedra*'s a meer Machine, a paſſive Vehicle, that ſerves purely for the more cleanly conveyance of theGoddeſſes malice. The unraveling likewiſe is perform'd by Machine, *Pallas* deſcends to clear the Innocence of *Hippolytus*, and accuſes *Venus*. In ſhort, the Action is all forc'd and unnatural, and of conſequence, the *Moral*, if any, muſt be ſtrain'd.

More artificial than the Hippolytus *of* Euripides.

Seneca has artfully avoided theſe inconveniences, by making the inceſtuous Love of *Phædra* ſpring from her own Infirmity, and the death of *Hippolytus*, the effect of her Revenge of his Scornfully rejecting her Paſſion, and her fear of his making a diſcovery of her Infamy to his Father. Her puniſhment by this means becomes juſt, which was not ſo in the *Greek*, and her Rage, Deſpair, Confeſſion and Death, are the natural reſult of her Guilt and Folly. From the unhappy *Cataſtrophe* of this Lady, matter of fair Inſtruction may be drawn to check ſuch licentious Flames in their firſt Birth, which if indulg'd draw after 'em ſuch fatal conſequences. And

The Moral.

from the raſh miſplac'd imprecation of *Theſeus*, Parents may be caution'd againſt too eaſie a credulity in ſuch extraordinary caſes, and to guard againſt ſuch violences of Paſſion, as may extort Curſes from 'em, that may return upon their own Heads, and involve themſelves in the concluſion.

This Plot, as it ſtands in *Seneca*, is one of the neateſt of Antiquity, and had the Author taken care to diſencourage himſelf as happily from *Neptune*, as he has from *Venus* and *Minerva*, I ſee nothing inartificial in the diſpoſition of it. But *Neptune* performing his part *extra Scenam*, this fault is the more pardonable, eſpecially ſince 'tis originally the overſight of *Euripides*.

The reſt choſe Copies from the Greek.

The reſt of this Author's Plays varying little or nothing in the Fable from the *Greek* Originals, (thoſe I mean, that we know, for the *Thyeſtes* of *Sophocles* is loſt) whatever the faults of 'em may be in that reſpect, the *Latin* Author is not ſo properly accountable for 'em. The

Octavia *illcontriv'd and inſipid.*

Octavia, being the only Tragedy of *Roman* Stock that remains to us, ſeems to challenge upon that Score ſome regard, whoſoever was the Author of it. But being

being rather a relation by way of Dialogue between the ſeveral Parties concerned of an unjuſt Tyrannick Action, in which there is neither Plot, Turn, Moral, nor Conſequence, it wou'd be time loſt to beſtow an Examination upon it here.

Having thus run through the Tragedies of Antiquity, perhaps ſomething more minutely, than may be thought requiſite upon this Article, I ſhall not make many reflections upon the whole, but leave 'em to the further conſideration of the Reader, after a Remark or two, concerning the Practice of the Ancients in general, in this reſpect.

General Reflections on the Ancient Tragedy.

It is obſervable, that the Ancients in the diſpoſition of their Fables, ſeem to have had ſuch very little regard to the Moral of 'em, they contented themſelves with delivering their Inſtructions in wiſe ſayings, ſcatter'd here and there up and down the Dialogue, or at the cloſe of all; and only ſought in their Fables matter and occaſion of moving the Paſſions, which was generally done by way of Narration; to which end they furniſh'd out their Dialogue with all the Force, Pomp, and Terrour of

Ex-

Expreſſion they could, in which how well they have ſuccceded, is not to the preſent purpoſe to take notice.

Ariſtotle's *diviſion of Tragedy.*

Ariſtotle had, no doubt, this practice of theirs in view, when he divided Tragedy into *Moral* and *Pathetick*. By this Diviſion of Tragedy (*ratione Subjecti*) *Ariſtotle* plainly indicates, not only that the Subjects of the Ancient Tragedy were not all *Moral*, but likewiſe that it was not neceſſary, that they ſhould be ſo. He inſtances in the *Phthiotides*, and *Peleus*, two Tragedies that are loſt, as examples of the *Moral* kind; and beſides this mention of 'em, I do not remember any notice that he has taken of this ſort of Tragedy. For all his Rules ſeem to be calculated for the ſervice of the *Pathetick* and *Implex* kinds.

Moral Plays not much encouraged at Athens.

From this ſilence of *Ariſtotle*, and the ſcarcity of 'em amongſt the remains of the *Greek* Tragedy, we may reaſonably collect, that this ſort of Tragedy was not much in uſe amongſt the Ancients themſelves. For of all the Pieces of Antiquity the *Alceſtis* of *Euripides* alone in my opinion deſerves the name of a *Moral* Tragedy. In this Play both *Admetus*, and his Wife *Alceſtis* are Per-

ſons

ſons of ſtrict Probity, and great Piety. *Alceſtis* out of a ſingular Piety, offers her ſelf to *Death* a voluntary Sacrifice, in lieu of her Husband. In the depth of *Admetus*'s grief while his Wife was yet in the Houſe, and the rites of Funeral unperform'd, comes *Hercules*, who obſerving the Family to be in Mourning, deſires to be excus'd from troubling his Houſe at ſo unſeaſonable a time. *Admetus*, unwilling to turn away ſuch a Gueſt, diſſembles the real cauſe of his Grief, and receives him nobly, but *Hercules* enquiring, and being inform'd of the Truth of *Admetus*'s loſs, combats *Death*, recovers *Alceſtis*, and reſtores her to her Husband.

The *Fable* of this Play is truly *Moral*. *Alceſtis* firſt by her Piety redeems her Husband from *Death*; and *Admetus* afterwards by his *Generoſity* and *Hoſpitality*, by means of *Hercules*, reſcues her from the Grave. Thus they reciprocally owe their lives to each others Virtue. But if this Play be remarkably *Moral*, it is on the other hand monſtrouſly unnatural, and conſequently on that account is incapable of affording any extraordinary Pleaſure, or Improve-

Alceſtis *of* Euripides *a* Moral *Tragedy.*

ment. This probably might be the reaſon, why this ſort of *Tragedy* was ſo little in requeſt.

Antients *careleſs of the* General Moral *of the Plays.*

From the whole it appears, that the *Antients* were not ſo careful of their Models, as Mr *Collier* pretends; but were on the contrary extremely negligent of the *Moral* in the *Fables* of their *Tragedies*. So that if one or two do afford a tolerable one, we may conclude by the ſlight notice they take of it, that they did not ſee it, or but caſually found it there, rather than induſtriouſly ſought it; and that we are more beholding to their luck, than Judgment or good Intentions for 'em. I grant this way of arguing not to be demonſtrative, but it is not therefore unconcluſive. For ſince the ſenſe of the *Antients*, is not any where (that I know of) delivered in expreſs terms concerning this matter, I take their Practice, backt by the Authority of *Ariſtotle*, to be a ſufficient warrant for any concluſions, that ſhall be drawn naturally from 'em.

Conſequence of Mr Collier's *looſe way of Writing.*

But if I wou'd indulge my ſelf in the Liberties of Mr. *Collier*, and charge the *Antiens* at that looſe rate, that he does the *Engliſh Dramatick* Poets, I might not

not only tax 'em with negligence of their Morals, but with maliciouſly diſcouraging Vertue, and induſtriouſly promoting Villany, and Impiety. Nor wou'd the Poets ſuffer alone, all the great Men of Antiquity, that have commended their works, muſt ſhare both the Guilt, and the Sentence; and *Ariſtotle* above the reſt wou'd be even capitally criminal, his *Art of Poetry* is an inexhauſtible Spring of Corruption, an everlaſting Source of Infection, that has diffus'd its Venome over the whole World, and poiſon'd Mankind almoſt univerſally with *Villany*, *Impiety*, *Lewdneſs*, and *Debauchery*, of all kinds, for above ſixteen hundred years together. This wou'd be high Treaſon among the Admirers of the *Antients*, yet 'tis nothing to one of Mr *Collier's* declamatory Rants, when he is in one of his Rhetorical Fits, and about to dreſs up a Character for *Ariſtophanes*, or any of the *Engliſh* Poets. After this diſingenuous rate 'twere eaſie to turn the Satyr upon Ages long ſince paſt, and railly in his own words, thoſe whom he himſelf recommends to the Imitation of our preſent Writers. An inſtance of this kind mayn't be amiſs to ſhew how eaſie 'tis to miſrepreſent the faireſt intentions, and to improve Peccadillo's into Crimes of the blackeſt Dye, to make a helliſh Plot of an overſight, and plunge Men over head and ears in Brimſtone,for Humane infirmities.

Turn'd upon the Antients. 'Tis *a Jeſt*, that the Antients wou'd make us believe, *that their deſign was Virtue and Reformation. In good time!*
P. 286. *They are likely to combat Vice with Succeſs, who deſtroy the Principles of Good and Evil.* Wou'd *Euripides* perſwade us that his aim is Virtuous, and his deſign Moral? Why then does he make choice of means ſo diſproportionate to the end he pretends to drive at? Why is Vice repreſented ſucceſsful, and Villany triumphant, but to encourage Men to the Practice of it? Why is *Medea*, the betrayer of her Father, and Country, a Poyſoner, a Sorcereſs, and a Murtherer, one that had run thro the whole compaſs, and meaſur'd all the Paces of Villany, ſuffer'd to make her eſcape? Or if ſhe muſt not be puniſh'd, why are the Gods engaged in the matter, and ſhe taken into the care of Providence, and furniſhed with means of Eſcape at the

the expence of a Miracle ? Why are *Orestes* and *Electra*, Parricides, taken immediately into the Protection of Heaven, under Despondency, and the lashes of a guilty Conscience ? Why are they encourag'd to bear up against the convictions of their own minds, and promis d prosperity from Heaven ? Why is *Hippolytus* maliciously persecuted, and no less then two Deities employ'd in his ruine, only for being chaste by vow ? unless it be to shew us, that the World has been mistaken in its notions of Providence, that wickedness is meritorious, and Innocence a Crime, that Virtue, and Vice, of which the Philosophers prate so much, are but the Whimseys of *Hypocondriacks*, the Dreams of speculative *Enthusiasts*. Are these the *Socratick* Dialogues, and this the result of the Philosophers Lectures ? Is this the Admirer of *Socrates*, that was reciprocally so admir'd by him, that he cou'd sit whole days with Patience at the recital of his Plays ? If we may judge of one by the other, the Scholar was an Atheist, and his Master little better. Why else did he not reprove him for his blasphemous Fictions, and making the Gods the Actors, and Patrons of Villany, and reprehend

prehend him for miſtaking the notions of Providence, confounding the Ideas of Virtue and Vice, and ſubverting the Maxims of Morality?

Socrates *by this means condemned.*

Thus we ſee at this rate of declaiming not only *Euripides*, who affected Philoſophy a little too much in his Poems, but even *Socrates* himſelf, the Boaſt of Antiquity, and the Glory of the Heathen World ſtands condemn'd, as an Abettour of *Murther*, *Inceſt*, and *Blaſphemy*. Let us ſee whether *Æſchylus* or *Sophocles* can acquit themſelves any better.

Æſchylus *arraign'd by Mr* Collier's *Precedent.*

If *Æſchylus* had taken due care of his deſigns, and built only upon Models of Virtue, we had never heard of his *Prometheus*. This Poet ſtrikes at the Root of all Moral Virtue. He ſcorns to trifle, and pluck it down piece-meal, but blows it up all together. *Philanthropy*, or Charity is the Ground and Foundation of all Morality. This in the *Prometheus* is made a Crime, and a God ſentenc'd to perpetual Puniſhment for his love to Mankind, which is all that is objected to him. This muſt needs create in Mankind a great Veneration, and impreſs a ſuitable

Reve-

Reverence for the Gods, who are ſo very tender of 'em, in return for their oblations, that 'tis high Treaſon to bear 'em any good Will. No doubt but Religion muſt ſhoot, and flouriſh mightily under ſuch a hopeful Proſpect of Reward.

Sophocles has been altogether as careful of Religion in his *Philoctetes*. That Spark, with his Carcaſs rotten, and full of aches and ulcers, hectors the Gods at a ſtrange rate, and they think it worth their while to cajole him into their ſervice. *Hercules* is ſent to make him a fine Speech, and large promiſes to invite him to obedience, and allure him over to their Party. *Oedipus* is made Virtuous, Juſt, and Wiſe, but unhappy thro a Fatality, againſt which his Virtue is no ſecurity; Juſtice requires that he ſhou'd be rewarded and encouraged, but Providence will have him afflicted, and puniſht with extremity of Rigour. Sophocles

Can any thing be more diſſerviceable to Probity and Religion, than theſe Examples of Injuſtice, Oppreſſion, and Cowardice in their Gods? *They cheriſh thoſe Paſſions, and reward thoſe Vices*, P. 287.

which 'tis the business of Reason to discountenance. They strike at the root of Principle, and draw off the Inclinations from Virtue, and spoil good Education: They are the most effectual means to baffle Discipline, to emasculate people's Sprits, and debauch their Manners. How many of the unwary have these Syrens devoured? And how often has the best blood been tainted with this Infection? What disappointments of Parents, what Confusion in Families, and what Beggary in Estates have been hence occasioned: And which is still worse, the Mischief spreads, and the Malignity grows more envenom'd. The Fever works up towards Madness, and will scarce endure to be touch'd.

Extravagance of this way of declaiming.

I doubt not but the sober admirers of the *Greek* Tragedy will think that the fumes of Mr *Collier*'s stumm'd Rant are got into my Head, and work me out of my Wits. And had he so far debauch'd my Judgment, as to make this my serious Opinion, I wou'd grant, that he and I were only fit to lead a Colony to settle at * *Anticyra*, and dyet upon *Hellebore*. But tho I have no such lewd thoughts of the great Men of Antiquity,

* *An Island famous for plenty of* Hellebore, *used in the cure of Madness.*

tiquity, yet ſo far I ſhall preſume to venture, (without treſpaſſing againſt Modeſty, or breaking rudely in upon the harmonious Judgment of the Learned for a long Succeſſion of Ages) as to ſay, that Mr *Collier*'s unreaſonable Satyr comes as full upon the Antients whom he admires and commends, as upon the Moderns, whom he vilifies and condemns.

The *Modern* Tragedy is a Feild large enough for us to loſe our ſelves in, and therefore I ſhall not take the Liberty of ranging thro 'em at large, but for the moſt part confine my ſelf to ſuch as Mr *Collier* has already attackt. Upon preſumption therefore that theſe are the weakeſt, if theſe can be defended, the reſt I ſuppoſe may hold out of themſelves.

I ſhall begin with *Shakeſpear*, whom notwithſtanding the ſeverity of Mr *Rhimer*, and the hard uſage of Mr *Collier*, I muſt ſtill think the *Proto-Dramatiſt* of *England*, tho he fell ſhort of the Art of *Johnſon*, and the Converſation of *Beaumont* and *Fletcher*. Upon that account he wants many of their Graces,

Shakeſpear *preferr'd to all the reſt of the* English Dramatics.

yet

yet his Beauties make large amends for his Defects, and Nature has richly provided him with the materials, tho his unkind Fortune denied him the Art of managing them to the best Advantage.

Censure of Hamlet *unjust.*

His *Hamlet*, a Play of the first rate, has the misfortune to fall under Mr *Collier's* displeasure; and *Ophelia* who has had the luck hitherto to keep her reputation, is at last censur'd for Lightness in her Frenzy; nay, Mr *Collier* is so familiar with her, as to make an unkind discovery of the unsavouriness of her Breath, which no Body suspected before. But it may be this is a groundless surmise, and Mr *Collier* is deceived by a bad Nose, or a rotten Tooth of his own; and then he is obliged to beg the Poets and the Ladies pardon for the wrong he has done 'em; But that will fall more naturally under our consideration in another place.

Fable of Hamlet, *before the commencement of the Action.*

Hamlet King of *Denmark* was privately murther'd by his Brother, who immediately thereupon marry'd the Dowager, and supplanted his Nephew in the Succession to the Crown. Thus far before the proper action of the Play.

The

Fable after the Action commences.

The late Kings Ghoſt appears to his Son young *Hamlet*, and declares how and by whom he was murther'd, and engages him to revenge it. *Hamlet* hereupon grows very much diſcontented, and the King very jealous of him. Hereupon he is diſpatched with Ambaſſadors to *England*, then ſuppoſed Tributary to *Denmark*, whither a ſecret Commiſſion to put him to Death, is ſent by 'em: Which *Hamlet* diſcovering writes a new Commiſſion, in which he inſerts the names of the Ambaſſadors inſtead of his own. After this a Pirate engaging their Veſſel, and *Hamlet* too eagerly boarding her is carried off, and ſet aſhore in *Denmark* again. The Ambaſſadors not ſuſpecting *Hamlet*'s Trick, purſue their Voyage, and are caught in their own Trap. *Polonius*, a Councellour to the King, conveying himſelf as a Spy behind the Hangings, at an enterview between *Hamlet* and his Mother, is miſtaken for the King, and killed by him. *Laertes* his Son, together with the King contrive the Death of *Hamlet* by a ſham Match at Foyls, wherein *Laertes* uſes a poyſon'd unrebated Weapon. The King, not truſting to this ſingle Treachery,

chery, prepares a poyſoned Bowl for *Hamlet*, which the Queen ignorantly drinks. *Hamlet* is too hard for *Laertes*, and cloſes with him, and recovers the envenom'd weapon from him, but in ſo doing, he is hurt by, and hurts him with it. *Laertes* perceiving himſelf wounded, and knowing it to be mortal, confeſſes that it was a train laid by the King for *Hamlet*'s Life, and that the foul Practice is juſtly turn'd upon himſelf. The Queen at the ſame times cries out, that ſhe is poyſoned, whereupon *Hamlet* wounds the King with the envenom'd weapon. They all die.

Poetick Juſtice exactly obſerved in this Play.

Whatever defects the Criticks may find in this Fable, the Moral of it is excellent. Here was a Murther privately committed, ſtrangely diſcover'd, and wonderfully puniſh'd. Nothing in Antiquity can rival this Plot for the admirable diſtribution of Poetick Juſtice. The Criminals are not only brought to execution, but they are taken in their own Toyls, their own Stratagems recoyl upon 'em, and they are involv'd themſelves in that miſchief and ruine, which they had projected for *Hamlet*. *Polonius* by playing the Spy meets a Fate, which was

was neither expected by, nor intended for him. *Guildenstern* and *Rosencraus*, the Kings Decoys, are counterplotted, and sent to meet that fate, to which they were trepanning the Prince. The Tyrant himself falls by his own Plot, and by the hand of the Son of that Brother, whom he had murther'd. *Laertes* suffers by his own Treachery, and dies by a Weapon of his own preparing. Thus every one's crime naturally produces his Punishment, and every one (the Tyrant excepted) commences a Wretch almost as soon as a Villain.

The Moral of all this is very obvious, it shews us, *That the Greatness of the Offender does not qualifie the Offence, and that no Humane Power, or Policy are a sufficent Guard against the Impartial Hand, and Eye of Providence, which defeats their wicked purposes, and turns their dangerous Machinations upon their own heads.* This Moral *Hamlet* himself insinuates to us, when he tells *Horatio*, that he ow'd the Discovery of the Design against his Life in *England*, to a rash indiscreet curiosity, and thence makes this Inference.

Moral of Hamlet.

Our Indiſcretion ſometimes ſerves as well,
When our dear Plots do fail, and that ſhou'd teach us,
There's a Divinity, that ſhapes our ends,
Rough hew'em how we will.

Tragedies of this Author generally moral.

The Tragedies of this Author in general are Moral and Inſtructive, and many of 'em ſuch, as the beſt of Antiquity can't equal in that reſpect. His *King Lear*, *Timon of Athens*, *Macbeth*, and ſome others are ſo remarkable upon that ſcore, that 'twou'd be impertinent to trouble the Reader with a minute examination of Plays ſo generally known and approved.

The other Tragedies upon which Mr *Collier* lets his indignation fall ſo heavy, are ſo recent, and ſo common in the hands of every Play Reader, that 'tis almoſt an affront to their memories to trouble 'em with too particular a Recapitulation. But ſince we have oblig'd our ſelves to make good the Comparative innocence of the Moderns by inſtances upon the Parallel, Mr *Collier* can never deſire fairer Play, than for us to undertake the defence of thoſe very Plays, which

which he himſelf has markt out, and aſſigned us ; of which the next in order is the *Orphan*, againſt which he enters the Liſts as the *Chaplains* Champion, in whoſe Quarrel and upon whoſe account he is moſt implacably enraged.

The Model of this Play is ſomething like that of *Oedipus*, except that in this the crime of *Polydore*, being voluntary, his guilt is real, and by conſequence *Poetick* Juſtice is obſerv'd in his puniſhment, which is juſt. In this Tragedy likewiſe *Acaſto*, *Caſtalio*, and *Monimia* are innocent, virtuous Characters, and their misfortunes undeſerv'd, which made 'em naturally objects of Pity and Commiſeration. The fatal conſequences of *Polydore*'s intemperate luſt, and baſe raſh action, afford matter of Terrour and Example. This Play is exactly conſtituted according to *Ariſtotle*, who requires only that Tragedy ſhou'd move Terrour and Compaſſion, which are the proper Springs, by which it works upon the Audience. In this it excells the Fable of the *Oedipus*, that it bears naturally a good Moral, and in the wretched Cataſtrophe of *Polydore*, and the miſeries

The Orphan.

The Moral *good*.

which

which his incontinence brought upon his Family, preaches Chaſtity to the Audience after the moſt effectual manner.

Mr Collier*'s Zeal for the* Pagan Prieſthood *injurious to the* Chriſtian Miniſtry.

But Mr *Collier*'s in the humour now, and he ſcorns to circumſcribe his kindneſs to the limits of the Chriſtian Prieſthood, whether Orthodox, or Heterodox. For even the *Mufti* is allowed the benefit of his Clergy, and ſhares his Patronage. He is furiouſly provok'd at Mr *Dryden* for ſaying that *Prieſts of all Religions are the ſame*, when he himſelf at the ſame time makes no diſtinction, but treats the Prieſts of God Almighty, *Mahomet* and *Anubis* with the ſame reſpect. He is for ſtrengthening his Party, and contracting an Alliance with all Faiths and Complexions; he ranſacks *Europe*, *Aſia*, and *Africa*, and enters into a religious League offenſive and defenſive with Sun-burnt *Africans*, and Monſters of the *Nile*. To this end, he labours hard to find out ſome relation between the *Mufti* and the Biſhops, and very dutifully ſtrains to extend the ſcandal from *Africk* to *England*, that what is ſaid of their Arch-Prieſt may reflect upon our Prelates. The moſt bigotted

Muſſul-

Muſſulman of 'em all cou'd not have acted more for the ſervice of their Prieſts, than to have ſhifted the reproach from them to ours. But I hope there is no ſuch Sympathy between 'em (as Mr *Collier* injuriouſly fancies) and that to break the *Mufti*'s wou'd not make our Biſhops Heads ach, or his black and blue be ſeen in their Faces. Thoſe worthy great Men, who are the honour of both our Church and Nation, have little reaſon to thank him for endeavouring to ally 'em to thoſe, that muſt of neceſſity, putting the mildeſt conſtruction upon their actions, be either groſs Fools or rank Knaves; Fools if they believe, and Knaves if they help on the cheat and impoſture of *Mahomet* without believing. Thus Mr *Collier* puts a groſſer affront upon our Religion and Clergy, than any Mr *Dryden* has done, and his reproof deſerves a ſeverer correction, than t'others fault. This perhaps is a liberty too great to be indulg'd in any one but Mr *Collier*'s dear ſelf, and therefore to chaſtize Mr *Dryden*'s Preſumption and Inſolence for but ſeeming to invade his fancied Property, he falls moſt outrageouſly upon his *Don Sebaſtian*.

Don Sebaſtian *a Religious Play.*

The Subject of this Play bears a very *Religious Moral*, and conſonant to the Tenour of the 2d Commandment ſhews, that the Puniſhment of Mens crimes, ſhall extend not only to their own perſons, but if unrepented ſhall reach their Poſterity likewiſe. In this Fable *Muley Moloch*, a Tyrant and an Uſurper, *Benducar* a crafty Villain and a Traytor, the *Mufti* a raſcally Hypocrite and a Traytor. Theſe three therefore are juſtly rewarded for their own proper Demerits. The Tyrant falls by Treachery, the treacherous Miniſter by publick Juſtice, and the Hypocrite is unmaskt, depos'd, and his Eſtate confiſcated. *Sebaſtian* and *Almeyda* are Characters of extraordinary Virtue, *Sebaſtian* appears juſt and brave, and *Almeyda* chaſte and conſtant to an Heroick Pitch. Their offence was involuntary, and a Sin of Ignorance, the unhappy conſequence of the tranſgreſſion of their Parents, and their Puniſhment is proportion'd very well to the nature of their Treſpaſs. For tho Inceſt be a Sin of a very black Dye, yet their Ignorance of the nearneſs of their Blood waſhes away their Guilt, and makes it their misfortune, not their Crime. In this

caſe

caſe a bare Separation wou'd be a ſufficient Juſtification of their Innocence. But a Judgment hanging over their heads for the ſin of their Parents, to divert that ſomething more mortifying was neceſſary, and therefore a voluntary abdication, exile, and a recluſe religious Life are thrown in by way of Pennance to make weight, and give the attonement its due complement. But leſt the true *Moral* ſhou'd eſcape the Audience, the Poet has taken care to fix, and ſumm it up in the four concluding Lines

> *Let* Sebaſtian *and* Almeyda'*s Fate*
> *This dreadful Sentence to the World relate,*
> *That unrepented crimes of Parents dead,*
> *Are juſtly puniſh'd on their Childrens heads.*

This Moral needs no defence, and wou'd plead ſucceſsfully for its Author, and excuſe many little Slips before any Judge leſs partially ſevere than Mr *Collier.*

The *Cleomenes* of the ſame Author ſtands indicted upon the ſame ſcore, that is, for being to free with the Prieſts

Reaſon of Mr Collier's *quarrel to the* Cleomenes.

of *Apis*. For tho that been't the only Allegation against this Play, 'tis apparently the sole ground. Thus Mr *Collier* as well as Mr *Dryden*, sets Priests of all Religions upon the same Foot. So they be but Priests, 'tis no matter to whom, he expects they shou'd be respected and reverenc'd; the compliment must be paid to their Livery, whether it be Christs or the Devils. Else why are the *Mufti*, and the Priests of *Apis* so much his Concern? Why all this heat in the cause of Infidels and Idolaters, and those none of the simple deluded Rout, but the Arch Jugglers, and Managers of the Cheat.

Moral *wanting to the* Cleomenes.

In this Play he has forgot, or overlook'd his greatest advantage, which is the want of *Moral*. His Passion had got the upperhand of his Judgement, and push'd him headlong on to the attack, no matter where. In this Play Poetick Justice is altogether neglected, Virtue is every where depressed, and calamitous, and falls at last unreveng'd in the ruine of *Cleomenes*, *Pantheus*, *Cleanthes*, *Cleonidas*, *Cratisiclea*, and *Cleora*. Vice revels all along, and triumphs

triumphs at length in the perſons of *Ptolomy*, *Caſandra*, and *Soſybins*. The Fidelity of *Cleomenes* to his Nuptial Vows is the deſtruction of himſelf and all his Friends, while the Luxury of *Ptolomy*, the Wantonneſs and Infidelity of *Caſandra*, and the Treachery of *Soſybius*, inſult in ſecurity unfortunate Virtue.

'Tis true, *Soſybius* in the cloſe ſeems to become a Convert, and pretends to pay extraordinary honours to the Body of the dead Hero. From whence we may draw this inference, *That Virtue has its altars tho neglected, even in the moſt profligate Breaſts, and that the moſt inveterate. of its Enemies will confeſs its Charms, when they no longer dread its power.*

Moral Inference.

Mr *Dryden* has confin'd himſelf a little too near the Story, had he aſſerted his right, and taken the Liberty of a Poet, he might have improv'd the *Moral* very much by ſending *Soſybius*, *Caſandra*, and *Ptolomy* to attend *Cleomenes* to the other World. For (with Submiſſion to Mr *Dryden*'s better Judgment) I ſee no neceſſity for *letting the Curtain fall* ſo immediately upon the Death

The Poet *too faithful to the* Hiſtory.

 of

of *Cleomenes*. The fall of his Hero ought to have drawn after it a train of Consequences fatal to the Contrivers of it; the ruines of a Hero of his size and weight ought to have crush'd those feeble *Ægyptians*. Had the rage and despair, that might naturally be supposed in a Woman of *Cassandra*'s furious temper, upon the disappointment of her licentious ungovernable Flame, been wrought up to the destruction of *Sosybius* and herself, *Magas* might have made his appearance in Person, to have finish'd the business, and dispatch'd *Ptolomy*. All this might have been done without unnaturally stretching, or making the action double. By this means *Treachery*, *Lust*, *Infidelity*, *Luxury*, *Cowardice*, and *Cruelty*, had all met their due reward. But the Poet by tracking too closely the Steps of the Historian has lost the *Moral*, which, had he been guided by, and depended absolutely upon his own Judgment, we had no doubt been indebted to him for.

Mourning Bride.

The next and last Tragedy I shall instance in is the *Mourning Bride*. I have had occasion already to say something of the Observation of Poetick Justice

Juſtice in this Play, but this being the proper place, I ſhall take it a little more particularly into conſideration.

The Fable of this Play is one of the moſt juſt, and regular that the Stage, either Antient or Modern, can boaſt of. I mean, for the diſtribution of Rewards, and Puniſhments. For no virtuous perſon miſſes his Recompence, and no vitious one eſcapes Vengeance. *Manuel* in the proſecution and exerciſe of his Cruelty and Tyranny, is taken in a Trap of his own laying, and falls himſelf a Sacrifice in the room of him, whom he in his rage had devoted. *Gonſalez* villanous cunning returns upon his own head, and makes him by miſtake kill the King his Maſter, and in that cut off, not only all his hopes, but his only Prop and Support, and make ſure of his own Deſtruction. *Alonzo*, his Creature and Inſtrument, acts by his inſtructions, and ſhares his Fate. *Zara*'s furious Temper and impetuous ungovernable Paſſion, urge her to frequent violences, and conclude at laſt in a fatal miſtake. Thus every one's own Wickedneſs or Miſcarriage determines his Fate, without ſhedding any

Fable very juſt and regular.

Malignity upon the Perſons and Fortunes of others. *Alphonſo* in reward of his Virtue receives the Crowns of *Valentia* and *Granada*, and is happy in his Love; all which he acknowledges to be the Gift of Providence, which protects the Innocent, and rewards the Virtuous. *Almeria*, whoſe Virtues are much of the ſame kind, and who Sympathiz'd with him in his afflictions, becomes a joynt Partner of his Happineſs. And *Garcia*, tho a Servant of the Tyrant, and Son of the treacherous, ambitious Stateſman, yet executing only his Soveraigns lawful Commands, and being untainted with his Fathers guilt, and his Principles undebauch'd, is receiv'd into *Alphonſo*'s favour.

Moral *excellent.*

All this as well as the *Moral* is ſumm'd up ſo fully, and ſo conciſely in *Alphonſo*'s laſt ſpeech, that 'twere injuſtice not to give it in the Poets own words.

(*To* Alm.) *Thy Father fell, where he deſign'd my Death.*
Gonſalez *and* Alonzo, *both of Wounds*
Expiring, have with their laſt Breath
Confeſt
The

The just Decrees of Heaven, in turning on
Themselves their own most bloody Purposes,
(*To* Garcia——— ——— *O* Garcia
Seest thou, how just the hand of Heaven has been?
Let us, that thro our Innocence survive,
Still in the Paths of Honour persevere,
And not for past, or present ills despair.
For Blessings ever wait on virtuous deeds;
And tho a late, a sure Reward succeeds.

These I think are all the *English* Tragedies, which Mr *Collier* has by name excepted against. Taking therefore our View of the Modern Tragedy from that quarter, which he has alotted to draw a Prospect of it in, I shall leave it to the Reader to judge, whether have raised the more beautiful structures. But if we can with these Forces, which our Enemies have raised for us, make head, and maintain our ground against the united strength of all Antiquity, what might have been done, had we had the listing, and sizing 'em our selves.

Advantages of the Moderns *over the* Antients *in the* Morals *of their* Fables.

I shall only take notice of two or three things which are apparently the indisputable advantage of the *Moderns* over the *Antients*, in respect of the General *Moral* of their Fables.

Providence not employed to promote Villany.

1st, That they never are at the expence of a Machine to bring about a wicked Design, and by consequence don't interest Providence in promoting Villany; as the Antients have notoriously done in many of their Plays; of which number are the *Electra* of *Sophocles*; the *Electra, Orestes, Hippolytus, Ion*, and *others* of *Euripides*, and the *Thyestes* of *Seneca*.

Nor to oppress Virtue.

2dly, That they never engage Providence to afflict and oppress Virtue, by distressing it by supernatural means, as the Antients have manifestly done, by making their Gods the immediate Actors in or directors of the misfortunes of virtuous persons, as in the *Prometheus in Chains* of *Æschylus*, the *Oedipus* of *Sophocles*, the *Hippolytus* and *Hercules furens* of *Euripides*, the *Oedipus* and *Hercules furens* of *Seneca*, and divers others of Antiquity.

Nor to protect Malefactors.

3dly, That their *Malefactors* are generally punished, which those of the Antients seldom were; but if they escape

cape, the Moderns don't provide 'em with a miraculous delivery, or have recourſe to ſuch extraordinary Methods as exceed the reach of Humane Force or Cunning, ſo as to entitle Providence to the Protection of 'em, which was the frequent Practice of the Antients; as in the *Electra* of *Sophocles*; the *Medea*, the *Oreſtes*, the *Electra*, and others of *Euripides*; the *Medea* of *Seneca*, &c.

Modern *Poets more Religious than the* **Antients.**

From this ſhort review of the different conduct of the Antient and Modern Tragedians, we may ſee with how much more reſpect to Providence, and the Divine adminiſtration, our Poets have behaved themſelves, than they; and how far the Ballance of Religion inclines to our ſide. I ſuppoſe no one can be ſo ſilly, as to think, that I argue here for the truth of their Faith, but the meaſure of it in their reſpective perſwaſions, in which the advantage is infinitely on the ſide of the *Engliſh* Stage.

The **Fable** *of the* **Poets** *diſpoſal.* **Characters** *and* **Expreſſions** *not ſo.*

The *Fable* of every Play is undoubtedly the Authors own, whenceſoever he takes the Story, and he may model it as he pleaſes. The *Characters* are not ſo; the Poet is obliged to take 'em from Nature, and to copy as cloſe after her, as he is able. The ſame may be ſaid for the *Thoughts* and *Expreſſions*, they muſt be ſuited to the Mouth and *Character* of the Perſon that ſpeaks 'em, not the *Poet*'s. It is not what is right or wrong in the *Poet*'s Judgment, but what is natural, or unnatural for a Perſon of ſuch a *Character* upon ſuch an occaſion to ſay, which he is to conſider, and for which he is accountable only, as well by the rules of *Moral* as *Poetical* Juſtice. When therefore we find any thing in Plays that ſounds amiſs, we muſt examine whether it be proper to the *Character* or not, before we condemn the *Poet*, whom we may otherwiſe arraign as *Mal a propos*, as a Judge wou'd the Kings Evidence, if he ſhou'd prefer an Indictment againſt 'em for ſpeaking Treaſon in their Depoſitions.

The Fable *if any, the Evidence of the* Poets *Opinion.*

The *Fable* therefore being the main ſpring of the Machine in Tragedy, and the *Poet*'s own proper Workmanſhip, 'tis by the temper and diſpoſition of that, that we are to feel the *Poets* Pulſe, and find out his ſecret affections., Not but that we may err ſometimes in our Judgments of the *Poet*'s *Morals* on either hand. For 'tis poſſible, that the

Poet's

Poet's Morals may be very good, yet the Man's ſtark naught, that is, that a man may be a good *Moral Poet*, yet a bad Man. So on the other hand we may falſly meaſure his Manners by his management, and impute to Malice and Deſign thoſe faults, which flow from want of Judgment or Indiſcretion. This is hard meaſure, but ſuch as Mr *Collier* has been very liberal of to the *Poets*. It wou'd be a very uncharitable Error, ſhou'd we at any time hear the ſacred myſteries of our Faith poorly explained, or weakly defended out of the Pulpit, if we ſhou'd conclude, that the Preacher played booty and betrayed the cauſe he pretended to plead for: And I doubt it wou'd fall heavy upon many, that now paſs for honeſt and good Chriſtians, I hope with juſtice, if their Faith were to be meaſured by their Performance, and their Integrity by their parts. But it wou'd be much more unjuſt to rate all the reſt of their order by the deficient Standard of a few. Yet thus Mr *Collier* proceeds againſt thoſe, to whom he thinks fit to oppoſe himſelf. And yet even thus they wou'd not have much occaſion to fear his malice, if he wou'd

Mr Collier*'s a falſe, and perverſe Meaſure.*

wou'd proceed against 'em the proper way, and not charge as their private and real sense, the Sentiments, which they are obliged sometimes to furnish Villains and Extravagants with in conformity to their Characters, while he denies 'em the benefit of those many excellent and pious Reflections abounding in their works.

The Fable *the Engine of greatest and most secret Execution upon the Audience.* P. 95.

Certainly had our Poets any such lewd Design of *confounding the Distinctions between Truth and Fiction, between Majesty and a Pageant*; of *treating God like an Idol, and bantering, the Scriptures like Homer's Elysium* and *Hesiod's Theogonia*, it wou'd appear in the Fable, which is the part, as we have observ'd, that discovers most of the Poets proper Opinion, and gives him the fairest opportunity of stealing it artificially in, and poys'ning the Audience most effectually with least Suspicion. For tho the Fable, if skilfully contriv'd, be the Part which operates most powerfully, yet it works after a manner least sensible. We feel the effects without suspecting the cause, and are prejudiced without looking after a reason. If the *Poets* have any such villanous Plot against

Virtue

Virtue and Religion, they are certainly the moſt negligent Fellows, or the moſt unexperienced in the world to overlook the only place of advantage upon the whole Stage for their miſchievous purpoſe, where they might work their Mines unmoleſted, aud ſpring 'em undiſcover'd to moſt, and do the greateſt execution with the leaſt alarm to the Enemy. But they make War like *Dutchmen*, and ſell their Enemies Ammunition to ſpend upon themſelves. For all their Fables are contriv'd and modell'd for the ſervice of Virtue and Religion, and levell'd againſt themſelves, if they be ſuch *great Enemies*, and ſo *remarkably diſaffected*, as Mr *Collier* ſays they are. But perhaps he may, either thro miſtake or malice, miſrepreſent the matter; and what was ſcoffingly ſaid by the *Turks* to the *Poles*, may be ſeriouſly applied to the caſe before us by both Parties, that *they did not know of any War betwixt 'em.*

Not abuſed to any ill end by our Poets.

From the management of the *Fables* of our Poets, which, being the Principal, and moſt Efficacious part of their Plays, undoubtedly employ'd moſt their care, 'tis plain that Mr *Collier* has given the

the World a falſe alarm, and endeavours to ſet 'em upon thoſe as Subverters' of Religion and Morality, that have with abundance of art and pains labour'd in their ſervice, and rack'd their Inventions to weave 'em into the moſt Popular diverſions, and make even Luxury and Pleaſure ſubſervient and inſtrumental to the eſtabliſhment of Moral Principles, and the confirmation of Virtuous Reſolutions.

Before I take leave of Tragedy upon this Head, I muſt take notice to the Reader, that in this Parallel betwixt the *Antient* and *Modern* Tragedy, I have not wreſted any thing to the unjuſt Prejudice of one, or favour of t'other. Nor, tho I find moſt of the Antient Fables defective in the general *Moral*, do I charge 'em with any deſign of undermining the Intereſt, or leſſening the credit and eſteem of Virtue. The *Moral* and the *Pathetic* were in their days diſtinct Branches of Tragedy (as we have already obſerv'd from *Ariſtotle*) of which their Poets in all probability made choice, according to the encouragement they obſerv'd 'em to meet with. If therefore we find few

Apology for the Antients.

Moral

Moral Plays amongſt the remains of thoſe extraordinary Perſons the *Greek* Tragedians, we may fairly preſume, that they did not take at *Athens*, otherwiſe they wou'd have been more cultivated. For this reaſon probably it was, that *Ariſtotle* took ſo ſlender notice of Moral Tragedy, as not thinking it worth while to lay down rules for the practice of that, which was no longer in uſe, or eſteem amongſt his Countrymen in his Time. Nor did this diſ-eſteem of *Moral* Plays proceed from any propenſity to, or Habit of Vice peculiar to that Age, which might give 'em a diſreliſh for Virtuous Entertainments. The contrary of this is evident from ſeveral of thoſe Tragedies, which ſucceeded at *Athens*, the Diſcourſe in which is frequently Moral and Inſtructive, tho the Fable it ſelf be not. But *Moral* Tragedy not admitting ſuch Incidents as were proper to move Terrour or Compaſſion, the Springs of Paſſion were wanting, and conſequently the Audience were but weakly affected with ſuch ſort of repreſentations.

Moral *Plays not eſteem'd at* Athens.

The *Moderns*, who were ſenſible of the uſe of one, and the power of t'other

Moral *and* Pathetick *reconciled, and united by the Moderns.*

Q ſort

ſort of Tragedy, have taken a happy Liberty of compounding 'em, and throwing the *ſimple* Tragedy quite aſide, ſtick altogether to an Implex kind, which is at once both *Moral* and *Pathetick*. Wherein they muſt to their honour be acknowledg'd, to have made a conſiderable improvement of Tragedy, and to have had a ſingular regard to Probity and Virtue; which (without injuſtice to Antiquity, I may venture to affirm) had very little Intereſt in the Fable before. Nor can the moſt par-

Poetick Juſtice neglected by the Antients *in general.*

tial Admirer of the *Antients*, with any colour of Juſtice deny this advantage to the *Moderns*; ſince neither *Ariſtotle*, nor *Horace*, amongſt all their excellent Rules, and Obſervations for Dramatick Writing, have taken the leaſt notice of Poetick Juſtice, which is now become the Principal Article of the *Drama*; which queſtionleſs they wou'd never have forgotten, had the Practice of the Stage in their own, or preceeding Ages, or even their own thoughts ſuggeſted the neceſſity of it. Nay ſo far is *Ariſtotle* from thinking it a requiſite condition, that he recommends * *the misfortunes of a Perſon unhappy thro his miſtake, not his*

* μήτε διὰ κακίαν ϗ μοχθηρίαν μεταβάλλων εἰς τὴν δυστυχίαν, ἀλλὰ δι᾽ ἁμαρτίαν τινά. Κεφ. 17.

his Fault, as the most proper Subject for Tragedy; which is directly opposite to this Rule, which requires, that the fortune of every one shou'd be adjusted to his Merit, whether good or bad. 'Tis true, *Aristotle* thinks, that 'tis inconsistent with the regard that is due to Mankind, to represent such revolutions in the Fortunes of Men, as shall make Persons eminently Virtuous unhappy, or notoriously wicked successful and prosperous. But I don't find that he made their proper Demerits the Standard, or immediate Rule for Squaring their future Fortune. And if we consider the examples he produces to his own Rule, we shall perhaps be induc'd to believe, that he did not insist upon a very rigorous observation of it. For of his two instances, *Oedipus* was (as we have already observ'd) a very virtuous Person, and *Thyestes*, according to the traditions remaining concerning him, a very wicked One. So that even while he is laying down his Rule, he seems to indulge a latitude in the observance, and to justifie any Liberties, that may be taken with it, by the Precedent of the best Play, not only of *Sophocles*, but of all Antiquity.

Monsieur Dacier's *exception to Monsieur* Corneille *answered.*

Monsieur *Dacier* (who, according the humour of most Commentators, will allow no slips in his Author) strains hard to reconcile the examples to the Rule. He charges Monsieur *Corneille* with making an unjust exception, for want of understanding rightly, the words ἁμαρτίαν τινά. I shall not undertake to Arbitrate the point of Monsieur *Corneille*'s Learning, but I think his observation just, and yet in full Force, and Monsieur *Dacier*'s answer, however Learned, no better than an Evasion. In ennumerating the good qualities, and summing up the Character of *Oedipus*, Mr *Dacier* omits his *Piety* towards his Country, and places the service of destroying the *Sphinx* to the account of his ambition, and the reward of the Crown tacked to it. His *Piety* I have already taken sufficient notice of elsewhere, and for his ambition let *Sophocles* answer, who tells us otherwise in the concluding Lines;

Οσ]ις ὁ ζήλῳ πολιτῶν, καὶ τύχαις ἐπιβλέπων.

Who affected not base Popularity, nor courted Fortune.

This

This may ſuffice to clear him from the imputation of Vanity and Ambition, with which Monſieur *Dacier* loads his Character, and added to the reſt, prove him an excellent Perſon; one that, according to *Ariſtotle*, was too good to ſuffer in ſo extraordinary a manner.

Poetick Juſtice a Modern Invention.

To digreſs no farther, I think we are obliged to the *Modern* Tragick Poets for the introduction of Poetick Juſtice upon the Stage, and muſt own, that they were the firſt that made it their conſtant aim to inſtruct, as well as pleaſe by the Fable. The *Antients* brought indifferently all ſorts of ſubjects upon the Stage, which they took from Hiſtory or Tradition, and were therefore more ſolicitous to make their ſtories conform to the relation, or to the publick Opinion, than to Poetick Juſtice, or the Propriety of Tragick Action. By this means all hopes of a *Moral* was cut off, or if by chance the ſtory afforded any, we are more obliged to the Poets luck for it, than to his Skill or Care. Thus the Moral, the higheſt, and moſt ſerviceable improvement that ever was, or ever can be made of the *Drama*, is of *Modern* Extraction, and may very well be pleaded in bar to all claim laid in behalf of the Antients, to preference in point of Morality, and service to Virtue, as likewise in answer to all Objections made to the Manners and Conduct of the *Modern* Stage in general.

Modern *Stage on this account preferable of the* Antient.

Thus the *Modern* Stage, against which Mr *Collier* maliciously declaims with so much bitterness, is upon this account infinitely preferable to the *Athenians*, which he commends and admires, and that which he rails at as the bane of Sobriety, and the Pest of Good Manners, is prov'd the most commodious instrument to propagate Morality, and the easiest, and most palatable Vehicle to make Instruction go down with effect. But the Violence and Partiality of some observe no bounds of Justice, and admit of no check from Modesty or Reason. But I shall take leave here, and pass on to the Fable of *Comedy*, against which Mr *Collier*'s spight is more particularly levelled.

Fable *of* Comedy *considered.*

The *Fable* of *Comedy* will give us very little trouble, if we consider rightly the Nature and Business of this part

of

of the *Drama*. *Comedy* deals altogether in Ridicule, and its Subject consequently must be such as affords matter of ridiculous Mirth. All its Machinations tend to the exciting that ill natur'd titillation, which carries scorn and contempt along with it. Its business is to correct, and hinder the spreading of Folly and Knavery, by making 'em ridiculous, and to reform Rascals and Coxcombs by exposing 'em. *Aristotle* therefore has has very judiciously defined Comedy Μίμησις φαυλοτέρων μὲν, οὐ μέντοι κατὰ πᾶσαν κακίαν ἀλλὰ τοῦ αἰσχροῦ ἐστι τὸ γελοῖον μόριον. *The Imitation of the baser sort of People, not in all kinds of Villany, but in the ridiculous part, which is one sort of Turpitude.*

The Action of *Comedy* must be suited to the Actors, who are *the baser sort of People*, and consequently can't be of any great importance either in its nature or effects, and therefore can afford no extraordinary *Moral*. By the *baser sort of People*, Persons of low Extraction or Fortune are not here meant, but Persons who by their practices and Conduct have expos'd themselves to Scandal and Contempt. From the Nature therefore, and quality of the Actors nothing great

In Comedy the Action and Persons low.

or generous can be expected from *Comedy*. The Duping of an old Knave, the cullying of a Coxcomb, the ſtealing of an Heireſs from a Mercenary Guardian, are the uſual exploits of Comedy; wherein tho Gentlemen are ſometimes concerned, yet they are, or ought always to be ſuch, as have ſome blemiſh, or other upon.'em, otherwiſe they are not fit for the buſineſs they are engag'd in. *Comedy* ſeems to be deſigned to teach Men Civil Prudence, and a convenient Management in reſpect of one another, rather than any thing of Morality; and their private duty. There their misfortunes and diſgraces are all the immediate reſult of their own Folly and Miſmanagement, and may therefore very well cauſe men to reflect upon that want of Wit and Caution, which cauſed themſelves or others to miſcarry, and teach 'em to be more wary for the future ; but it wou'd hardly confer any Grace, or mend their Principles.

The correction of Folly *the proper buſineſs of* Comedy.

The buſineſs of *Comedy* being ridicule, thoſe Vices only fall under its correction, that are capable of being made ridiculous, and thoſe only after ſuch a manner as may raiſe Scorn and Con-

Contempt. For this reaſon *Comedy* ſeems to be more naturally diſpoſed for the cure of Mens Follies, than their Vices, thoſe running more naturally into ridicule than theſe, which are more apt to raiſe Indignation and Averſion, and are the proper inſtruments of Tragedy. Not but that Vice too may ſometimes be ſeaſonably corrected in *Comedy*, but then it muſt be join'd with, and wear the Livery of Folly, to help to make it ridiculous, and the object of Scorn, rather than Indignation.

Perfect Virtue excluded the Comick Stage.

Hence it will appear, what ſort of Perſons are moſt proper to be employed in *Comedy*, which dealing altogether in Stratagem and Intrigue, requires Perſons of Trick and Cunning on one hand, and eaſie credulous Folks on the other, otherwiſe the Plot will but go heavily forward. By this means all Characters abſolutely perfect are excluded the *Comick* Stage. For what has a Man of pure Integrity to do with Intrigues of any kind? He can't aſſiſt in the execution of any deſign of Circumvention without forfeiting his Character; and to bring ſuch a Character upon the Stage to be practic'd upon, is ſuch

an

an outrage to Virtue, that the most licentious of our Poets have not dar'd to venture upon it.

Some Infirmity required to qualifie a Character for Comedy.

I grant that 'tis neither necessary, nor convenient, that all the Characters in *Comedy* shou'd be vicious, that were to abuse mankind, with a scandalous representation. But I maintain, that they ought all to have some failing or Infirmity, to qualifie 'em for the business of the Place. Men of Honour may be made use of to punish Knaves, as Knaves to cure Fools, but their honour ought not to be too strait-laced, too squeamish and scrupulous. They must be Persons of some Liberty, that out of an over-niceness will not balk a well laid design, and spoil a Project with too much honesty. Men of Hononr may be men of Pleasure; nay, and must be so too, or we do 'em wrong to make 'em appear in such Company, as *Comedy* must bring 'em into.

No Gentlemen but men of pleasure fit for Comedy.

What other natural occasion can be assigned for embroiling a Gentleman of Quality, with Usurers, Pimps, Sharpers, Jilts and Bullies, but the extravagance of his Pleasures? which they may all serve in their several capacities.

The

The Usurer with his Wife, his Daughter, or his Money; the Pimp in his Intrigues; the Jilt, the Sharper, and the Bully in their respective Offices may assist his Revenges, and be useful Engines in those designs, where 'tis not proper for himself to appear. That no Gentlemen but of this sort shou'd be brought upon the *Comick* Stage, I think, is so plain, as well from *Aristotle*'s Definition, as from the Nature and Business of the Place; that he that disputes it forfeits all Pretence to Judgment in these matters. I mean no Gentlemen of Wit and Sense, but such as these. For Fools of what Quality soever are the proper Goods and Chattels of the Stage; they are the wrecks of understanding, which Poets, as Lords of the Mannor of Wit from immemorial Prescription, have an uncontested Title to, and may dispose of, as they see fit.

Comick *Poetry and* Droll *Painting compar'd.*

A true *Comick* Poet like a good Droll Painter, ought not to make his whole Piece ridiculous, and consequently ought not to draw any Face that is so regular, as not to have something amiss either in Feature or Complextion. To

put

put a Gentleman of ſound Senſe and perfect Morals into *Comedy*, wou'd be as unnatural, as to draw *Cato* dancing amongſt the Boors at a Dutch Wedding. It does not therefore follow, that none but Rakes and Scoundrels muſt paſs for Gentlemen in *Comedy*. A Gentleman of Wit and Honour may be judiciouſly introduced into it, but he muſt be a man of wild unreclaim'd honour, whoſe Appetites are ſtrong and irregular enough, to hurry him beyond his diſcretion, and make him act againſt the Conviction of his Judgment on the return of his Reaſon. Such a Character as this no more is unnatural, than to ſee a drunken Gentleman frolicking with the Mob, or kiſſing a Link-Boy.

Such Characters real and common.

Nothing is more frequent than to meet in our common Converſation, and affairs of Life, with Gentlemen of this ſort, who, tho they may be Men of excellent Parts, Temper, and Principles, yet in the heat of their Blood, and Pride of their Fortunes, are apt to be byaſſed a little towards Extravagance, and not to conſult the ſeverity of Reaſon, or the exactneſs of Juſtice on many occaſions,

ſions, eſpecially in matters relating to their Pleaſures.

What therefore is ſo common and obvious in the World, can't be unnatural upon the Stage, but by uſing it improperly. To put a Gentleman upon the Office of a Villain or a Scoundrel, or to make a Man of Senſe a Bubble or a Cully in the Conclusion, is an abuſe to the Character, and a treſpaſs againſt the Laws of the *Drama*. If therefore the Poet employs any of this Character, he is obliged to give him Succeſs, notwithſtanding the blemiſhes of his Character. For, with all his Faults, he is the beſt, as well as the moſt conſiderable Perſon, that 'tis lawful for him to make bold with. And if he is at laſt brought to a Senſe of his Extravagance and Errours, and a reſolution of amendment, the Poet has exerted his Authority to the utmoſt extent of his Commiſſion; and the Laws of Comedy exact no more.

Mr Collier's *miſtake concerning the Nature of* Comedy.

Had Mr *Collier* known and conſider'd ſufficiently the nature of *Comedy*, I am apt to think, that we had never ſeen his whole fourth Chapter, which runs altogether upon this miſtake

ſtake, *That no Liberties are to be indulg'd in Comedy, and that the principal Characters ought to be in all reſpects exemplary, and without Blemiſh.* That this a miſtake I hope is very plain from what has been already ſaid. But becauſe Mr *Collier* has taken the pains to back, and aſſert this erroneous Opinion with a tedious Harangue, and ſome ſeemingly plauſible Arguments, it may not be amiſs to abſtract one from t'other, and conſider the latter diſtinctly, without amuſing our ſelves about his Pompous expreſſions, and Formal Rhetorick.

Heads of Mr Collier's *charge againſt* Engliſh Cody.

The whole Summ of Mr *Collier*'s long extravagant charge againſt the *Engliſh* Poets, eſpecially the preſent Comick Poets, againſt whom this Chapter ſeems to be particularly levelled, may be reduced to theſe two heads.

1ſt. That by making their Protagoniſts, or chief Perſons Licentious or debauched they encourage Vice, and Irreligion, and diſcourage Virtue.

2dly. That the rich Citizens are often repreſented as Miſers and Cuckolds; and the Univerſities as Schools of Pedantry; and thereby Learning, Induſtry and Frugality ridiculed.

Mr

Mr *Collier*, whoſe buſineſs all thro his Book is Invective, not Argument, lays himſelf forth with all thePomp of Formal Eloquence, and vehemence of Expreſſion, that he is able, to aggravate the crime,and amplifie the guilt of thePoets not to prove it. He is more ſollicitous to poſſeſs his Reader, than convince him, and for that reaſon lets ſlip the circumſtance of proof as not very material, becauſe he found it wou'd tye him up to ſtrict Argument, and cloſe Reaſoinng, which is not for his purpoſe, and inſiſts upon the General charge of Debauchery and Impiety; which allowing him all the Liberties of Declamation and Harangue, give him ample Field-room to publiſh, and diſplay his Parts, and his Malice together; which he does moſt egregigiouſly, and Flouriſhes moſt triumphantly. Never did learned Recorder inſult poor *Culprit* in more formidable Oratory, than he does the Poets.

'Tis true, he offers ſeveral inſtances in confirmation of his Aſſertion, which he draws from divers of our *Engliſh* Comedies, which, with the untoward gloſs he puts

upon

upon 'em, seem to favour his malicious purpose. These I shall consider in their proper places, as far as is absolutely requisite to our purpose, and leave the farther justification of 'em to the Gentlemen more immediately concerned, who I suppose will not be wanting to their own necessary defence.

His first Article examined.

We shall therefore proceed to the examination of the main Branch of his accusation, contained in the first Article, which is *the neglect of Poetick Justice, the encouraging of Vice with Success, and the Discouraging of Virtue.*

The whole weight of this Objection turns upon this hinge, that the *Protagonists*, or chief Persons in *Comedy* are generally vicious and successful, which he pretends to be against the Law of Comedy, which is to reward Virtue and punish Vice. This objection, as he observes, was started by Mr *Dryden* against himself in his *preface* to his *Mock-Astrologer*. But he objects against the answer, which Mr *Dryden* there makes to it. *That he knows no such Law constantly observed in Comedy, either by the Antients or Moderns.*

This

This Mr *Collier* calls a *lame Defence*, and I agree with him, tho we go upon different grounds. For I think Mr *Dryden* has clogg'd his anſwer with an unneceſſary reſtriction, and by the over Modeſty of it weakned the ſufficiency of it. I grant, that the neglect, or contempt of a Law, does by no means deſtroy the Authority of it. But I ſhall carry it ſomething farther, and ſay that no ſuch Law ever was at all obſerv'd, or ſo much as preſcrib'd to *Comedy*. Nor do I herein truſt to the Strength of my own Memory, or preſume upon the extraordinary reach and extent of my Enquiries. But I draw this Concluſion from the nature of *Comedy* itſelf, which will admit of no ſuch Rule in the latitude Mr *Dryden* propoſes, and Mr *Collier* maintains it. *This Rule repugnant to the Nature of Comedy*

Comedy, which deals altogether in ridicule, can take no cognizance of, and give no correction to thoſe Vices and Immoralities which it cannot expoſe on that ſide. For this reaſon, the Sallies of Youth, and the Licentiouſneſs of men of Senſe and Fortune, unleſs they be ſuch as bring their underſtandings into queſtion, and make 'em ridiculous, how *Reaſon why.*

ever unjuſtifiable, immoral, and offenſive they may be to ſober people, eſcape the cenſure of *Comedy*, becauſe they can't be tried in her way.

Indulgence of Plautus *and* Terence *to vicious young People miſplaced by Mr* Collier. *P.*149.

This Conſideration it was, that induc'd *Terence* and *Plautus* to indulge their Young Men ſo far as they did, and afford ſo many inſtances of Favour to vicious young people, as Mr *Collier* allows they did. He is miſtaken, when he fancies, *that* becauſe *thoſe Poets* had *a greater compaſs of Liberty in their Religion*, and that *Debauchery did not lie under thoſe diſcouragements of Penalty and Scandal with them, as it does with us*; therefore their Poets indulg'd themſelves in thoſe Liberties, which otherwiſe they durſt not have taken. *Plautus* and *Terence*, eſpecially the latter, were nice Obſervers of Mankind, and greater Maſters of their own Art, than to take an Improper Liberty, only becauſe 'twas not dangerous. But their Religion, falſe as it was, and the Laws of their Country, which were very ſevere at *Rome* in this caſe, requir'd ſtrict Morality, and Regularity of Life. If therefore they had ſuſpected, that theſe Indulgences had tended any ways to the Debauch-

Debauching of their Youth, and the Corrupting of their Manners, they durst not have ventur'd 'em into publick view. Nor wou'd their Magistrates, to whose Censure they were particularly submitted, have suffer'd examples of such ill consequence to have been produc'd openly. Besides, *Cato*, whose Virtue was as sowre and austere, and perhaps as great as Mr *Collier*'s, was a great encourager of 'em, which 'tis not proba- he wou'd have been, had he smelt any such dangerous Plot in 'em. So that the Authority of these *Precedents* may stand, and be of service, notwithstanding the wide difference betwixt *Heathenism*, and *Christianity*, and Mr *Collier*'s Opinion to the contrary.

Plautus *and* Terence *faithful Copyers from Nature.*

But *Plautus* and *Terence* have taken no such unjustifiable liberties, as he imagines. They have copyed faithfully from Nature, and their Draughts come incomparably near the Life. No outrage is done to the Original, by enlarging or contracting the Features, in order to entertain the Audience with Monsters or Dwarfs, but Humane Life is depicted in its true and just Proportion. If therefore the Images, which their Plays reflect, displease any froward *Cynic*, the Fault is in the Face, not the Glass which gives a true representation; and he quarrels with Providence, whose Creature Mankind is, if he dislikes the sight. Any liberties therefore, which these Poets have taken, wherein Nature is not wrong'd, descend undoubtedly to all those that succeed 'em upon the *Comick* Stage, who have a right to all the Priviledges of their Predecessors upon the same terms.

But *Plautus* and *Terence* made their young fellows, as Nature frequently does, wild and extravagant; at which Mr *Collier* is scandaliz'd, and appeals from their Judgment to

Opinion of Horace *enquir'd into.* P. 149.

Horace, *who* (he says) *was as good a Judge of the Stage, as either of those* Comedians, *yet seems to be of another opinion.* Let us see how far the Precept of *Horace* for the drawing of youth in general differs from the Practice of those *Comedians*. *Horace* tells us, *that the young Squire, as soon as he has shaken off the yoak of a Tutor, is for Dogs and Horses*, (and Whores too, as appears by the sequel of his Character) *that he is*

Cereus

Cereus in vitium flecti, monitoribus asper Art. Poet.
Utilium tardus Provisor, prodigus æris,
Sublimis, cupidusque, & amata relinquere pernix.

Prone to Vice, Impatient of Reproof, Careless of things necessary, Prodigal, Proud, Eager, and Inconstant in his Desires.

This is not a bare character, a simple description of the humours of young people; but 'tis a Precept, a Rule for Artists to draw 'em by. And therefore ought to include nothing contingent, or unnecessary; but every thing contain'd in it ought to be the inseparable Adjunct of the Species, such as a true Idea of the Generality cannot be given without, tho perhaps some Individuals may be met with, that want it. Upon this rule let Mr *Collier* arraign these Authors if he can. For tho they wrote before *Horace*, and consequently can't plead his Precept in their defence, yet the observation of Nature was common to them with him, and the reason of the rule as well known to 'em. I suppose therefore, if *Horace* be made their Judge in this case, they must be acquitted, otherwise he will condemn himself.

This not a bare Character but a Rule.

P. 149. But Mr *Collier* tells you, *that* Horace *condemns the obscenities of* Plautus, *and tells you that Men of Fortune and Quality, in his time, wou'd not endure immodest Satire.*

Sense of Horace *in this place mistaken, or perverted by* Mr Collier.

This I believe is a discovery of Mr *Collier*'s own, for I don't find any such accusation in *Horace*; he tells us, *that he did by no means admire the Versification and Raillery of* Plautus, *as their Ancestors had injudiciously done, that his Numbers were not true, nor his Wit Gentile.*

At nostri Proavi Plautinos, & numeros, &
Laudavere Sales; nimium patienter utrumque,
(Ne dicam Stultè) mirati: si modo ego, & vos
Scimus inurbanum, lepido seponere dicto,
Legitimumq; sonum digitis callemus, & arte.

Here he excepts against the Numbers, and Raillery of *Plautus*, and arraigns the Taste, and Judgment of their Ancestors, that approved 'em. But I don't find that he lays Immodesty, or Obscenity to his charge.

But

But this ſeems to be a ſtrain in emulation of his famous Predeceſſor Mr *Prynne*, whoſe Arguments and way of Reaſoning Mr *Collier* inherits as well as quarrel, with a double portion of his Spirit. Mr *Prynne* was offended at the appearance of Actreſſes upon the Stage, and in the Fervour of his Zeal finds it forbidden in Scripture; *Becauſe*, ſays he, *St Paul expreſsly prohibits Women from ſpeaking publickly in the Church*. Mr *Collier* in a fit of Criticiſm ſomething like this, takes occaſion from this Paſſage of *Horace*, to ſhew how apt a Scholar he is; and not to be behind hand with Mr *Prynne*, for a Reaſon, has recourſe to his uſual method of conſtruction, (in which we have already ſeen he has a ſingular dexterity) and converts *Horace*'s charge of inharmonious Verſe and Clowniſh Jeſts, to *Obſcenity* and *Immodeſt Satyr*.

Parity of reaſoning betwixt Mr Prynn *and Mr* Collier.

To cover this piece of Legerdemain, he confounds this Paſſage with another as little to his purpoſe. *Horace* from talking of *Tragedy* proceeds to lay down ſome Maxims for the better regulation of the *Satyræ*, then in uſe upon the *Roman* Stage. Theſe *Satyræ* were a ſort

Another outrage to Horace.

of Interludes introduced betwixt the Acts in Tragedy to refresh, and divert the Audience. The Persons represented were the *Satyri* or *Fauni*, or train of *Bacchus* or *Pan*; Persons supposed to be of very loose and virulent Tongues, and Rustick Behaviour. And accordingly the matter of these Poems was generally scandal, and Clownish raillery, in which to gain the applause of the Mob, they often took such sawcy Liberties in point of Scandal and Undecency, that the People of better Quality were offended at 'em. And *Horace* assures us, that the Quality and Mob cou'd never agree in their Verdict about 'em.

Art. Poet. *Sylvis deducti caveant (me Judice) Fauni,*
Ne, velut innati triviis, ac pene forenses,
Aut nimium teneris juvenenter versibus unquam,
Aut immunda crepent, ignominiosaque dicta
Offenduntur enim, quibus est Equus, & Pater, & res:
Nec, siquid fricti ciceris probat, & nucis emptor,
Æquis accipiunt animis, donantve corona.

But

But what's all this to *Plautus* and *Comedy*, who never had any Dealings with these *Satyræ*.

After this notable exploit, he launches out into the wide Sea of Poetry, and flourishes with the Character that *Horace* gives of the first Poets, *Orpheus*, *Amphion*, *&c*, whom he celebrates as the civilizers of Mankind; but as that affords little matter either of Honour or Reproach to these, that came so long after them, when the Muses, tho they might have kept their Virtue, yet had lost very much of their Power, and instead of commanding the Passions of their Auditors, were forced on many occasions to comply with and submit to their Whimsies, and humour their capricious Appetites: It will be impertinent (whatever licence Mr *Collier* may assume) to insist any longer upon a case no way Paralell. For this Character, which *Horace* bestows upon those Poets, was intended as a complement to Poetry in general, but not to reflect any honour upon the *Drama* in particular, (much less *Comedy*, the more recent branch of it) which was not invented till long after the time of *Orpheus* and *Amphion*.

His

Use of a Chorus *according to* Horace.

His next uſe that he makes of the Authority of *Horace*, he draws from his Inſtructions about the Office of the *Chorus. The Chorus* (*Horace* tells us after *Ariſtotle*) *ought to bear the part of an Actor, and take care to ſay nothing incoherent, or incongruous to the main deſign, but to make his Song of a piece with the whole. From hence* (Mr *Collier* infers that) *'tis plain, that* Horace *wou'd have no immoral Character have either Countenance or good Fortune upon the Stage.*

Objection.

But here he foreſees an Objection, that the *Chorus* was left off in *Comedy* before *Horace*'s time, and that theſe directions muſt needs therefore be intended for *Tragedy*. To which

Mr Collier's *anſwer.*

He *anſwers, that the Conſequence is not good. For the uſe of the* Chorus *is not inconſiſtent with* Comedy. *The Antient* Comedians *had it.* Ariſtophanes *is an Inſtance. I know 'tis ſaid the* Chorus *was left out, in that which they call* New Comedy.

Reply to Mr Collier's *anſwer.*

Had Mr *Collier* conſider'd who 'twas that ſaid this, he ought to have acquieſc'd in his Authority; but ſince he is ſo unwilling to confeſs, he muſt be convicted, and therefore we ſhall endeadeavour to prove the validity of the consequence upon him. I shall trouble the Reader with the Depositions of but one Evidence, but he shall be, like Conscience in this case, *Mille Testes*. *Horace* tells us, *that the* Old Comedy *grew so intolerably abusive and scandalous, that a Law was made to curb it, and that from that time the* Chorus *was silenc'd.*

Successit vetus his Comœdia, non sine multâ Art. Poet.
Laude, sed in vitium libertas excidit, & vim
Dignam lege regi. Lex est accepta, Chorusque
Turpiter obticuit, sublato jure nocendi.

This testimony of *Horace* is full against Mr *Collier*, and a plain argument that he never intended his directions for a *Chorus* for the use of *Comedy*. The *Chorus* in the *Old Comedy* had the greatest freedom of Speech, and took the boldest liberties of any part of the Play, and consequently gave the greatest offence, and stood most in need of Correction. And *Horace* seems to insinuate, that the *Chorus* was not only scandalously offensive, but that it was express-

Chorus *in* Old Comedy.

preſsly ſilenc'd by Law, when he ſays,

—Lex eſt accepta, Chorusque
Turpiter obticuit, ſublato jure nocendi.

As if the whole Buſineſs of the *Chorus* in *Comedy* had been Scandal, and the Law levell'd againſt the *Chorus* only. The event juſtifies this Expoſition; For after the Publication of the Laws againſt the Liberty of Scandal, which was grown ſo rampant in the *Old Comedy*, the *Chorus* vaniſh'd, and appear'd no more upon the *Athenian* Stage in *Comedy*, that we know of.

Plutus *of* Ariſtophanes. P. 150.

This Mr *Collier* denies, and fortifies himſelf and his Aſſertion with matter of Fact. *For* Ariſtophanes *his* Plutus *is* New Comedy *with a* Chorus *in't.*

Double miſtake of Mr Collier.

In this Aſſertion there are two miſtakes, which being Critical ones, I don't much wonder at, becauſe they contribute towards making the Book Uniform, and preſerve the Integrity of the Piece. Yet he building with ſo much aſſurance upon 'em, 'twill be but Charity to let him ſee, that his Foundation is too weak to ſupport the weight of the ſuperſtructure he has laid upon it.

The

The first of these is, that the *Plutus* of *Aristphanes* is not *New Comedy*.

2dly. That in the *Plutus*, there is no *Chorus*.

The Learned (whom I suppose Mr *Collier* means by *they*) divide the *Greek Comedy* into three *Classes*, the *Old*, the *Middle*, and the *New*; not to mention that the *Old Comedy* it self is subdivided into two Ages; the latter of which commences with *Cratinus*, who first distinguisht the Parts, disposed the Acts, and fixt the number of Actors; and comprehends *Eupolis*, *Aristophanes*, and the rest of the Comick Poets till the conclusion of the Popular Authority, and the beginning of the Oligarchy, from which time to the time of *Alexander*, that which is now called the *Middle Comedy* flourished, till *Menander*, and the Poets of his time, *Philemon*, *Diphilus*, *Apollodorus*, and others, quite altered the Face of the *Comick Stage*, and introduc'd that which is now call'd the *New Comedy*.

Tripartite Division of the Greek Comedy.

By this Division, which is both just, and accurate, the *Plutus* falls to the share of the *Old Comedy*; to which, notwithstanding the deviations therein

By this the Plutus Old *Comedy*.

from

from the former Practice of *Ariſtophanes*, it does moſt properly belong. But if Mr *Col lier* will have the *Plutus* of *Ariſtophanes* to be the firſt ſtep towards the Reformation of *Comedy* at *Athens*, I ſhall not much diſpute the matter with him. Becauſe he has in that abridged himſelf of much of that Liberty, which he has uſed in his former Plays. But granting even this, *Ariſtophanes* can at moſt but lead up the Van of the *Middle Comedy*; and is very far diſtanc'd by the *New*.

Fable *of* Old *Comedy of what kind.*

For tho *Ariſtophanes* has in ſome meaſure altered his Conduct in his *Plutus*, yet he retains abſolutely the Form and ſtamp of the *Old Comedy*, and retrenches only ſome offenſive Liberties. The Fable of the old *Comedy* was altogether Chimerical, and the Characters Romantick and Whimſical, neither of 'em drawn from the Obſervation of Nature, or the buſineſs of Humane Life, but pumpt out of the extravagance of the *Poets* Brain. The Spirit of theſe Entertainments conſiſted in the Piquancy of the Raillery and Jeſts, and the boldneſs of the Scandal, in which they took exceſſive Liber-

ties

ties with particular Perſons, eſpecially the *Chorus*, and to which the ſucceſs of 'em was wholy owing. *Cratinus* is ſaid to have been very bold, and to have taxed people freely by their names, without miucing the matter, (I had almoſt ſaid without Fear or Wit) and charged them with all ſorts of Crimes, without reſpect to Perſons. *Eupolis* was ſomewhat more diſcreet, couching real Crimes and Perſons under ſham Names, and laſhing his Fellow Citizens on the backs of feigned Offenders. *Ariſtophanes* was frequently no leſs plain than *Cratinus* in reſpect to Names, but his Wit was of another ſort, leſs Sullen and Chagrine. He turned all into Jeſt, and bantered thoſe things, which the others reprehended after a manner more ſerious aud ſevere.

Characters of Cratinus, Eupolis, *and* Ariſtophanes *how differenc'd.*

Menander and the *New Comedians* formed their Models after a very different manner. For having particularly Scandal, which had given ſo much Offence in the *Old Comedy*, they began to furniſh themſelves from Obſervation and Experience, rather than Invention, and to employ their Judgments more than their Fancies. They raiſed the

New Comedy *how differing from the* Old.

ſtructure of their Plays upon the Foundations of Nature, and made the Intrigues of the World, and the common Affairs of Life the Subjects of 'em, and the different orders of Mankind. A hard Father, a difficult Maſter, a wild Son, a crafty Servant, an impudent Pandar, a Mercenary Courtezan, and a Captive Virgin, were the moſt uſual Characters; which being oppoſite to, and concerned with one another, ſet the Plot naturally to work, and give occaſion to ſet all the Wheels of the Machine a going.

Plutus *not* New *Comedy.*

This may ſuffice to give us an Idea of the difference between the *Old Comedy* and the *New*, and to convince us that the *Plutus* of *Ariſtophanes*, which deals altogether in unaccountable Deſigns and ſurprizing Events, and works by Unnatural Machines to a Chimerical, Romantick end, is not *New Comedy*; tho the Poet contrary to his Cuſtom makes uſe of Feigned Names, and lays aſide the *Chorus*. For tho theſe Innovations be here made in *Comedy*, yet both the matter and the Form (wherein conſiſted the main difference between the *Old Comedy* and the *New*) remaining

ing still the same with the rest of his Plays, it can by no means be admitted into the *New*, both matter and form of which were different, if not directly opposite to the former. For in the *Old Comedy* they proceeded from Generals that were Chimerical and false, to argue particulars that were real and true. In the *New* from Particulars that were imaginary and false, they reprehended Generals that were real. The *Old Comick Poets* generally devised some extravagant and unnatural, or at least improbable tale, into which they took occasion to thrust particular Facts and Persons that were real, and well known. The *New* made use of such Intrigues and Persons as were frequent and familiar amongst Mankind, and thereby corrected the common Faults, such as Avarice, Fraud, *&c.* but copyed neither the Actions, nor Manners of Individuals; and so reflected not particularly upon any One. The first resembled a Limner, that cou'd copy the Features of a Face, but cou'd only draw Individuals like, ye cou'd not design; the latter a true Historical Painter, that aim'd rather at expressing the Manners, and Passions

Satire of the Old *Comedy particular of the* New *general.*

of Mankind than the countenances. In whose pieces you shou'd not amongst a Thousand meet one Face, that you distinctly knew, yet none but what were natural and significant, and such as you must acknowledge you saw every day. The difference therefore betwixt the *Old Comedy* and the *New* is as great and evident, as betwixt the Paintings of *Raphael Urbin*, or *Michael Angelo*, and those of Sir *Anthony Vandike*, or Sir *Peter Lely*. I shall not therefore insist upon those lesser differences of *Phrase* and *Metre*, those already given, being sufficient to inform a very indifferent Judge.

Aristophanes *the Beginner of the* Middle Comedy.

However, as *Aristophanes* has in this Play varied his Conduct in some things from the Practice of the rest of the *Old Comedians*, and of himself in his former Pieces, he seems to challenge the first place in the *Middle Comedy*, which the Learned have found it necessary to distinguish both from the *Old* and the *New*. Because several alterations were made in *Comedy*, of which perhaps the Omission of the *Chorus* was none of the least considerable, yet neither the Model or Design were

were totally changed till the time of *Menander*, and his Cotemporaries.

Mr *Collier*'s second mistake in relation to the *Plutus* of *Aristophanes* is, *that it has a Chorus in't*. If he means that there is a part in this Play, which is sustained by a *Person* or *Persons* under the name of *Chorus*, Matter of Fact is directly for him. But if he thinks that there is any such thing as a true *Chorus* in it, it is as plain against him. This matter will easily be decided, if we consider the Nature, and Office of a *Chorus* in the *Old Comedy*.

No Chorus in the Plutus.

The *Chorus* in *Comedy*, was a Person consisting of divers, either Men or Women, or both, and assisted in two Capacities. One as an Actor, or Party concern'd to promote and carry on the main design, and help forward the Action of the Play, which is common to the *Chorus* with the other Actors, and does not distinguish it from 'em. The other, as the *Poet*'s Representative, to make the *Parabases*, or Transitions from the Actors, (with whom only as an Actor the *Chorus* is concern'd) to the *Gods*, or to the *Audience*. To the *Gods*, to invoke their Aid, or celebrate

Office of the Chorus *in* Comedy.

their Praiſes, as the occaſion ſuggeſted. To the *Audience*, to inform 'em of what was ſuppos'd to paſs *extra Scenam* behind the Scenes, to make the Action of the Play entire, or to make reflections on what paſs'd upon the Stage for the Inſtruction of the Audience, and to tax the evil Practices of ſuch Citizens, as were obnoxious to the *Poet*, and the Publick. This was the part by which it at leaſt gave offence, by the diſorderly liberties which it took; and ſometimes to acquaint the Audience with the Poet's hopes and fears, his acknowledgments and complaints, which laſt part of the buſineſs of the *Chorus* is anſwer'd by the *Prologue* among the *Romans*.

The parts Eſſential to a Chorus *omitted in the* Plutus.

I ſhall not trouble the Reader with the *Grammatical* diviſion of the parts of the *Chorus*, (*viz.*) *Ode*, *Antode*, *Strophe*, and *Antiſtrophe*, &c. which ſignify nothing to the point before us. But I ſhall deſire the Reader to take notice that in the *Plutus* of *Ariſtophanes*, this part which alone conſtitutes the Office, and Buſineſs of a *Chorus*, and which only diſtinguiſhes it from a common Actor is entirely omitted. The *Chorus* in in this Play appears but as an ordinary Actor, and addresses itself to the other Actors only, comes on, and goes off without once singing or speaking apart from the rest. The *Chorus* therefore, as it is called, in this Play might more properly have been personated by a single man, and called by any other name, since it performs nothing of the Office.

The Observation of this defect of the Essential part of the *Chorus*, made the Learned * *Julius Scaliger* think, that this Play had been castrated, and that the *Chorus* (which he confesses to be wanting) was not omitted, but taken away since the writing of it. But whether it were, as *Scaliger* suspects, taken out after it was finish'd, or omitted in the writing, is not very material; 'tis plain we have it not, and 'tis very probable that 'twas the Author's own fear of offending, that depriv'd us of it; the want of which caution in his Βάπται cost *Cratinus* his Life. For had the *Chorus* of the *Plutus* ever been made publick, I see no reason why that, as well as the rest of his *Chori*, should not have been transmitted to us. I would

*Etiam in ejusdem Pluto Chori desiderantur, quod & alibi monebamus: ita tamen ut non omissus, sed exemptus videatur. Poetic. lib. I. cap. viii.

advise Mr *Collier* in the next *Greek* Play he cites, to read farther than the List of the Persons of the *Drama*. For 'tis apparently negligence, that has led him into this Errour, and made him think, that because he found a *Chorus* there, it must needs be in the Play, which he would not have allow'd to be a legitimate *Chorus*, had he read the Play, and known the business of a *Chorus*. 'Tis yet in his Election which excuse shall stand for him.

Mr *Collier*'s Instance therefore signifies nothing to his Argument, because it does not prove a *Chorus* consistent with the *New Comedy*.

1st, Because the *Plutus* in which he instances is not *New Comedy*.

2dly, Because (tho it were *New Comedy*) it has no *Chorus*.

So that, I suppose, we may lay the Authority of *Aristophanes* aside in this case.

We shall not trouble the Reader with a particular of the Fables of *Aristophanes*, which are so extravagantly Romantick, that 'tis impossible they should be edifying. And therefore I suppose Mr *Collier* will not play the Morality of of the *Greek Comedy* upon us from that Quarter.

But he proceeds to prove the continuance of the *Chorus* in *Comedy* by an oblique Inference from *Aristotle*, *who lived after this Revolution of the* Stage, (yet) *mentions nothing of the omission of the* Chorus. But in Mr *Collier's* opinion, *rather supposes the continuance of it, by saying the* Chorus *was added by the Government long after the Invention of* Comedy.

Unconclusive Inference from Aristotle.

P. 150.

Here the Silence of *Aristotle* concerning the omission of the *Chorus* in *Comedy*, is made an Argument of the Continuance of it ; and by an odd sort of Sophistry, he concludes, that because he has taken notice of the first Institution of it, he must needs do the same for the disuse of it, had he been acquainted with it.

Silence of Aristotle *no argument in this Case.*

By the same way of arguing he might have prov'd, that *Aristophanes* was the the last of the *Comic Poets* before *Aristotle*, because he has made no mention of any that succeeded him ; and yet we are sufficiently inform'd, that there were divers between *Aristotle* and *Aristophanes*.

Reason of Ari-ſtotle's *ſilence in this point.*

But if at this diſtance we muſt needs be conjecturing at reaſons, for that which paſs'd ſo long ago, a much more natural account may be given of this Silence, than that which Mr *Collier* ſtrains ſo hard for. *Ariſtotle* was a man of extraordinary Capacity and Judgment, and did not talk ſo impertinently as Mr *Collier* ſuppoſes he would have done, if he had had opportunity. *Ariſtotle*, in his Treatiſe of *Tragedy*, gives a very brief account of the Riſe and Progreſs of the *Drama*, and as his ſubject obliged him, tells us, that the two Branches, *Tragedy* and *Comedy*, aroſe both from the ſame Spring, *viz.* the *Hymns* to *Bacchus*, the former from the *Dithyrambi*, which contain'd his Praiſes and Exploits, the latter from the τὰ φαλλικὰ, a ſort of obſcene Songs compos'd of the ſame Deity, which in conformity to the Law were ſtill continued his time in the Villages.

His account of the Riſe of the Drama.

Cap. 4.

* ἁ δὲ ἀπὸ τῶν τὰ φαλλικὰ ἔτι ϗ νῦν ἐν πολλαῖς τῶν πόλεων διαμένει νομιζόμενα.

In the next Chapter he proceeds to the Definition of *Comedy*, in order to illuſtrate the difference betwixt that and *Tragedy*; and then informs us, that the firſt ſteps towards the reducing *Comedy* to Form and Order, were made in

Progreſs of Comedy *obſcure.*

in the dark, and the marks of'em too far obliterated to be trac'd backwards, through publick neglect, that 'twas long e're it came to be Acted at the Expence of the Publick. For that's the meaning in this place, of the Magistrates giving the *Chorus*, that is paying the *Actors*. For he immediately subjoyns, that all before that time *were Volunteers* in this Service, that is, acted *gratis*.

Brevity of Aristotle.

In this account of the growth of *Comedy*, *Aristotle* according to his usual Method, is very concise, and does not make one step out of his way to gratifie any Curiosity, which he foresaw that some of his Readers might have. But Mr *Collier*, who reasons after a manner very different from the Philosopher, wou'd lead him a Wild Goose Chase quite out of his road, to tell when the *Chorus* in *Comedy* was silenc'd, tho 'twas nothing to his purpose, and a long way from his Text ; or force him to confess against his Conscience that he knows nothing of the matter. But *Aristotle*, who was a better Judge than Mr *Collier* of what was proper and necessary to his subject, reserves this point to ano-

ther

ther occaſion, and in the preceding Chapter reprimands the unſeaſonable Curioſity and Impatience of thoſe, that require deciſions out of Time and Order. Which had Mr *Collier* carefully read, this Argument probably had been ſuppreſs'd.

Cap. 4.

A particular Treatiſe of Comedy *written by* Ariſtotle, *but loſt.*

However, to oblige him with a little ſcratching where it itches, I muſt deſire him to take notice, that at that time *Ariſtotle* had actually written, or deſign'd at leaſt to write another Book concerning *Comedy* in particular, and therefore prudently forbore to uſe thoſe Materials here, which he knew wou'd be more ſerviceable in another place. This Book has been long loſt, and therefore there lies no Appeal to it on this occaſion. Yet becauſe he has ſuch a mind to make *Ariſtophanes* the Father of the *New* Comedy, we'll ſtretch a point farther than we are bound by the Laws of *Polemicks*; and to ſhew that we are fair Adverſaries, point him out a Play, that may perhaps ſerve his turn ſomewhat better than the *Plutus*. The *Cocalus*, one of the laſt Plays of *Ariſtophanes*, which is loſt, is ſaid by ſome learned men to have been the Model,

which

which *Menander* copyed exactly, and took his design of the *New* Comedy from. If this be true, *Aristophanes* may in some sense claim the *New* Comedy as his Issue. But then Mr *Collier* must not say a word more of the *Chorus*. For 'tis certain that *Menander* used none, and very probable, that the *Cocalus* had none neither, if that were his Model.

By this it may appear, that whether a *Chorus* be consistent with *New Comedy* or not, it was not used in it by the *Antients*. Nor was it indeed fit to be used according to the liberties of *Aristophanes*. And we may conclude from the practice of all Ages and Nations ever since, that they thought those Freedoms essential to the *Chorus* of *Comedy*, when they chose rather to lay it wholly aside than to reform it. If *Moliere* has, after two thousand years discontinuance, ventur'd to bring a Chorus again upon the *Comick* Stage, I don't find that his performances of that kind have any extraordinary effect, or that they stir up many Imitators to follow his Example. *Moliere* was arrived at the second Infancy of his *Poetry*, and might want those

Chorus *not used in the* New Comedy.

thoſe helps to keep his Plays upon their Legs, which by the firſt *Comick Poets* were made uſe of to teach theirs to go upright. His more vigorous productions ſcorn'd thoſe Crutches, which the Iſſue of his old Age, that brings the Infirmities of its Parent along with it into the world, is forc'd to have recourſe to for its ſupport.

Chorus *altogether improper for the* Comick *Stage in* England.

But to what end wou'd Mr *Collier* introduce the *Chorus* into the *Engliſh Comedy* ? We have no *Hymns*, no *Anthems* to be ſung upon the *Stage* ; nor no *Muſic*, or *Dancing*, but what is as well or better perform'd by the ordinary Method now in uſe, than it could be by a *Chorus*. The main buſineſs of a *Chorus* is cut off by our Religion, and the reſt render'd uſeleſs and unneceſſary, by the method and diſpoſition of our Comedies. Something like it we have ſtill in uſe, tho not in our *Theatres*, yet at our *Puppet Shews* ; where *Chorus* ſtands before the *Scenes*, and explains to the Spectators what they ſee, and informs 'em what ſhall happen afterwards, makes his Wiſe reflections on what is paſt, and ſometimes enters into Dialogue with his little *Actors*, as a Party concern'd,

Uſed at Puppet *Shews.*

concern'd, and talks to the purpose like one of them. This is exactly the Office of a *Chorus*, and therefore I don't see why the fellow that discharges it mayn't wear the Title ; except it be, that the Authors of that sort of *Drama*, are generally too illiterate to know from whence they originally fetcht their Precedent. Here is nothing of the duty of a *Chorus* omitted, except the *Singing*, *Dancing*, and *Idolatrous Part*, which, as we have already observ'd, are all either better supply'd otherwise, or absolutely inconsistent with our Religion and Stage.

Mr *Collier* indeed seems to assign the *Chorus* another Office. He wou'd have it to be a sort of *Monitor*, or *Chaplain* to the Play, to preach to the Audience, and correct the Disorders of the Stage. This is a new Function, for which I doubt he can produce no warrant from *Aristophanes*, or Precedent from *Moliere*. 'Tis an Office of his own creating, and therefore he wou'd do well to execute it a while himself, to instruct the *Players*, and teach 'em the knack of Preaching, in which they are yet unexercis'd.

Function assigned the Chorus *by* Mr Collier.

But

Original Errour of Mr Collier.

But all this Torrent of Misreasoning and false Rhetorick flows from one Spring, one Original Error has branch'd itself out thus amply. Mr *Collier* knows, that *the business of* Comedy *is to instruct by example*; and he mistakenly imagines, that these ought to be Examples for Imitation. Whereas, if he considers the nature of *Comedy*, he will find just the reverse of this fancy to be true. For, as we have already taken notice, it can employ no perfectly upright Characters, and consequently can afford no Examples, but for Caution.

Loose Characters in Comedy no Encouragement to Debauchery.

Nor is *Comedy* therefore to be thought imperfect, any more than the Law, which makes no other provision for the encouragement of Virtue and good Actions, than by punishing Vice and Villany. What Mr *Collier* objects in this case is groundless, that the Poets, by dressing up an imperfect, or debauch'd Character, with the embellishments of Wit and Sense, and other good Qualities, and crowning it with Success at last, pave the way to Licentiousness and Debauchery. For, whether the Poet brings such a Character to a solemn Resolution of Reforming at last,

laſt, or not, which yet they generally do, 'tis evident, that the ſucceſs which attends it, is not given to the Licentiouſneſs, but to the Wit and Senſe, or other good Qualities, which are predominant in the Character. He therefore that can take Succeſs ſo beſtow'd, and circumſtantiated as it is uſually in *Comedy*, for an encouragement to Debauchery muſt have a very deprav'd Apprehenſion.

But Mr *Collier* is implacably enrag'd at the *Poets*, for mixing ſuch Beauties and ſuch Blemiſhes in one Piece; and is in a Pannick Fear, leſt the Beauty of the whole ſhou'd tempt Folks to ape the Deformities of it. This is as ridiculous an Apprehenſion, as if any awkard Fellow ſhou'd ſee a *Beau* in all his Glory with dirty Shoes, and ſhou'd fancy that he made that ſplendid Figure purely by virtue of the dirt upon his Shoes, and reſolve never to have his own clean'd again. A fine Face, with a caſt of the Eyes, may move the *Beau*'s and the Ladies to wiſh for ſuch Features, and ſuch a Complexion, yet it wou'd ſcarce win 'em to endeavour to ſquint like it. Whatever Mr *Collier* may

Ridiculous Fear of Mr Collier.

may think, the Underſtanding of our Youth is not ſo very depreſs'd and low, but they can very readily diſtinguiſh between the obvious Beauties, and Defects of a Character, and are not to be fool'd like *Dottrels* into a vicious Imitation. If a Man ſhou'd know a *Pick-pocket* that was an excellent Accountant, or a *Forger* of falſe Notes that was an incomparable Writing-maſter, it were very eaſie, and very commendable, for any one to imitate their good Qualities, without receiving any taint or impreſſion from their Rogueries.

Theatres wrongfully accuſed by him.

However, Mr *Collier* obſerves abundance of Licentiouſneſs and Impurity in the world, and is reſolv'd to lay it all at the doors of the Theatres. He ſees up and down a great number of figures like thoſe that are expos'd upon the Stage, and he wiſely concludes, that the Models muſt needs be taken from thence, and that theſe men are but the Players apes, which is directly contrary to the Truth. For theſe are the Originals, of which thoſe upon the Stage are but the Copies, the Images, which that, like a Glaſs, reflects back upon 'em

Cha-

Chorus, or no *Chorus*, Mr *Collier* pushes still forward upon the mistaken Authority of *Horace*; and maintains that *Horace having expressly mentioned the Beginning and Progress of Comedy, discovers himself more fully. He advises a* Poet *to form his work upon the Precepts of* Socrates *and* Plato, *and the Models of Moral Philosophy. This was the way to preserve Decency, and to assign a proper Fate and Behaviour to every* Character. *Now if* Horace *wou'd have his* Poet *govern'd by the Maxims of Morality, he must oblige him to Sobriety of Conduct, and a just Destribution of Rewards and Punishments.*

Sense of Horace *again perverted.*

P. 151.

To try the validity of this Argument, we must have recourse to the Original, which will shew us some misapplication, and some mistake of *Horace*'s meaning in this short Paragraph. Mr *Collier* links this advice of *Horace* immediately to his account of the Rise and Progress of *Comedy*; and that he may appropriate it solely to *Comedy*, skips over a transition of twenty lines, by which the Poet artificially passes from the particular of *Comedy* to *Poetry* in

 general;

general ; and takes occasion to say, that *a good Poet ought to be a wise Man, and acquainted with the Writings of the Philosophers.* For *Socrates* appears in this place as the *Representative* of the whole Body of *Moral* Philosophers, and not for himself and *Plato* only, as Mr *Collier* imagines.

Hor. Art. Poet.

> *Scribendi recte sapere est Principium & Fons.*
> *Rem tibi Socraticæ poterunt ostendere chartæ.*

The reason of this he immediately subjoyns, which will also make the application for us. For, says he, *The man that knows what is due to his Country, and his Friends, his obligations to Parents and Kindred, the Laws of Hospitality, and the duty of a* Senator, *a* Judge, *and a* General, *knows enough to enable him to do Justice to every* Character.

Ibid.

> *Qui didicit Patriæ quid debeat, & quid amicis :*
> *Quo sit amore Parens, quo Frater amandus & Hospes,*
> *Quod*

Quod sit Conscripti, quod Judicis officium, quæ
Partes in bellum missi ducis: ille profecto
Reddere personæ scit convenientia cuiq;.

This List of Qualifications seems prepar'd only for *Tragick* and *Epick* Poetry. *Comedy*, which concerns none but the lesser Intrigues of Mankind, and the private Affairs of particular Families, or Persons, has no dealings with the Publick, or its Magistrates; and therefore does not seem to be comprehended in the aim of these directions.

Yet, if Mr *Collier* will have it included, he ought to have shewn how far it was affected in particular upon a fair exposition. But that method wou'd not serve his turn. For *Horace* in this passage, does not advise the Study of *Morality*, but *Politicks*, which could best satisfy demands of this nature. He did not expect that the *Poets* shou'd tye their *Characters* up to severe duty, and make every one act up to the strict Rules of Morality, and be guided by the dictates of right Reason and Justice, or otherwise to punish 'em always in propor-

This Advice Political, not Moral.

proportion to the Deviations they made from 'em, as Mr *Collier* insinuates. All that he requir'd was, that a Poet shou'd know how it became the several orders of men to behave themselves in civil Societies, according to their respective Ranks, Degrees, and Qualities; that they might thereby be qualify'd to give distinct Images of every kind, whether good or bad, without mixing of Characters, or confounding Ideas. *Rectum est Index sui, & obliqui*, was his Rule in this case, and 'tis a true one, a right notion of things will certainly discover a false one. For this he advis'd his *Poet*, to consult the *Philosophers*, and to dive into the political Reasons of these matters, without which their view of 'em wou'd be but superficial and confus'd.

Yet after all he gave him very large Priviledges, and extended his Charter, as far as the observation of Humane Nature, he allow'd him the liberty of saying any thing that Providence laid before him, provided he kept close to the Original. To this end he bids him *look upon the Examples that men set him in their Lives and Manners, and thence*

thence learn to draw true pictures of Mankind.

Respicere exemplar vitæ, morumq; jubebo.
Doctum Imitatorem, & veras hinc ducere voces.

The *Mores*, or *Manners* here mentioned by *Horace*, are the *Poetical*, not *Moral*, the distinction betwixt which Mr *Collier* very well knows, as appears by his making use of it, when 'tis for his turn, tho he wilfully over-looks it in many other places, where the notice of it would be more natural, but less for his malicious purpose. However, since he has given a sort of definition, tho an imperfect one, of *Poetical Manners*, I shall give it the Reader in his own words. And because 'tis the only Statute Law of *Parnassus*, by which the Poets can fairly be tried for any misdemeanour, either of Character or Expression, I shall supply the Defects of Mr *Collier*'s report of it from *Aristotle*, who is more full and clear. Manners *here signified* Poetical *not* Moral.

Manners, *in the Language of Poetry*, is a propriety of Actions and Persons. *To succeed in this business there must be* *Mr* Collier's *description of* Poetical Manners

P. 165. *a regard had to* Age, Sex, and Condition: *And nothing put into the mouths of Persons, which disagrees with any of these circumstances. 'Tis not enough to say a witty thing, unless it be spoken by a likely Person, and upon a proper occasion.*

Defective and Equivocal. In this account I observe many things deficient, something equivocal, which I shall first take notice of, and then proceed to supply the Defects. The three things, Mr *Collier* recommends to a *Poet*'s, or *Reader*'s careful observation, and regard, are *Age, Sex, and Condition.* Of these, the first and the last, *Age* and *Condition*, are equivocal terms. The Author has not taken care to explain, whether he means by *Age*, the Age of a *Person*, or the Age of the *World*, which he is suppos'd to live in. For to both these great regard is to be had, because they difference the *Characters* equally. A noble *Roman* of four and twenty in the first Ages of the Commonwealth, was no more like one of the same Age under the Emperors, in humour and inclinations, than either of 'em was like his Grandfather of Fourscore. As great, or greater is the Ambiguity of the word *Condition*, whereby

whereby he has not signify'd whether he means Condition, as to *Estate*, *Quality*, *Understanding*, or *Circumstances, as to the Action of the Play, at the juncture when the person does or says any thing*. Yet these have all an equal share in the propriety both of Words and Actions, and ought to be consider'd, otherwise the Manners can never be preserv'd in their Propriety and Integrity. But by supplying the Defects of this Account, we shall remedy the danger of mistakes from the equivocal Expressions contained in it.

Aristotle requires four conditions to the perfection of *Poetick Manners*.

Aristotle's *description*.

1st, *That they be good*.

By the *Goodness* of *Manners* the Philosopher does not here understand any *Moral* Goodness; for he declares in this very Article, that he means only * that they should be expressive of the Character, and carry both in words and actions, the distinguishing marks of the Humour and Inclinations of the person, whether they be *morally* Good or Bad. So that if the Humour or natural Inclinations of the persons be sufficiently markt in the words and actions, the Man-

* Ἕξει δὲ ἦθος μὲν, ἐὰν, ὥσπερ ἐλέχθη, ποιῇ φανερὸν ὁ λόγος, ἢ ἡ πρᾶξις προαίρεσίν τινα φαῦλον μὲν, ἐὰν φαύλην χρηστὸν δὲ ἐὰν χρηστῇ.

Manners are good, according to *Ariſtotle*, let 'em be never ſo vicious. *Horace* underſtands *Manners* the ſame way, when he tells us, *that ſometimes Plays of little Elegance, without Ornament, or Art, yet wherein the Manners were well expreſs'd, took better than others, wherein they were neglected for Tinſel and Bombaſt.*

Hor. Art. Poet.

Interdum ſpecioſa locis, morataq; recte
Fabula, nullius Veneris ſine pondere & Arte
Valdius oblectat Populum, meliuſq; moratur,
Quam verſus inopes rerum, Nugæq; canoræ.

2dly, * *That they be proper.*

* τὰ ἁρμόττοντα.

Propriety of Manners requir'd.

Wherein this propriety conſiſts *Ariſtotle* has not told us, except in one Negative Inſtance, *that Courage is a Quality improper, or unbecoming a Woman.* Mr *Collier*'s account of *Poetical Manners* above-cited, relates to this particular Condition only, yet is both defective and equivocal in that. *Horace* has been very full upon this, and takes care to deſcribe at large the different humours of man in the ſeveral Stages of his Life.

The

The ſame he does to the ſeveral orders and degrees of men, according to their reſpective Capacities, either Natural or Political, and gives the Poets a great Charge not to confound 'em. To repeat his words upon this occaſion wou'd be tedious, upon the ſcore of length. However, I ſhall endeavour to give the Reader as good an *Idea* of this *Poetical* Propriety, as the narrow compaſs I am oblig'd to will permit. The propriety of *Manners* conſiſts in an exact conformity both of words and actions to the ſuppoſed *Age* both of the perſon and the world, to the *Humour*, *Fortune*, *Quality*, *Underſtanding*, and preſent *Condition*, as to the buſineſs of the Play, of the perſon acting or ſpeaking. *Horace* as well as *Ariſtotle*, has expreſs'd all this in one word, *Convenientia*, both which I have render'd *Proper*. This place does not afford me room for inſtances for each particular, and therefore I ſhall deſire the Reader's patience, till the Subject calls for 'em in their proper places.

Wherein it conſiſts.

3dly, *That they be like.*

This Condition relates only to *Characters* taken from Hiſtories, or *Poetical* Tra-

Similitude *of* Manners *what.*

Traditions very well known. When the *Poet* makes uſe of Names, or Stories with which the Audience is well acquainted, he muſt be ſure to make 'em conform to the receiv'd opinion. Otherwiſe the Audience, who will not endure to have their own Notions contradicted, will never acknowledge 'em to be the Perſons they wou'd be taken for. For this reaſon *Horace* bids his Poet, *Follow common Fame*, *Famam Sequere*. And if he meddled with known Names, to keep to the known Characters, and Accounts of 'em.

Hor. Art. Poet.

—Honoratum ſi forte reponis Achillem;
Impiger, iracundus, inexorabilis, acer;
Jura neget ſibi nata, nihil non arroget armis.
Sit Medea ferox, invictaq; flebilis Ino,
Perfidus Ixion, Io vaga, triſtis Oreſtes.

The likeneſs here deſign'd, is not a *Natural*, but a *Hiſtorical* likeneſs. However monſtrous a Character were, if it was form'd upon, and adjuſted to common *Fame*, the *Poet* was juſtify'd.

4thly,

4thly, *That they should be equal.*

Equality *of* Manners *what.*

Here likewise *Aristotle* puts in his *Caveat*, lest any one by *Equality* of *Manners* shou'd understand such a steadiness of Temper and Resolution, as would exclude from the Stage the uncertainty of Fickle Humours, which he very well knew to be the case of a very great part of mankind. All that he requir'd was, that they should be all of a piece, that there might be no dismembring of Characters, no repugnancy to themselves in any part of 'em. *Horace*, his best Interpreter, says, *Let the character be maintain'd, and let the person appear the same at his exit, that he did at his entrance, and be consistent with himself.*

——Servetur ad imum
Qualis ab incepto processerit, & sibi constet.

Art. Poet.

The Philosopher did by no means intend to cut off so considerable a Branch from the revenue of *Comedy* as *Levity*; than which nothing deserves her Correction more, nothing fits her purpose better. But he cautions the *Poets*, whenever they make use of any of of theſe *Unequal*, or *Uncertain* Tempers, to repreſent 'em * *equally*, or *alike unequal* thro the whole Piece; and not to make 'em Fickle and Inconſtant in one Act, and Reſolv'd and Steady in another.

* ὁμαλῶς ἀνώμαλον δεῖ εἶναι.

Upon theſe Rules we may proceed to try the *Characters*, and *Expreſſions* of our *Poets*, either in conjunction with the *Antients*, or ſeparately by themſelves.

Faults of Characters *what.*

The *Characters* and *Expreſſions* have ſuch a natural dependance upon one another, that they can't be examin'd apart, each being juſtifiable or condemnable upon the Evidence of the other only. The *Character* may offend two ways; *firſt*, by being unnatural, and conſequently Monſtrous; *2dly*, by being Inconſiſtent with itſelf, and not all of a Piece. Theſe Faults, when committed, are likewiſe two ways diſcoverable, by the *Actions*, and by the *Expreſſions*, when any thing is done, or ſaid unnatural, or improper, a Fault is committed againſt *Character*, which is thereby broken, and becomes double.

Faults of Expreſſion *manifold.*

The Faults of Expreſſion are as various as the circumſtances againſt which it may offend, which are already ſumm'd up up under the head of Propriety, which may again be every one ſubdivided into ſo many Branches, that it would be endleſs to particularize the ſeveral ways of treſpaſſing in this kind. I ſhall therefore content my ſelf to take notice of 'em ſeverally, as occaſion ſhall preſent it ſelf, and wave any further notice of thoſe which ſhall not be found to my preſent purpoſe.

Mr *Collier* might unqueſtionably have found our *Poets* remiſs enough in the obſervation of theſe Rules, and conſequently guilty of faults deſerving his or any one's correction. But he choſe rather to brand 'em with crimes of a blacker dye, tho with leſs Juſtice and Truth, and like an *Iriſh* Evidence, by his forwardneſs to charge, and the monſtrouſneſs of his allegations, deſtroys the credit of his depoſitions.

His charge againſt our *Stage* for the miſmanagement of their *Characters* conſiſts of three general heads. *Some heads of Mr* Collier's *Charge.*

1. *Miſrepreſentation of* Women.
2. *Abuſe of the* Clergy.
3. *Rude treatment of the* Nobility.

To

To all these I shall say something general, with regard to the Argument, without entring into a discussion of the Merits of those particular Instances which he brings to back his Assertions. Not but I think many of 'em easily to be Apologiz'd for, or rather to be justify'd ; but because it would spin out this discourse to an unreasonable length, and likewise because there are those whose Abilities in this dispute are as much greater than mine, as their Interest in it, to whom I leave it.

P. 8, 9, 12. *The* Poets (says Mr *Collier*) *make* Women *speak smuttily.* They *bring 'em under such misbehaviour, as is violence to their Native Modesty, and a misrepresentation of their Sex. For Modesty, as Mr* Rapin *observes, is the Character of Women. They represent their single Ladies, and persons of Condition, under these disorders of Liberty. This makes the Irregularity still more monstrous, and a greater Contradiction to Nature and Probability.*

This point mistaken. Here again, according to his usual method, Mr *Collier* mistakes his point, and runs away with a wrong scent ; however he opens, and cries it lustily away, that the Musick may atone for the

the mistake, and draw all those that are not stanch in Partners to his Error. Mr *Rapin observes that the Character of Women is Modesty*, and therefore Mr *Collier* thinks, that no *Woman* must be shewn without it. *Aristotle* has given *Courage* or *Valour* as the *Characteristick* or Mark of distinction proper to the other *Sex*, which was a notion so *Antient*, and so universally receiv'd, that most Nations have given it a denomination from the Sex, as if peculiar to it. The *Greeks* call'd it Ἀνδρεία, we *Manhood*. Yet 'tis no Solecism in *Poetical Manners* to represent Men sometimes upon the Stage as Cowards; nor did any man ever think the whole Sex affronted by it; how near soever it might touch some Individuals.

Faults of particular *no reflection upon the* Sex *in* General.

If the *Poets* set up these Women of Liberty for the Representatives of their whole Sex, or pretended to make them the Standards to measure all the rest by, the Sex wou'd have just reason to complain of so abusive a Misrepresentation. But 'tis just the contrary, the Sex has no Interest in the Virtues or Vices of any Individual, either on the Stage, or off of it; they reflect no honour or dis-

grace

grace on the Collective Body, any more than the Neatneſs and good Breeding of the *Court* affect the Naſtineſs and ill Manners of *Billingſgate*, or are affected by 'em.

Univerſals *and* Individuals *improper* Characters.

In Plays the *Characters* are neither *Univerſal* nor *General*. Marks ſo comprehenſive are the Impreſſes and Signatures of Nature, which are not to be corrected, or improv'd by us, and therefore not to be meddled with. Beſides, they give us no Idea of the perſon characteriz'd, but what is common to the reſt of the ſpecies, and do not ſufficiently diſtinguiſh him. Neither are they ſo *Singular*, as to extend no farther than ſingle *Individuals*. *Characters* of ſo narrow a Compaſs wou'd be of very little uſe, or diverſion. Becauſe they wou'd not appear natural, the Originals being probably unknown to the greateſt part, if not the whole Audience; nor cou'd any of the Audience find any thing to correct in themſelves by ſeeing the Infirmity peculiar to a particular man expos'd. This was indeed the method of the *Old Greek Comedy*; but then they pick'd out publick perſons, whom they dreſs'd in Fools Coats and expos'd upon the Stage, not in their own own Shapes, but thoſe of the Poet's Fancy; an Inſolence, that never would have been endur'd in any, but a Popular Government, where the beſt of Men are ſometimes ſacrificed to the Humours and Caprices of a giddy multitude. Yet even by them it was at laſt ſuppreſſed.

The *Characters* therefore muſt neither be too general, nor too ſingular, one loſes the diſtinction, the other makes it monſtrous, we are too familiar with that to take notice of it, and too unacquainted with this to acknowledge it to be real. But betwixt theſe there is an almoſt infinite variety; ſome natural and approaching to Generals, as the ſeveral *Ages* of the World, and of *Life*, *Sexes* and *Tempers*; ſome Artificial, and more particular, as the vaſt Varieties and Shapes of *Villany*, *Knavery*, *Folly*, *Affectation* and *Humour*, *&c.* All theſe are within the *Poet*'s Royalty, and he may ſummon 'em to attend him, whenever he has occaſion for their ſervice. Yet tho theſe make up perhaps the greateſt part of Mankind, he is not fondly to imagine, that

What Characters proper.

he has any Authority over the whole, or to expect homage from any of 'em, as the Publick Reprefentatives of their Sex.

Two forts of Refemblances in Poetry.

Yet even granting to the *Poets* fuch an unlimited Authority (which I fhall not do) Mr *Collier*'s Argument falls to the Ground neverthelefs. For as in *Painting*, fo in *Poetry*, 'tis a Maxim as true as common, that there are two forts of Refemblances, one handfome, t'other homely. Now *Comedy*, whofe Duty 'tis not to flatter, like Droll Painting. gives the Features true, tho the Air be ridiculous. The Sex has its *Characteriftick* Blemifhes as well as Ornaments; and thofe are to be copied, when a Defective Character is intended, as the others are for a perfect one. And yet, for the reafons already given, when the Virtues or Vices of any particular Women are reprefented, the Sex in general have no fhare either in the Complimeut or the Affront. Becaufe any particular Inftances to the contrary notwithftanding, the Sex may be in the main either good or bad. So that Mr *Collier*'s charge of mifreprefenting the Sex in general is groundlefs.

But

But he pursues his Argument to particulars, and takes notice, that even Quality it self is not excepted from these Mismanagements.

Quality not just reason for exemption.

If Dignities conferr'd true Merit, and Titles took away all Blemishes, the *Poets* were certainly very much in the wrong to represent any Person of Quality with failings about her. But if Birth or Preferment be no sufficient Guard to a weakly Virtue or Understanding. If Title be no security against the usual Humane Infirmities; I see no reason, why they mayn't as well appear together upon the lesser Stage of the Theatre, as upon the grand one of the World. But this will be more properly consider'd in another place.

Mr Collier's collectin from the Antients very loosely made.

From these more general exceptions, he descends to particular *Expressions*. Which, that he may render the more inexcusable, he flies out into extravagant Commendations of the *Antients* upon the score of their Modesty, and the Cleanness of their *Expressions*. In this employment he bestirs himself notably, and pretends not to leave one exceptionable Passage unremarked. But either he has had a Prodigious Crop, or is a very ill Husband; for he leaves very large gleanings behind him. We ſhall make bold to walk over the ſame ground, and pick up ſome of his leavings, (for all wou'd be too bulky to find room in this place) and reſtore 'em to their Owners, whether left by him out of negligence or deſign.

One thing I muſt deſire the Reader to take notice of, which is, that I don't charge theſe paſſages as faults, or immoralities upon the *Antients*, but only inſtance in 'em, to ſhew the partiality of Mr *Collier*, who violently wreſts the Words and Senſe of the Moderns, only to make that monſtrous and unſufferable in them, which he either excuſes or defends in the others. Nor do I here pretend to preſent the Reader with a compleat Collection of the kind. I aſſure him, that I ſhall leave untouch'd ſome hundreds of thoſe inſtances which I have actually obſerv'd amongſt the *Greek* and *Latin Dramatiſts*, and only give him ſo many, as are indiſpenſably neceſſary to ſhew how unjuſtly Mr *Collier* has drawn his parallel. For ſince both *Antients* and *Moderns*, as *Poets* are ſubmitted to, and ought

ought to be govern'd by the ſame Laws, 'tis but reaſon, that one as well as t'other, ſhou'd be allow'd the benefit of 'em.

Shakeſpear's *Ophelia* comes firſt under his Laſh, for not keeping her mouth clean under her diſtraction. He is ſo very nice, that her breath, which for ſo many years has ſtood the teſt of the moſt critical Noſes, ſmells rank to him. It may therefore be worth while to enquire, whether the fault lies in her Mouth, or his Noſe. *Objection to Ophelia.*

Ophelia was a modeſt young Virgin, beloved by *Hamlet*, and in Love with him. Her Paſſion was approv'd, and directed by her Father, and her Pretenſions to a match with *Hamlet*, the heir apparent to the Crown of *Denmark*, encouraged, and ſupported by the Countenance and Aſſiſtance of the *King* and *Queen*. A warrantable Love, ſo naturally planted in ſo tender a Breaſt, ſo carefully nurſed, ſo artfully manured, and ſo ſtrongly forced up, muſt needs take very deep Root, and bear a very great Head. Love, even in the moſt difficult Circumſtances, is the Paſſion naturally moſt predominant in young Breaſts *Character of Ophelia.*

but when it is encouraged and cheriſh'd by thoſe of whom they ſtand in awe, it grows Maſterly and Tyrannical, and will admit of no Check. This was poor *Ophelia*'s caſe. *Hamlet* had ſworn, her *Father* had approved, the *King* and *Queen* conſented to, nay, deſired the Conſummation of her Wiſhes. Her hopes were full blown, when they were miſerably blaſted. *Hamlet* by miſtake kills her Father, and runs mad; or, which is all one to her, counterfeits madneſs ſo well, that ſhe is cheated into a belief of the reality of it. Here Piety and Love concur to make her Affliction piercing, and to impreſs her Sorrow more deep and laſting. To tear up two ſuch paſſions violently by the roots, muſt needs make horrible Convulſions in a Mind ſo tender, and a Sex ſo weak. Theſe Calamities diſtract her, and ſhe talks incoherently; at which Mr *Collier* is amaz'd, he is downright ſtupified, and thinks the Woman's mad to run out of her wits. But tho ſhe talks a little light-headed, and ſeems to want ſleep, I don't find ſhe needed any *Caſhew* in her Mouth to correct her Breath. That's a diſcovery

of

of Mr *Collier's*, (like ſome other of his) who perhaps is of Opinion, that the Breath and the Underſtanding have the ſame Lodging, and muſt needs be vitiated together. However, *Shakeſpear* has drown'd her at laſt, and Mr *Collier* is angry that he did it no ſooner. He is for having Execution done upon her ſeriouſly, and in ſober ſadneſs, without the excuſe of madneſs for Self-murther. To kill her is not ſufficient with him, unleſs ſhe be damn'd into the bargain. Allowing the Cauſe of her madneſs to be *Partie per Pale*, the death of her Father, and the loſs of her Love, which is the utmoſt we can give to the latter, yet her paſſion is as innocent, and inoffenſive in her diſtraction as before, tho not ſo reaſonable and well govern'd. Mr *Collier* has not told us, what he grounds his hard cenſure upon, but we may gueſs, that if he be really ſo angry as he pretends, 'tis at the mad Song, which *Ophelia* ſings to the Queen, which I ſhall venture to tranſcribe without fear of offending the modeſty of the moſt chaſte Ear.

Objection groundleſs & frivolous.

 To

Mad Song.

To morrow is St Valentine's *day, all*
in the morn betimes,
And I a Maid at your Window to be
your Valentine.
Then up he, he arose, and don'd his
Cloaths, and dupt the Chamber door,
Let in a Maid that out a Maid
Never departed more.
By Gis, *and by St* Charity :
Alack, and fie for shame !
Young men will do't, if they come to't,
By Cock they are to blame.
Quoth she, before you tumbled me,
You promis'd me to wed :
So had I done, by yonder Sun,
And thou hadst not come to bed.

Foolish but inoffensive.

'Tis strange this stuff shou'd wamble so in Mr *Collier*'s Stomach, and put him into such an Uproar. 'Tis silly indeed, but very harmless and inoffensive ; and 'tis no great Miracle, that a Woman out of her Wits shou'd talk Nonsense, who at the soundest of her Intellects had no extraordinary Talent at Speech-making. Sure Mr *Collier*'s concoctive Faculty's extreamly deprav'd, that meer Water-Pap turns to such virulent Corruption with him.

But

But Children and Mad Folks tell truth, they ſay, and he ſeems to diſcover thro her Frenzy what ſhe wou'd be at. She was troubled for the loſs of a Sweet-heart, and the breaking off her Match, Poor Soul. Not unlikely. Yet this was no Novelty in the days of our Fore-fathers; if he pleaſes to conſult the Records, he will find even in the days of *Sophocles*, Maids had an itching the ſame way, and longed to know, what was what, before they died.

Antients *more faulty then this.*

Antigone, whom he has produc'd as an inſtance of the Temperance, and Decency of the *Ancients* in this reſpect, may upon the Parallel ſerve us as an example of the contrary. The diſtinguiſhing Parts of this Ladies Character, are Piety and Reſolution, and ſhe makes both ſufficiently appear, ſhe buries her Brother, tho ſhe knew ſhe muſt die for it. And when ſhe receives her Sentence from *Creon*, which was immediately to be put in execution, ſhe makes light of Death, and inſults the Tyrant. But as ſhe is led to Execution, ſhe is unexpectedly concerned about the Toy her Maidenhead; 'tis her great Affliction, that

Inſtance in the Antigone *of* Sophocles.

that ſhe muſt go out of the world with that great Burthen about her. Upon this occaſion ſhe is very clamorous, and that it may be taken notice of as her main grievance, ſhe repeats it divers times over, and chews the Cud upon it liberally.

—— οὔθ' ὑμεναίων
ἔγκληρον, οὔτ' ἐπινυμφίδιος
πω μέ τις ὕμνος ὕμνησεν,
ἀλλ' ἀχέροντι νυμφεύσω ——

Poor Girl, ſhe does not reliſh her Sentence half ſo well as an *Epithalamium*. She thinks a ſoft Bed, and a warm Bed-fellow more comfortable by abundance, than a cold Grave. And who can blame her ? But Matrimony runs ſtrangely in her head. For a little after ſhe's at it again, complaining of her want of a Husband, and is very ſorry that ſhe muſt croſs the *Styx*, and viſit her Parents with her Maiden-head about her.

πρὸς οὓς ἀραῖος, ἄγαμος ἅ
δ' ἐγὼ μέτοικος ἔρχομαι.

And immediately after ſhe's at it again.

—— ἀνυμέναιος

Un-

Unmarried is ſtill the burthen of the Song. Nay, ſhe is ſo full of it, that ſhe can't forbear talking of a ſecond Husband , in caſe ſhe were a Widow.

πόσις μὲν ἂν μοι κατθανόντος, ἄλλος ἦν.

This thought of a ſecond Husband is ſuch a Refreſhment to her, that ſhe can't forbear dilating upon it. One wou'd think by the odd Frolickſomeneſs of her complaints, and the whimſical Comforts ſhe finds out, that ſhe was only going to dance bare-foot at a Siſters VVedding. But within a few lines, ſhe relapſes again into her agonies of deſpair, and is more afraid of leading Apes in Hell, than e're a hopeleſs Antiquated Damſel within our Bills of Mortality. She is not ſo much concern'd at dying, but to go out of the world,

ἄλεκτρον, ἀνυμφέαιον, οὔτε τοῦ γάμου
μέρος λαχοῦσαν.

and not to have one Honey Moon, not ſo much as a merey Bout before ſhe went, was a hardſhip ſhe cou'd not bear with any temper. VVe

VVe may find by this Lady's complaint, that ſhe was very deſirous to diſpoſe of her Maiden-head; but for any thing that appears from her complaint or behaviour, ſhe was very indifferent to whom. 'Twas a Burthen ſhe long'd to be rid of, and ſeem'd not to care who eas'd her; for ſhe does not mention her Contract with *Hæmon*, which ſhe decently might, but laments her want of a Husband in general terms, without giving the leaſt hint of an Honourable Love for any particular perſon.

Theſe are extraordinary Speculations for a dying Perſon. However, Mr *Collier* admires the *Poets* conduct in this caſe, and were he *Ordinary* no doubt but we ſhou'd have theſe Flowers tranſplanted in great plenty to the laſt Speeches of his dying Females. He thinks 'tis out of pure regard to Modeſty and Decency, that *Antigone* takes no notice of *Hæmon* in her complaints. I ſhall not diſpute, whether 'twere the faſhion in the days of *Sophocles* or not; but I am ſure 'tis accounted but an ill Symptome of Modeſty in our Age, when a young Lady ſhews an impatience to be married, before ſhe has made a Settlement of

her

her Affection upon any Individual Man.

However, *Antigone*'s Carriage is not singular; *Electra*, another Lady of much the same Quality and Character, (tho not under those immediate apprehensions of Death) declares her self of the same Opinion. She's in great distress too for want of a Husband, and complains very heavily upon that score.

Instance in Electra *of the same Author.*

—— ἄτεκνος,
τάλαιν' ἀνύμφευτος, αἰὲν οἰχνῶ
δάκρυσι μυδαλέα.

Nor is *Euripides* a whit more tender in this point. The Royal *Polyxena*, just before she was to be led away as a Victim to the *Manes* of *Achilles*, harps upon the same string. It lies very heavy upon her Spirits, that she must go out of the World in ignorance.

—ἄπειμι δὴ κάτω
ἄνυμφος, ἀνυμέναιος, ὧν μ' ἐχρῆν τυχεῖν.

This Princess's complaint is yet more unreasonable than either of the former, and more unbecoming the Modesty of her Sex, and the greatness of her Birth

and

and Courage, as 'tis both before and afterwards shew. Shewn as a Captive, a part of the Plunder of the sack'd City, one that besides her own unhappy Destiny, which hung immediately over her head, had the Ruin and Miseries of her Country and Family fresh in view, to put all wanton thoughts out of her head. Besides, she cou'd not expect to ascend the insolent Conquerors Bed any otherwise than as his Vassal, the Slave of his Lust and Pleasure, which, as it was below her to comply with, but upon Force, so it must be a Slavish Baseness, as well as Wantonness and Incontinence, to desire it under her Circumstances.

It were easy to bring many Instances more of this kind, but I think it wou'd be tedious and unnecessary to multiply instances in a plain case. I think it likewise a labour altogether as superfluous to spend more words to shew the vast disproportion between the innocent Extravagance of *Ophelia*'s Frenzy, and the sober Rants of *Antigone*, *Electra*, and *Polyxena*. To suppose the Reader cou'd over-look that, were to affront his Understanding.

But

But before I part with *Antigone*, I ſhall beg leave to make one obſervation more. Mr *Collier* takes notice, that *Caſſandra, in reporting the misfortunes of the* Greeks, *ſtops at the Adulteries of* Clytemneſtra *and* Ægiale. *And gives this handſome reaſon for making a halt.* P. 35.

Σιγᾶν ἄμεινον τ᾽ αἰσχρά.
Foul things are beſt unſaid.

From whence he obſerves, that *Some things are dangerous in report, as well as practice, and many times a Diſeaſe in the Deſcription. This* Euripides *was aware of, and manag'd accordingly, and was remarkably regular both in Stile and Manners.*

This was indeed an extraordinary piece of niceneſs in *Euripides*, more I think by a great deal, than he was oblig'd to, and I am ſure more than he has ſhewn upon other occaſions. *Caſſandra* might have foretold the Diſcovery of the Adulteries of *Clytemneſtra* and *Ægiale*, without any Indecencies of Language, or ſhocking the moſt tender Ear, had the Poet ſo pleas'd.

Antigone *in* Sophocles *not so nice.*

Sophocles, who was as good a Judge and as careful an obſerver of decency as *Euripides,* gives his *Antigone* more liberty; tho had he thought it indecent, he might with better reaſon have excus'd her. 1ſt, Becauſe what *Antigone* ſays is no way neceſſary, being neither provok'd by any thing that preceeded, nor of uſe to the promoting of the Action, or the Information of the Audience. 2dly, Becauſe ſhe thereby revives the Infamy of her Parents, and refreſhes the ſcandalous impreſſions, which her own Inceſtuous Birth muſt needs have made upon the Audience to her diſadvantage.

> Ἰὼ ματρῷαι λέκτρων
> Ἆται, κοιμήματ' αὐτογέννητα
> Ἀμῷ πατρὶ δυσμόρου ματρὸς
> Οἵων ἐγώ ποθ' ἀταλαίφρων ἔφυν.

If *Antigone* might be thus free with her own Family without breach of Modeſty, I can't ſee why *Caſſandra* ſhou'd be ſo tender of an Enemy, whom ſhe was juſt going to ſupplant in her Bed; and in the divulging of whoſe Faults, as well as Misfortunes, ſhe might be allow'd to take ſome

Plea-

Pleasure, as a sort of anticipation of the satisfaction, which she took in the Revenge of the Destruction of her Family, which she foresaw was to come. But *Casandra* lov'd doing better than talking. For in the Speech foregoing to this, which Mr *Collier* commends so much for the Modesty of it, *Casandra* runs almost mad for Joy, that *Agamemnon* wou'd take her to his Bed, and calls in an Enthusiastick manner upon *Hymen*, upon *Hecate*, and *Apollo* to grace the Ceremony She desires her *Mother*, and the miserable *Phrygians* about her to adorn themselves, be merry, and dance, and sing,. as if her Father were in the heighth of his prosperity. The *Chorus* hereupon desires *Hecuba* to curb her, and keep her from running voluntarily to the *Grecian* Camp. Her Mother accordingly reprimands her, and tells her she thought their Calamities might have made her more modest, that Tears better became their Fortune, than Nuptial Songs or Torches.

Casandra *not so nice as Mr* Collier *pretends.*

——Οἴ μοι τέκνον,
Ὡς ὐκ ὑπ' αἰχμῆς, ὐδ' ὑπ' ἀργείου δορὸς,

Γάμους γαμεῖσθαι τούσδ' ἐδόξαζον ποτε.
Παράδοτ' ἐμοὶ φῶς. οὐ γὰρ ὀρθὰ πυρφορεῖς
Μαινὰς θοάζουσ', οὐδέ σ' αἱ τύχαι τέκνον
Σεσωφρονήκασιν, ἀλλ' ἔτ' ἐν ταὐτῷ μένεις.
Εἰσφέρετε πεύκας, δάκρυά τ' ἀνταλλάσσετε
Τοῖς τῆσδε μέλεσι Τρῳάδες γαμηλίοις.

Extravagance of Casandra.

This Reproof has a ſtrange Operation upon *Caſandra.* For inſtead of reclaiming and reducing her to reaſon, it makes her ten times madder. She falls to croſs purpoſes with her Mother, and as if ſhe had been Pandreſs in the caſe, calls upon her to crown her victorious head, and wiſh her Joy of her Royal Match. She bids her lead her, and if ſhe does not make haſt enough, ſhe wou'd have her puſh violently on.

Μᾶτερ, πύκαζε κρᾶτ' ἐμὸν νικηφόρον,
Καὶ τοῖς ἐμοῖσι βασιλικοῖς γάμοις,
Καὶ πέμπε τε, κἂν μὴ τ' ἀμά σοι πρόθυμά γ' ᾖ
Ὤθει βιαίως.

Is this the Modeſt, the baſhful *Caſandra,* ſo demure, that ſhe can't name adultery, tho in an Enemy, and yet ſo forward to act it, that no reſtraints of Shame or Miſery can keep her within bounds.

It

It may perhaps be objected in Defence of *Casandra*, that her Joy and Transport springs not from any Pleasure or Satisfaction, that she shou'd take in this Match, but from the Prospect she had of revenging the Quarrel of her Family, and the Ruine and Destruction which she foresaw shou'd thence come upon the House of *Atreus* her mortal Enemies.

Admit this to be true. Yet *Casandra* pushes her Resentments too far, when she sacrifices her Virtue and Modesty to her Revenge. Had *Casandra* been represented as a Woman of a furious vindicative Spirit, she might in a sudden fit of Rage have rashly sacrificed all Considerations to the Violence of her present Fury. But then if the Character be virtuous in the main, such Outrages are not offered to Modesty, till after prodigious struggles, and racking Convulsions of Mind. Passion must not triumph over Reason and Honour, but with vast labour and difficulty, and in those Breasts only, where it is the ruling, uncontrollable Power, and where the prospect of its success is great, and immediate, and is *Indecency against Character.*

in Women provoked as well by Appetite as Inclination.

But this is none of *Casandra's* case. She shared indeed amongst the rest the common Fate, and became a Slave, and a Prey to the victors Lust and Avarice. This might naturally make her wish the utter confusion of the Destroyers of her Country and Family; but not at the expence of her Fame and Virtue. 'Twas all she had left to comfort her; and as *Andromache* in the same Play cou'd inform her, of infinitely more worth, than the wretched remainder of a servile Life. This therefore shou'd not have been parted with at any rate, much less upon a slender consideration. Had she submitted to necessity only, and comply'd as a Slave with reluctance to the desires of *Agamemnon*, as *Andromache* does to *Pyrrhus*, she had saved hes Modesty, and secured her Revenge ev'ry whit as well. The Disasters of *Agamemnon* and his House, interpreted as a Punishment of her's, and her Family's wrongs, tho they were only Prophetically fore-known by her, had given a sullen sort of Comfort, and afforded a reason for her resignation of her self

to

to the Conquerors Pleaſure. But if the Poet deſigned her for ſo implacable a Character,as to take ſuch great ſatisfaction in, and purchaſe at ſo dear a rate a Proſpect only of Revenge at ſuch a diſtance, by which ſhe herſelf muſt be cruſhed, and all her Friends either dead, or ſo diſperſed as to have no intereſt in the accompliſhment of it: he ought to have prepar'd the Audience for ſo unaccountable an extravagance, by ſome notice of the Violence of her Temper, either by ſomething from her own mouth or Conduct previous to this,or from the mouth of ſome Friend of her's, that might have abated the ſurprize of ſuch a reſolution. Eſpecially ſince he was reſolved ſhe ſhou'd appear no more by her future modeſt behaviour to qualify the Scandal of this Miſdemeanour.

This Lady being ſet up by Mr *Collier* as the Standard of Modeſty, I have examined her Conduct the more at large; and am very willing to leave it to the deciſion of the Reader,whether *Caſandra* or *Ophelia* wou'd beſt become the Cloyſter, or moſt needs the Diſcipline of the Nunnery in *Moorfields*.

Misbehaviour of Hecuba.

We have seen how this Lady can behave her self upon occasion. Let us examine her Mother, that corrected her wantonness so seasonably upon this occasion. She as older shou'd have more wit, and yet she forgets herself extreamly too sometimes. In the Play that bears her name, *Hecuba* comes to *Agamemnon*, complains of the murther of her Son *Polydorus* by *Polymestor*, and to move him to Compassion begins a wanton Discourse of the Pleasures of Love to him, tho she thinks at the same time, that 'tis impertinent, yet she's resolv'd it shall out.

> Καὶ μὴν ἴσως μὲν τοῦ λόγου κενὸν τόδε,
> Κύπειν προβάλλειν. ἀλλ' ὅμως εἰρήσεται.

As an old Woman she had the priviledge of tattling.But as a Prudent Woman, she ought to have handled her Daughters disgrace a little more tenderly. The good old Lady ne'r minces the matter, but outs with all roundly, and is concerned, that any thing shou'd abate of the satisfaction *Casandra* might have in so good a Bedfellow.

> Πρὸς σῇσι πλευρῇς παῖς ἐμὴ κοιμίζεται,
> Ἡ φοιβὰς, ἣν καλοῦσι Κασάνδραν Φρύγες.
> Ποῦ τὰς φίλας δῆτ' εὐφρόνας δείξεις, ἄναξ,
> Ἢ τῶν ἐν εὐνῇ φιλτάτων ἀσπασμάτων
> Χάριν τίν' ἕξει παῖς ἐμή.

This is plain dealing, but ſomething below the Dignity of the Queen of *Aſia*, at the loweſt ebb of her Fortune. What follows is fit only for the Mouth of a Drunken Midwife at a Chriſtening in *Wapping*.

Ἐκ τοῦ σκότου γὰρ, νυκτέρων τ᾽ ἀσπασμάτων,
φίλτρων ἁμοῦ τε, τοῖς βροτοῖς πολλὴ χάρις.

Love and Tenderneſs uſed by the Moderns. *Luſt and Violence by the* Antients.

After theſe remarkable Inſtances of the regularity of *Euripides*, both in Stile and Manners, I ſuppoſe our Poets may venture to ſhew their Faces in his Company, without danger of putting him to the bluſh with their want of Modeſty. But the Antients, it ſeems, had very little *Love* or *Courtſhip* in their Plays. Perhaps ſo. But they had Luſt and Violence, which Mr *Collier* thinks more eligible. The fault of the Modern Lovers, it ſeems, is too much tenderneſs and fooling away their time in idle Talk. The vigorous Antients went more roundly to work, their's were like *Spaniſh* Intrigues, two words ſtruck the bargain betwixt 'em.

Numerous instances of this kind to be found in Euripides.

'Twere easie to multiply instances of this nature from *Euripides*, were that my Design. But I love not to rake into the Ashes of the Dead for that which isn't worth finding. Yet that the Reader, if he has the curiosity, may have the satisfaction, I shall refer him to the Places where they are to be found; where he that has a mind to a more ample Collection, may be abundantly furnished.

Some referr'd to.

Hermione rails at *Andromache* in terms very misbecoming her Sex, Quality, and Years. *Andromache* reproves her for it in terms yet less beseeming a sober Matron, and casts a scandalous aspersion upon her whole Sex. *Creusa* makes a foul relation of her rape by *Apollo*, and descends nauseously to particulars with her Servant. *Ion* her Son civilly questions his Mother, whether she had not play'd the Whore with some base Groom, and to cover her disgrace laid her Bastard (himself) falsly to *Apollo*'s charge. *Electra*'s manners are much of the same size and complexion; when she is urging her Brother *Orestes* to the murther of *Ægisthus*; she bids him ring in his Ears the who-

ring

ring of her Mother, and tell him, that ſince he had a Whore of her he muſt expect ſharers in her, and be the Cuckold of other Men, as her Father had been his. That he was notorious for her Cully all the Town over. This ſort of ſtuff ſhe lets run over without regard to Decency, and rambles as wantonly thro the Infamy of her Family, as is if 'twere only Scandal pickt up at a Goſſipping, in which they had no particular Concern.

Whoever conſults theſe and divers Paſſages, as well in *Sophocles* as *Euripides*, will find the moſt exceptionable Paſſages in our Poets, whether Comick or Tragick very excuſable, upon a fair Conſtruction, let it be never ſo ſevere within the Bounds of Juſtice.

Seneca has received Abſolution, and is pronounced clear of the ſin of Uncleanneſs. Yet with Mr *Collier*'s leave, ſince he is introduced to vilify and depreciate the Moderns, he is bound to confront 'em, and anſwer for his own Conduct, before he takes upon him magiſterially to cenſure and correct others. But ſince 'tis not ſo much his act as Mr *Collier*'s, who has ventured to be

Seneca *examin'd upon this Article.*

be his Godfather, and anſwer for him, a ſlight Inquiſition ſhall excuſe him. We ſhall not require ſo ſevere a Proof of his Chaſtity as the Ordeal Tryal. It ſhall be ſufficient for him to enter his Proteſtation againſt what has been done in his Name.

Miſcarriage of Phædra. In his *Hippolytus*, *Phædra* is poſſeſſed with a ſcandalous, inceſtuous Paſſion, and ſhe indulges it at as looſe, a ſcandalous rate. She enters firſt with her Reſolution, as ſtrong as her Deſires. She is not concerned at the Nature or Conſequences of ſo vile a Paſſion, but at the difficulty of ſatisfying it. She appears at firſt ſight full grown and confirm'd in Wickedneſs, and inſtead of condemning and endeavouring to ſtifle ſo lewd, a licentious Flame, ſhe animates her ſelf to the accompliſhment of her deſign by a recrimination upon her Husband, and rips up, amongſt others, even thoſe of his Faults, to which herſelf had been acceſſary, and the ſole occaſion of his Guilt. But what is more ſtrange and unnatural, ſhe draws matter of Comfort and Encouragement from the monſtrous Lewdneſs of her Mother, and the Infamy of her Houſe. But what's what's most wonderful of all, she's come to this heighth of Impudence, before she well knows what ails her; she is but just arrived at the Discovery of her Malady. She can neither Eat, Sleep, Work, nor Pray; but she burns, and boils inwardly like *Ætna* it self, and is all agog on the sudden for hunting and handling the Boarspear: She knows not why, till at length she finds, that she's her Mother's own Daughter, and so the Mystery comes out.

Quo tendis anime? quid furens saltus amas?
Fatale miseræ matris agnosco malum,
Peccare noster novit in Sylvis amor.
Genetrix, tui me miseret, infando malo
Correpta pecoris efferi sævum ducem
Audax amasti. Torvus impatiens juge
Adulter ille, ductor indomiti gregis.
Sed amabat aliquid: Quis meas miseræ Deus,
Aut quis juvare Dædalus flammas queat?
Non si ille remeet arte mopsopia potens,
Qui nostra cæca monstra concluset domo,
Promittat ullam casibus nostris opem.
———— Nulla Minois levi

De-

Defuncta amore est: jungitur semper nefas.

'Twas the fate of her Family, it seems, and she was by no means for contending with her destiny, and therefore surrenders upon the first Summons of her passion. Her Mother, she thinks, was much oblig'd to *Dædalus*, whose ingenuity brought her and her horned Lover together. But alas! Poor Soul, She's hard put to't. Her Mother's Bull was a gentle tender-hearted Gallant, to her Savage obdurate Son-in-law; and she, good woman, had no such necessary helps for her Consolation. What must she do? Her Nurse advises her to strangle this Incestuous Brat, her Passion, in the Birth. But she bravely resolves to push on, whatever comes on't.

Quemcunq; dederit exitum casus, feram.

Is this the modest *Phædra*, whose Language is under such discipline? Can she be so free with the Infamy of her House, make such fulsome descriptions, and envy her Mother the caresses

of

of a Bull? But the Nurſe mends the matter, and reproves her ſeverely. Here therefore we may expect a ſample of ſtrict and exemplary modeſty, and chaſte expreſſion.

Sed ut ſecundus Numinum abſcondat favor
Coitus nefandos—and immediately after
————*Metue concubitus novos.*
Miſcere thalamos Patris, & Nati apparas,
Uteroq; prolem capere confuſam impio.

Is this the diſciplin'd Language Mr *Collier* boaſts of? Such we have indeed ſometimes under the diſcipline of *Bridewel* and *Bedlam*, but ſeldom elſewhere. The moſt accompliſh'd Diſciple that ever came out of the late famous Academy of the virtuous Mrs *Meggs* of notable Memory, cou'd not have been more free in her Language, as well as Thoughts. The *Antients*, good Men, did not puzzle their Heads about double *entendre*'s to ſcreen a foul thought, or labour for Allegories and Alluſions, but honeſtly called a Spade, a Spade, whenever they had occaſion. I believe theſe

theſe Ladies wou'd be better company for *Joan* of *Naples*, than Mr *Dryden*'s *Leonora*, if fulſome Deſcriptions be ſo toothſome to her.

Modeſty of Lycus *conſider.*

But Mr *Collier* is mightily pleaſed, that *there is no courting, except in the* Hercules Furens, *where the Tyrant* Lycus *addreſſes* Megara *very briefly, and in modeſt remote Language.* Here he has pointed us a Specimen of what he calls *modeſt* and *remote.* The Tyrant had courted *Megara*, the Wife of *Hercules*, to no purpoſe, ſhe obſtinately repulſed him; and therefore he turns him about, and *modeſtly* (as Mr *Collier* thinks) thus addreſſes himſelf to *Amphitruo. You have Pimpt for* Jupiter *to your Wife, and ſhall do as much for me to your Daughter-in-Law, having ſo expert a Maſter it can be no novelty either to her, or her Husband, to be civil to their Betters. But if ſhe obſtinately refuſes to comply, I'll force her, and beget a generous Race.*

Jovi. dediſti conjugem, Regi dabis.
Et te magiſtro non novum hoc diſcet Nurus,
Etiam viro probante, meliorem ſequi,
Sin copulari pertinax tædis negat,

Vel

Vel ex coacta nobilem partum feram.

This, according to Mr *Collier*, is Distance and Modesty,. Old Stile. If he will make these allowances to our *Poets*, I'll engage to prove there never was an immodest thing said upon the *English Stage*; a task I shou'd be loth to undertake upon any other terms, as much as I am perswaded of their comparative Innocence.

But 'tis not in his Judgment only, that Mr *Collier* can be partial; his Memory can be favourable too upon occasion. For tho he does *non omnibus dormire*, yet he can wink at the Faults of his old Friends, while he sees ev'ry slip of the Moderns double. He says, that *Seneca* has no courting but this of *Lycus*; but I suppose, he wilfully forgets the shameful solicitations which *Phædra* uses to corrupt her Son-in-Law *Hippolitus*, against the Charter of her Sex, and the rules of Decency. They, whose curiosity invites 'em to a further enquiry, may find matter in abundance for their speculations, in the *Agamemnon*, particularly in the *Scenes* between *Clytemnestra* and her *Nurse*,

References to other instances.

Ægisthus

Ægisthus and *Clytemnestra*, *Electra* and *Clytemnestra*; and in divers others places of the rest of the Plays of that Collection.

These Faults less pardonable in Tragedy, *than* Comedy.

If we should examine the *Ancient Comedy* with the severity that Mr *Collier* uses to the *Moderns*, we should let in such a torrent of Citations, as wou'd almost over-whelm us. But for the reasons already given, there are grains of allowance to be made to *Comedy*, to which *Tragedy* can lay no claim. *Tragedy* deals with persons of the highest Condition, by and before whom the strictest severity of Manners and Decorum is to be observ'd. The business is of great importance, and requires serious consideration, and gives no opportunity for wantonness, or light indecencies. Whenever therefore the *Poet* suffers such persons to talk such Fooleries themselves, or others to talk 'em to 'em, he stoops 'em below their Characters and Business. But in *Comedy* the case is quite different, both the persons and business are little, and exact neither State nor Ceremony. Most of the persons are such, as either don't know, or don't regard Forms and

we

Punctilio's of good Breeding. This we have a plain Proof of in all the Comedies of Antiquity, whether of the old or new Cut. The Slaves ate ſo familiar with their Maſters, that by the freedoms they take, 'tis hard to diſtinguiſh one from t'other, except that the Slave bears the Character of Advantage, and appears generally to have more wit than his Maſter, whom he is to aſſiſt if he be young, and cheat if he be old. Accordingly we find 'em almoſt always bantering, quibbling, drolling, and jeſting upon their Maſters, when they are together. Their employment is uſually to purchaſe their young Maſter a Miſtreſs, with the Hunks their Old Maſters money. By this means the Slaves become the Principal Character in the *Antient Comedy*, and are the main Spring, by which the whole Machine of the *Fable* is ſet a going. The reſt, which are uſually in the new Comedy, a covetous old Fellow, an extravagant young one, a Bawd, a Whore, a ſtolen Virgin, are but the under Wheels, whoſe motions are regulated altogether by thoſe of the Slave, who is the Man of Intrigue, and carries all the Brains the

Slaves *the top Characters of the* Roman Comedy.

Poet can ſpare about him. The old Man is froward, ſuſpicious, ſevere, and cloſe-fiſted; and ſometimes he is repreſented eaſy and indulgent, but has a ſcolding, turbulent, griping Wife, a churliſh, parſimonious Brother, or Relation, or conceited Wiſe Friend, that takes upon himſelf to correct and govern him. The young Fellow is in Love, extravagant, and in want of Money. The *Bawd*, whether Male, or Female, is faithleſs, impoſing, and acted only by preſent profit. The *Whore*, if an experienc'd one, is altogether Mercenary, if raw in her Trade, ſhe is dotingly fond and loving, but under the care of the Bawd. The ſtoln Virgin is always next to a Mute.

Very little variety in their Plots.

Their *Plots* are confined to as narrow a compaſs, as their *Characters*. The young Man is in Love with a Slave, and wants money to purchaſe her of the *Bawd*, who is about to ſell, or proſtitute her to another. The young Man in this exigent has recourſe to a crafty Servant, who helps by ſome Stratagem to ſqueeze the money out of the old Spunge his Father, or to cheat ſome other Body. A diſcovery at length is made

made to his Father, who is vehemently provoked at his Sons folly and extravagance, and threatens to disinherit him. Young Master and Man are at their wits end, to reconcile themselves to the old Man, and no fetch, no contrivance left to bring themselves off, when in comes some Merchant or Stranger, who discovers that this Maiden is a Citizen, and well born; which pacifies the Old Fellow, the young Man thrives in his amours, a match is struck up by consent of all Parties, and all's well again.

Greater Liberty taken by Aristophanes.

'Tis true, *Aristophanes* took a much greater compass, and brought not only *Mankind*, but *Gods*, *Brute Animals*, and even *inanimate Bodies* within the Pale of the *Stage*. This, as it inlarg'd his walk, encreas'd his Liberty, which he sometimes abuses at a scandalous unjustifyable rate. Mr *Collier*, to obviate all objections that might be rais'd from the practice of *Aristophanes*, whose *Comedies* are the only pieces of that kind remaining of the *Greek* Stage, by way of prevention excepts against his Credit, and endeavours to invalidate his Evidence by accusing him of *Atheism*.

Aristo-phanes whether an Atheist or not nothing to the pur-pose.

But tho I think Mr *Collier*'s Arguments to prove him an Atheist to be of no validity, as I could easily shew, were it not an impertinent digression in this place; yet I shall wave the particular refutation of 'em, because I think it not material to the point in hand, whether he were so or not. For tho we should grant, that the Poet himself was an Atheist, yet Mr *Collier* himself will not pretend that his Audience, the people of *Athens* were so too. On the contrary it appears that they were as arrant Bigots, as Mr *Collier* himself could wish to trade with. They put *Socrates* to death, only because he would not be cullied out of his reason, and be the Priest's Fool, to countenance and encourage a senseless extravagant superstition. This made some Christian Fathers reckon him among the *Martyrs* for the *Unity* of the *Deity*.

But Mr *Collier*, who has a much better hand at supposing than proving, takes a very odd method to clear the reputation of that great man from the suggestions of *Aristophanes*, and the censure of his Country, by whom he was condemn'd for *Atheism*. That

That Socrates *was no* Atheiſt *is clear from Inſtances enow. To mention but one. The confidence he had in his Dæmon or Genius, by which he govern'd his Affairs, puts it beyond diſpute.*

That *Socrates* held, and believ'd the exiſtence of *Dæmons* or *Genii*, may be an argument, that he was no *Atheiſt*. But that he pretended to have any Familiarity, or hold any Correſpondence with ſuch a *Dæmon* or *Genius*, gives me but a very indifferent notion of his Faith and Integrity. It ſmells rank of Impoſture, and muſt needs make but a bad Impreſſion upon men of Integrity, and Underſtanding of thoſe Principles, which want the ſupport of ſuch diſhoneſt ſhifts. But this was *Plato*'s report of him, and perhaps was neither the real practice nor opinion of *Socrates*, whom therefore we ſhall diſmiſs, as having been brought in only to ſhew how unluckily Mr *Collier* is gifted for Argument.

This Argument conſidered.

But if the *Athenians* could proceed with ſuch Rigour againſt a man ſo much rever'd for his Virtue and Wiſdom, and ſupported by the favour of their beſt and greateſt men only, for holding O-

Rigour of the Athenians *to* Socrates *a ſort of Acquitment of* Ariſtophanes.

pinions contrary to their Notions of Religion, 'tis not to be imagin'd, that they who were so very tender in this case, so extreamly sensible of any affront to the Common Faith, would with so little concern, or rather so much satisfaction, have heard it publickly insulted by *Aristophanes*. They shew'd in the case of *Socrates*, that their Blood could rise and ferment upon such occasions as high as any people's. How comes it then, that they who were so outrageous and impatient with *Socrates*, are so tame, and passive as to bear much greater Provocations of the same Nature from *Aristophanes* without the least sign of Resentment? Was the interest of the *Poet* so much superiour to the *Philosophers*, that what was capital in one shou'd deserve no manner of correction, or notice in t'other? No such matter, for he was call'd in question, and took his Tryal for a thing of much less moment, *viz.* For assuming the Liberties of a Citizen of *Athens* being a Foreigner. Now there is no doubt, but his Enemies who had the malice and the power to get him thus arraign'd, would have strengthen'd their Charge, with an Article

ticle ſo conſiderable as *Atheiſm*, and *Blaſphemy* againſt their *Gods*, before ſuch ſuperſtitious bigotted Judges as the *Athenians*, had there been any ground or colour of ſuſpicion. The Power and Malice of *Cleon* wou'd have reach'd, him, had there been any plauſible pretence, to have fixt the guilt of a Crime ſo unpopular upon him.

Mr *Collier* pretends to maintain his aſſertion by divers inſtances of irreverent paſſages in relation to their Gods, to be found in the Plays of *Ariſtophanes*. I grant there are ſuch paſſages, even more than Mr *Collier* has cited, tho many of thoſe which he has ſelected to prove his Allegation by, will by no means bear the weight of ſuch a Charge. But the people of *Athens*, who were in theſe matters much more delicate, than Mr *Collier* ſeems to be, had the niceneſs to diſtinguiſh juſtly between the *Private Sentiments* of the *Man*, and the *Publick* one's of the *Poet*. In this latter capacity almoſt all ſorts of Characters belong'd to him, and he muſt of conſequence be frequently neceſſitated to make uſe of Thoughts and Expreſſions very contrary to his own

Mr Collier's no proof of his aſſertion.

The Opinion of the Man *not meaſured by the Expreſſions of the* Poet *at* Athens.

proper opinion. The *Athenians* therefore did not lay these Liberties of the Stage, which they knew the nature of those Characters which he represented must of course oblige him to, as blemishes either in his Faith or Morals, to his Charge. Had Mr *Collier* been Master of as much Understanding and Justice, as these *Heathens*, not only *Aristophanes*, but our *English Poets* too had met with a fairer Adversary, and found civiller and honester treatment. 'Twere easie to enlarge in the Justification of *Aristophanes*; but Mr *Collier* gives him up, and therefore we need no parallel between him, and the *English Comick Poets*, to prove the comparative modesty of the latter; for which reason we shall proceed directly to *Plautus* whom he justifies upon the comparison.

Liberties of Plautus *greater than those of the* English *Stage.* *P.* 15.

Plautus, by reason of the narrow Circle that he moves in, affords no great variety, yet there is plenty enough in him, to make Mr *Collier* blush for his defence, if it were all produc'd at large. For what he calls *very moderate*, and says, *that our single Plays shall far outdo all this put together*, wou'd in his

Mi-

Microſcopical way of obſerving appear monſtrous, and infinitely exceed the moſt malicious collection he can make out of the *Engliſh Poets*. But he preſumes upon the ignorance of his Readers, and impoſes arbitrarily and magiſterially what ſenſe he pleaſes upon every thing, and deſpotically coins Citations, which he forces upon 'em for genuine, upon no better warrant than his own Will and Pleaſure. But to proceed to inſtance.

Inſtances from the Amphitruo.

In the *Amphitruo*, *Mercury*, after a long ſcene of groſs Drollery upon *Amphitruo*, bids him be gone, and not diſturb his Maſter's pleaſure with his Wife.

> *Abſcede moneo, moleſtus ne ſies, dum Amphitruo,*
> *Cum uxore modo ex hoſtibus adveniens, voluptatem capit.*

Upon this *Amphitruo* asks, What Wife? and is anſwer'd *Alcumena*. This does not ſatisfy his curioſity, but he muſt know whether *he lies with her* or not; and is not contented till he has doubl'd the Queſtion, and muſt be inform'd, whether they lie in the ſame room both or or not. Hereupon *Mercury*, to cut the debate ſhort, gives him this plain anſwer.

Corpore corpus incubat.

Upon this *Amphitruo* bewails his miſery, and *Mercury* in mockery ſays,

Lucri'ſt, quod hic miſeriam deputat. Nam uxorem uſurariam
Perinde eſt præbere, ac ſi agrum ſterilem fodiendum loces.

The man's a gainer by what he calls his miſery. For 'tis as profitable to have ones Wife, as ones Field till'd by another.

Remarkable Circumſtances of this Paſſage.

At this rate *Mercury* drolls on; wherein there is this remarkable, beſides the quality of the perſons, one a God, t'other a Heroe, that the words laſt cited are ſuppos'd to be ſpoken aſide out of the hearing of *Amphitruo*; and conſequently are immediately addreſs'd and peculiarly recommended to the Audience, as containing ſomething very edifying or very entertaining.

The Diſguiſe under which Mercury *appears no excuſe for his misbehaviour.*

I defy Mr *Collier* to prove any ſuch licentious freedoms upon the *Engliſh*

Am-

Amphitruo, as angry as he is with it. But perhaps Mr *Collier* thinks the disguise of *Sosia*, may excuse the ribaldry of *Mercury*. But this excuse won't serve his turn. For *Mercury* is under no disguise to the Audience, to whom this last Speech is particularly addrefs'd.*

But left he should think *Mercury* a Mad God, and allow him the liberty of Ribaldry, let us hear how cleanly *Jupiter* will express himself. It the last Scene this Soveraign of the Gods appears in state, owns his Quality and Intrigue, and bids *Amphitruo* receive his Wife. For, says he, Jupiter *not more modest.*

Mea vi subacta'st.

Mr *Collier* knows the meaning of the word *Subigo* in this case, and must strain as hard in this place, as he thinks *Lambin* has done in another, if he will defend it.

The *Asinaria*, the next Play in order, affords besides the Scene betwixt *Cleæreta* the Bawd, and *Argyrippus*, (which Mr *Collier* confesses to *border upon rudeness*, and I think down-right Bawdy in several places) two more, one betwixt *Instances from the* Asinaria.

Argy-

Argyrippus, *Philenium*, *Leonida*, and *Libanus*, which is very looſe, and another, which is ſingularly inſtructive, between *Argyrippus* and *Demænetus* his Father. The old man, like a *good* Father, purchaſes a Whore for his Son, upon condition that himſelf may come in for ſnacks, and withal tells him, that it becomes a young man to be modeſt, and let his Betters go before him, that he had provided a Miſtreſs for him to ſolace himſelf with all the year, if he could but be content, to let his Father be his Taſter. This is wholeſom Doctrine, and ſeaſon'd with ſuch grave Morality, no doubt very edifying. This Mr *Collier* finds no fault with, and therefore we may very well paſs it by; ſince, if it will bear the Teſt of his Hypotheſis, it will unqueſtionably of ours. Tho, had this been of *Engliſh* growth, it had found no favour, but had ſmarted unmercifully under his diſcipline.

Inſtance of ſingular Morality.

One thing 'tis neceſſary to take notice of before we go any further, and that is, that whether *Plautus*'s Lovers talk Love, or not, they act it very plainly and vigorouſly before Folks, where-

Plautus's Lovers more active than talkative.

where-ever they come together. An instance of this kind we have in * the *Curculio* at the meeting of *Phædromus*, and *Planeſium*, (who by the by is ſuppos'd to be a modeſt Virgin). At their purchas'd opportunity of coming together, they are ſo active and boiſterous, that *Palinurus* the Slave ſtands amaz'd, and cries out,

Inſtanced from the Curtulio.

———uterq; inſaniunt.
Viden' ut miſere moliuntur , nequeunt complecti ſatis.

Theſe words are more expreſſive of Action than Paſſion, though indeed they imply both. *Planeſium*, to mend the matter, expreſſes her diſcontent, that the Servant did not withdraw, but ſtaid to be a check upon 'em.

Jam huic voluptati hoc adjunctum odium eſt.

The Servant replies with indignation, and reprimands his Maſter for behaving himſelf ſo immodeſtly,
---*Ut immodeſtis hic te moderere moribus*

Comparative Modesty of the Virgins of the Antient *Stage hence to be observed.*

I mention this only to shew how much even the modest Virgins of the *Antient* Stage valued an opportunity. This, according to Mr *Collier*'s *Hypothesis*, would have been a Capital misdemeanour upon the *English* Stage, whatever it was upon the *Roman*. Many more instances of this kind, and more plain ones might be produc'd, but I have not room for 'em here. However, this may serve to shew what sort of *Nun*'s Flesh Mr *Collier* wou'd be at, when he makes *Vestals* of such Lasses as this.

Mr Collier's *own exceptions taken notice of.*

Mr *Collier* is so very fond of the Sobriety of *Plautus*'s Plays, that he defends even the Conduct of the *Pandars* and *Slaves*, and maintains, that they don't misbehave themselves before Women. He is sure at least, that *there are but four instances* to the contrary, *as he remembers*, *Olympio, Palæstrio, Stratilax* and *Dordalus are the persons. And the Women they discourse with, are two of them Slaves, and the third a Wench.*

P. 17.

His instance in Olympio *grosly mistaken or misrepresented.*

I'm sorry Mr *Collier*'s memory is so bad, when he has so much occasion for a better. He takes notice of but three Women thus freely dealt with, two whereof

whereof, as he tells us by way of mitigation of damages , were Slaves, and the third a Wench. From whence he ſeems to infer, that before Women of Modeſty and Condition, theſe *Slaves* and *Pandars* were more cautious and reſerv'd in their Language. But *Olympio*, whom he has ſubpæna'd as an Evidence for himſelf, will tell him otherwiſe. The perſons he plays *his Gambols before*, are *Cleoſtrata* and *Murrhina*, two principal Citizens Wives, Matrons of as great Quality and Virtue as any, that e're trod the *Roman* Stage in *Comedy*; *Alcumena* excepted. Theſe Matrons had ſhamm'd him with a man in woman's Cloaths for a Bride, and big with the expectation of the Iſſue of their jeſt, fell to catechizing him about the buſineſs. The Clown, without regard to their Quality, which was the more conſiderable in *Cleoſtrata*, becauſe ſhe was his proper Miſtreſs, and might ſeverely chaſtiſe any rudeneſs, yet the Clown, I ſay, makes a very rank deſcription, and what's worſe, the women were pleaſed with it, and urge and prompt him forward.

Ol.

Casina Act 5 Scen. 2.

Ol.——*illa haud verbum facit, & sepit veste, id qui estis,*
Ubi illum saltum video obseptum, rogo, ut altero sinat adire.
Enim jam magis jam appropero, magis jam lubet in Casinam irruere.——

This, instead of rebating the edge of his Mistresses Appetite, inflames her curiosity yet more; she's impatient till he proceeds.

Cl. *Perdis, quin pergis.*
Cl. ——*continuo stricto gladio: atat babæ papæ.* Cl. *Quid papæ.*
Ol. ——*Gladium ne haberet metui, id quærere occæpi*
Dum gladium ne habeat quæro, arripio capulum,
Sed quem cogito non habuit gladium, nam id esset Frigidius.

Here the Booby began to mince the matter; and his Mistress, that lov'd plain-dealing, corrects him for it, and bids him speak out, but he is asham'd, he says,

Cl. *Eloquere.* Ol. *At pudet.*

The

The Slave however has ſome grace. His Miſtreſs can't be ſatisfy'd ſo, ſhe's for every thing in as proper terms, as if he was giving evidence in a Court of Record. But not prevailing that way, ſhe prompts and pumps him with Interrogatories as looſely as a waggiſh Councel at a Bawdy Tryal.

Cl. *Nam radix fuit? Num cucumis?*

The Woman, 'tis plain, had a true apprehenſion of the matter, but ſhe did not like his clowniſh Baſhfulneſs. Still the fellow boggles at naked Imagery; however he improves, and comes on apace.

Ol. *Profecto non fuit quicquam olerum*
Niſi quicquid erat, calamitas profecto attigerat nunquam:
Ita quicquid erat, grande erat.
Volo, ut obvortat cubitiſſim,
Verbum ullum mutit,
Surgo ut ineam.

If we meaſure the Converſation of *Plautus*'s Ladies of Quality by this Standard, the Ladies of our Stage, taking even the loosest, need not be asham'd of their Breeding. Nay, they wou'd blush for their company if they were brought together.

Instance from the Asinaria. But *Cleostrata* and *Murrhina* are not singular. In the *Asinaria*, *Artemona*, upon the discovery of her Husbands intrigue, reflects upon his Failings towards her, and makes a very odd discovery of her own wants.

Art. ——— *Ego censeo*
Eum etiam hominem Senatui dare operam, aut Clientibus
Ibi labore delassatum noctem totam stertere.
Ille opere foris faciundo lassus noctu advenit.
Fundum alienum arat, incultum familiarem deserit.

He was (says she) *so taken up with tilling another's ground, that he let his own lye fallow.*

This frankness of the Lady's complaint gave the Slave her Informer the boldness to put a very homely question to her.

Possis

Possis si forte accubantem tuum virum conspecteris
Cum corona amplexum amicam, si videas cognoscere?

Cou'd you know your Husband, if you shou'd see him and his Mistress in a posture that wou'd not shew his Face.

This passage (to use a Phrase of Mr *Collier's*) I have translated *softly*, but very fairly. Yet even thus the Image, which in the Original is express'd in the proper vulgar terms, appears too gross and plain, and is such as wou'd not be endur'd upon our Stage, as lewd as Mr *Collier* thinks that and the Age.

Slaves not *the only Offenders of this kind in* Plautus.

However, *The Men who talk intemperately are generally Slaves*, says Mr *Collier*; and he can't find any Gentleman guilty of an indecent expression, except *Lusiteles*, who is once *over airy*. I shall help him to another, out of a great number, that are ready upon demand, which is the more authentick, because it comes from a grave old Gentleman in no very airy mood, but while

 he

he is correcting another for his Lewd ness and Debauchery. In the *Miles Gloriosus*, *Periplectomenes* asks *Pyrgopolinices* the Souldier,

Miles Gloriosus.

Cur es ausus subagitare alienam uxorem, impudens?

The Gravity of the man here makes the grossness of the Expression the more remarkable. After these instances I hope Mr *Collier* may upon second thoughts have a better opinion of the Gentlemen and Ladies of our Stage, than heretofore, at least that he will do em more Justice in his next Parallel.

His Prologues *and* Epilogues *not always inoffensive.*

P. 17.

But Mr *Collier* has one hold to retreat to yet, from whence he must be driven before we part. Plautus *his* Prologues *and* Epilogues *are inoffensive.* If this can be maintain'd, he has gain'd a great point; but here, as in other places, he triumphs before Victory. The *Prologue* and *Epilogue* are properly the Speeches of the *Poet*, and 'tis in them, if any where, that we discover the *Morals* of a *Comick Poet. Lambin* finds a double *entendre* in the *Prologue* to the *Pænulus*; Mr *Collier thinks there is a strain in the* con-

construction. I must own my self of *Lambin*'s opinion ; but, since Mr *Collier* does not here deliver himself after his usual dogmatical way, I shall not insist upon this passage, but proceed to instances, which no violence of Construction can wrest to a wrong sense.

Here let us return to the *Casina*, to which the *Poet* gives a very smutty conclusion, and a more smutty *Epilogue*. *Grex*, that speaks the *Epilogue*, advises the Audience to *clap lustily and give the Poet his due, and to those that did it, he wishes as many Whores as they pleased, unknown to their Wives ; but to those that did not clap, he wishes a He-Goat besmear'd with the Filth of a Ship for a Concubine.*

This prov'd from the Epilogue *to the* Casina.

Nunc nos æquum est, manibus meritis meritam mercedem dasfre,
Qui faxit, clam uxorem ducat scortum semper quod volet.
Verum qui non manibus clare, quantum poterit, pluserit,
Ei pro scorto supponetur hircus unctus nautea.

Epilogue to the Asinaria *an Encouragement to Lewdness.*

Here we have a Sample of the *Poet's Morals*, which Mr *Collier* has warranted, as we have already seen. In the *Epilogue* to the *Asinaria*, if we may take *Plautus*'s word, we may have a Taste of the *Manners* of his *Age* and *Country*, which Mr *Collier* is likewise very fond of. From both which put together, we may give a reasonable guess at Mr *Collier*'s own Palate in such matters. *Demænetus his Wife* had caught him in a Bawdy-house, whoring in his Son's company, and rated him home, which concludes the Action of the Play. Hereupon *Grex* by way of application thus accosts the *Audience*.

Hic senex siquid clam uxorem suo animo fecit volupe,
Neq; novum, neq; mirum fecit, nec secus quam alii solent,
Nec quisquast tam ingenio duro, nec tam firmo pectore
Quin ubi quicquam occasionis sit, sibi faciat bene.

Here the *Poet* justifies *Whoring*, even in an old married man, and pleads the common practice in defence of it. He thinks

thinks no man can withſtand a fair temptation *to do himſelf good.* For with that Phraſe, he ſweetens the buſineſs and qualifies the offence.

Let Mr *Collier* compare theſe two *Epilogues* with thoſe *Engliſh* ones to which he refers, and then condemn them, and abſolve theſe if he can. Nay, even the Play of which *Plautus* himſelf makes his boaſt, *That 'twas written up to the ſtricteſt rules of Chaſtity; that few ſuch Comedies were to be found, by which thoſe that were already good, might be made better,* has a very broad touch of Smut in the *Epilogue,* even at the time he is valuing himſelf upon his Modeſty, Captivi.

Spectatores, ad pudicos mores facta hæc
fabula eſt. Epilogue to the Captivi.
Neq; in hac ſubagitationes ſunt———
Hujuſmodi paucas Poetæ reperiunt Comædias,
Ubi boni meliores fiant———.

Such Inſtances as theſe crowd themſelves ſo upon us almoſt every where in *Plautus,* that 'tis hard to paſs 'em over, and endleſs to take notice of 'em. But

 having

having already far tranſgreſſed the intended limits of this diſcourſe, I ſhall treſpaſs no farther upon the Reader's patience on this head.

Complaint of the Abuſe *of the* Clergy *not well grounded.*

His next complaint is *the abuſe of the Clergy*. Were this complaint juſtly grounded, it would merit not only his, but all honeſt men's Indignation, and Reſentments. But this Charge does not ſeem to be ſufficiently made out. For 'tis raiſed upon a very weak foundation, a miſtaken Notion, that Prieſts above all the reſt of Mankind, are by priviledge exempted from having their faults taken notice of this way; His reaſon for this ſhall be conſider'd by and by. I ſuppoſe, if Mr *Collier*'s Band hung awry, or his Face was dirty, he would uſe the aſſiſtance of a Glaſs to make all right and clean. Why then does he reject the uſe of that which might do the ſame office for his mind, and help him to correct the follies and management of his Life? The caſe is plain, he is blind to his own Faults, and mad that any one elſe ſhould ſee 'em. This makes him call the ſhewing any of their failings, expoſing the Clergy, as if thereby only they

they became publick, not conſidering that the Glaſs ſhews our Faults to our ſelves only; other people can ſee 'em as plainly and as readily without its help. But Mr *Collier*, who takes every thing by the wrong handle, looks upon a correction as a reproach, and had rather a Fault ſhould paſs unmended, than be taken notice of. But beeauſe he pleads a peculiar Charter for the exemption of the Prieſthood, let us ſee how he makes out his Title. The Conſiderations, upon which he founds it, are three.

Firſt, *Becauſe of their Relation to the Deity.*

This *Relation to the Deity* he ſwells to a monſtrous ſize, and blows himſelf preſumptuouſly up in his own conceit, to a Condition ſomething above mortal. He pretends to no leſs, than to be one of the *Principal Miniſters of Gods Kingdom*, to *repreſent his Perſon*, to *publiſh his Laws*, *Paſs his Pardons*, *and Preſide in his Worſhip.* Mr *Collier's* Pride has here hurried him into prodigious Inſolence and Folly. To raiſe his own Character, he has made a *Pope* of every individual Prieſt, and given that

Their Relation to the Deity to conſidered.

P. 127. 128.

that to the meaneſt of 'em, which the moſt *Orthodox* part of the Chriſtian World deny to the pretended Succeſſor of St *Peter*? Is not the whole world God's Kingdom? What then, are its Kings, Princes, and Rulers, if every Prieſt be before 'em in Authority? Mr *Collier*, I believe, is the firſt bold Mortal, that ever pretended to repreſent the perſon of God Almighty ſeriouſly. This to me ſounds more like Blaſphemy, than any thing in the moſt profane *Poet*. The *Pope* indeed preſumes to ſtile himſelf *Chriſt*'s Vicar general, but he does not preſume to be the Repreſentative of his Perſon. As Mr *Collier* has aſſum'd a higher Title, ſo, I ſuppoſe, he expects more reverence. 'Tis ſtrange that Enthuſiaſm ſhould ſhoot to ſuch a heighth in our cold Climate, which it ſcarce ever reach'd in *Rome* its Native Place. But Mr *Collier* keeps a hot Bed, where he forces up violent Notions, in ſpight of the oppoſition of an unnatural Soil and Seaſon.

Perſonal Repreſentation of Deity abſurd.

But I ſhould be glad to know, wherein this perſonal Repreſentation conſiſts. Does he pretend, like the *Pope*, to poſſeſs

ſeſs any of the Divine Attributes? Infallibility, even of the Church itſelf, has been long ſince juſtly exploded by all ſober Chriſtians, that know, and dare to uſe their Reaſon in the guidance of their Conſciences. And the *Pope* himſelf in the heighth of his Pride and Uſurpation, never pretended to more. But in what does this vain Creature reſemble his Creator? Can a groveling Mortal ſuſtain the Majeſty and Figure of Omnipotence.

The Power of the Church not lodged with the Prieſt.

If notwithſtanding all theſe Magnificent expreſſions of himſelf, and his order, Mr *Collier* means no more, than than that a Prieſt derives a ſubordinate Authority from the Church, to exerciſe his Function in Spiritual matters conformably to her directions, then all this inſolent profane Bombaſt dwindles to nothing. For tho a very great power and truſt is repos'd in the Church, yet I don't find, that this Power was ever lodg'd entire with the Prieſt, or any other ſingle perſon whatſoever. And therefore Mr *Collier* graſps at too much, when he claims the ſame reſpect, and deference for every Prieſt, that is, or ought to be paid to the Church,

Church, and the Governours of it.

Mission of St. Paul, *and the Apostles what and how circumstantiated.*

But Mr *Collier* finds, that St. *Paul* calls himself and the rest of the *Apostles* *the Ambassadors of Christ*, and thinks himself thereby sufficiently warranted to take upon him to represent the *person of God*. The word which St *Paul* employs, 2 *Cor.* 5. 20. is πρεσβεύομεν, which signifies to come by commission from another, and consequently may probably enough be render'd, *We are the Embassadors*, tho it does not always import so much. Mr *Collier* lays hold of the word Embassadour, and fancies himself in the highest, and most honourable post that can be, under God Almighty, that is, *to represent his Person, to publish his Laws, Pass his Pardons, and Preside in his Worship*. All this indeed, except the *Personal Representation*, was the Office of St *Paul*, and the rest of the *Apostles*. But without affronting, or lessening the Authority of the Clergy, I think I may lawfully question whether Mr *Collier*'s Commission be of equal Extent or Validity with theirs. They were call'd to the Ministry immediately by God himself, endued with supernatural and miraculous

Fa-

Faculties, and Powers both of Difcerning, and Operation by Infpiration from the Holy Ghoft himfelf. They were to plant in the World a new Faith, which had not yet been heard of, except in a very fmall part of the world. Their Doctrines were reveal'd immediately to themfelves, and had no other Evidence than their own Affirmation, and the Works that they did, to back and confirm what they taught. They had occafion for a Spirit more than naturally difcerning to be affur'd of the fincerity of their Converts, and for a Commiffion and Power extraordinary, to remit the fins of thofe that they found to be true Penitents, and to fupport themfelves and their Profelytes againft the Oppreffions of the Civil Power.

Difference betwixt their Commiffion and that of the prefent Miniftry.

Thefe circumftances, as I take it, make a very wide difference between the Miniftry, and Commiffion of the Apoftles, and the other immediate Difciples of our Saviour, and the Chriftian Miniftry at this time. For firft, They have now no immediate call to the Miniftry, whatever fome Enthufiaftick or Knavifh Sectaries may pretend. Secondly, They have no natural Gifts above other men,

to

to warrant a Pretence to an extraordinary Miſſion. Thirdly, They have now no peculiar Revelation, nor any other Rule of Faith, or Source of Doctrine, which is not common to all mankind with them. The Scriptures lie open for all that will look into 'em, and our Clergy pretend to no ſupernatural Gift of Expoſition above the Laity, and conſequently can offer no new matter of Faith. Fourthly, They pretend to no Spirit of Diſcerning above the condition of meer humanity to enable 'em to ſee into mens hearts, and judge of the ſincerity of their repentance, and conſequently muſt diſpoſe of Pardons blindfold, if they exerciſe any ſuch power, otherwiſe than conditional, and upon the terms expreſs'd in Scripture. But the pronouncing an Abſolution on thoſe terms, is not paſſing a Pardon, any more than allowing the benefit of the Clergy to a Malefactor in a Court of Judicature is an act of Grace in the Bench. Laſtly, Since the World became Chriſtian, thoſe extraordinary Commiſſions, which the Apoſtles and Primitive Chriſtians had, ceas'd with the reaſons of 'em. For when the

Princes

Princes and Rulers of the World became the Proſelytes and Protectors of Chriſtianity, there was no further occaſion to propagate the Goſpel by extraordinary methods, which had the Civil Power on its ſide. By this means the care of the Church devolv'd upon the State, and the Prieſthood became ſubordinate to it. For tho no State or Prince can make any thing a Rule of Faith, which was not ſo before in its Nature, or by ſome higher obligation, yet in matters of Practice in things indifferent towards which the Scriptures leave us at liberty, they have in all Countries (not under the uſurpation of the Pope) aſſerted their Authority by ordering and directing the Forms and Models of Church Government, and appointing the Perſons of the Governours, who are therefore undoubtedly ſubordinate to thoſe, by whoſe Authority they govern.

From theſe differences 'tis plain, that the Miniſtry at preſent ſtands upon quite another foot, than it did in the time of the Apoſtles; and that Mr *Collier* challenges a relation to the Deity which he has not, and in right of that a greater Reverence and respect than is due to him.

Importance of their Office no exemption.

His second consideration is, *The Importance of their Office.* What that is, has been in great measure laid down in the preceding Article. How far they are concerned in publishing Gods Laws, and passing his Pardons has been already examin'd. There was indeed a time, when the Priests had a Monopoly of Faith and Salvation, and retail'd out Articles and Indulgences to the Laity, who repair'd to the Bank of Implicit Faith and Merit for as much as their occasions requir'd. But the weakness of their Fund being discover'd, that Bank is broke long since in *England.* and the Laity have taken their Consciences into their own Custody again, to Mr *Collier's* great Disappointment. However they preside (he says) in the Worship of God. If he means by presiding, Officiating, he presides over his Congregation, as a Clerk in Parliament presides over the House, because he reads the Bills, Petitions, *&c.* to 'em. That to officiate in the House of God is an Employment of great Importance and honour, I shall readily grant. And as

they

they that perform their duty in that ſtation conſcientiouſly and well deſerve all due reſpect and honour ; ſo on the other hand, thoſe that proſtitute their Character to baſe ends, and make the Caſſock a Cover for *Pride*, *Ambition*, *Avarice*, *Hypocriſie*, *Knavery*, or *Folly*, deſerve to be corrected, and expos'd to the Publick. The importance of the Office, which Mr *Collier* pleads in bar to any Lay Cenſure upon 'em, is a ſtrong Argument for it. For in proportion to the weight of the truſt, ought to be the check upon it.

There may be many Faults amongſt the inferiour Clergy, which eſcape the notice, or do not fall properly under the cognizance of the Ordinary, which 'tis convenient ſhou'd be amended, for the reputation of the Order, and the good of the Offenders themſelves. Mr *Collier* thinks otherwiſe, he owns that they ought not to be ſeen, but he would have the People's Eyes put out, rather than the Offence remov'd. A Blot's no Blot till 'tis hit ; ſo the reputation of the Clergy be ſafe, 'tis no matter for their Manners ; for the Sin lies in the Scandal. Elſe why is he ſo angry with the *Poets*,

Some faults not cognizable by the Ordinary.

 for

for taking notice, that there is ſuch a thing now and then to be ſeen in the world as a Faulty Clergy-man ? The Order does not pretend to be any more exempt from failings, than other men. Then where's the Offence in ſhewing what thoſe Frailties are, to which they lie moſt expos'd ? 'Tis true, this can't be done in the Dramatick way, without the appearance of the Offender by his Proxy ; which ſtirs Mr *Collier's* Blood, who would have the Laity believe 'em abſolutely without Fault. 'Twere well if they were ſo indeed, but ſince they are not, I think it not juſt nor reaſonable, that the Laity ſhou'd be cheated into ſuch a belief. The man that labours too much to conceal his Faults, ſhews that he aims rather at Impunity than Repentance. For men ſeldom think of Reformation, while they can run on in a proſperous courſe of undiſcover'd Villany.

Upon this account Mr *Collier's* reaſoning appears very odd and ſingular. For if the concealing and covering of Men's Vices, be the means to advance and promote their corruption, he ſeems to take a ſort of retrograde way to Reformation.

But

But his fear is, that the Vices of ſome few thus publickly ſhewn, ſhou'd reflect upon the whole Order, and weaken their Credit and Authority in the Miniſterial Function. This objection is already anſwered in the article of the *Miſrepreſentation of Women*; what has been there ſaid holds good here, and needs no repetition. It can therefore be of no ill conſequence; For thoſe that are juſt, and Conſcientious in the exerciſe of their Functions will loſe no Credit or Authority; and thoſe that are not, have too much, if they have any.

Prieſts not miſrepreſented unleſs faultleſs.

If Prieſts be without Fault, then to paint 'em with any is a Miſrepreſentation, and an abuſe, a malicious ſlandering of the Order. But if they be not, 'tis fit that the rotten Sheep ſhou'd be mark'd and driven from the Flock, to prevent the contagion, whether of the Diſeaſe or the Scandal, which are equally catching. But Mr *Collier* has learnt Politicks of *Hudibras*, and wou'd have Prieſts whipt by Proxy; their Faults ſhou'd be chaſtiſed on Laymens Backs. We thank him for his kindneſs, and are very willing to be his Deputies, provided he can prove that the Physick will have its effect that way. I have been told, that a Purge given to a wet Nurse, wou'd operate with the Child; but I never heard of a Med'cine that wou'd work *Vice versa*. I grant, that they ought not to be corrected on the Stage for Lay Follies. Their Characters must be proper, in order to which, whether they play the Fool or the Knave, it must be seasoned with a cast of the Profession; otherwise they are Lay Fools and Knaves in Masquerade. But as the Characters ought not to be so general, as to represent whole Bodies of Men, so neither ought they to be so particular, as to stigmatize Individuals, as they did in the *Old Comedy*. If this Caution be observed, not only the Collective Body of the Clergy, but every individual Man amongst 'em is safe from scandal from that Quarter. If the *Poets* have not observ'd it, Mr *Collier* in vindication of the Clergy has a just Provocation to lash 'em severely. But if they have, then Mr *Collier* does 'em wrong, and the *Poets* ought to resume the Whipcord, and return the Compliment.

His

His laſt, and, as it appears by his dilating ſo largely upon it, his ſtrongeſt Conſideration is, that *They have Preſcription for their Priviledge. Their Profeſſion has been in poſſeſſion of eſteem in all Ages and Countries.* That it has been in Eſteem, and that it ought ſtill to be ſo, more than it is, I believe the *Poets* themſelves will allow. But that it has always been eſteemed ſo ſacred, that the *Antient Poets* durſt never ſuffer any of their *Perſons* of the *Drama* to make bold with it, I deny; and I think I ſhall demonſtrate the contrary.

His Plea from Preſcription examined.

I ſhall confine my ſelf to the *Dramatick Poets*, and only obſerve, that ſo the Prieſt be well treated 'tis no matter how his God is ſerved. For *Homer* is careſſed at a high rate, for putting a Crown upon *Chryſes*'s head, tho he uſes the whole Tribe of the Gods like Scoundrels. The firſt *Poet*, that I ſhall produce is *Sophocles*. In the cloſe of his *Ajax* the *Chorus* gives us the Moral of the Play in theſe words; *Experience teaches us much, but before the Event is ſeen, ne'r a Prophet of'em all can tell what things will come to.*

Inſtance to the contrary from Sophocles.

Ajax Flagellifer.

Χο. Η πολλὰ βροτοῖς ἐςὶν ἰδοῦσι
Γνῶναι· πρὶν ἰδεῖν δ' ὐδεὶς μάντις
Τῶν μελλόντων ὃ, τι πράξει.

This is a plain reflection upon the Profeſſion, and ſo remarkably circumſtantiated, that there is no doubt, but 'twas the *Poets* real ſenſe. For 'tis ſpoken by the *Chorus*, and made the *Moral* of the Play.

I ſhall paſs by the reproaches which *Oedipus* makes *Tireſias*, becauſe Mr *Collier* ſays they relate only to his Perſon, tho he himſelf in his *Defence* will allow no diſtinction betwixt the Man and the Prieſt. *If you make the Man a Knave, the Prieſt muſt ſuffer under the Imputation.* However in the ſame Play; *Jocaſta* ſays, *She wou'd not give a Ruſh for Divination.*

Oedipus Tyrannus.

ὥς' ὐχὶ μαντείας γ' ἂν, ὔτε τῇδ' ἐγὼ
βλέψαιμ' ἂν ὕνεκ', ὔτε τῇδ' ἂν ὕςερον ——

In the next Play *Creon* amongſt other reproaches tells *Tireſias*, that *They were all a Pack of Mercenary Corrupt Fellows.*

Τὸ μαντικὸν γὰρ πᾶν φιλάργυρον γένος. Antigone.

We have not room to multiply inſtances ſo far, as we might, but theſe may ſuffice to ſhew, that *Sophocles* was not ſo much afraid of a Prieſt as Mr *Collier* pretends.

Euripides is not a whit more tender of 'em, *Agamemnon* calls the *whole tribe of 'em a vain-glorious raſcally Race.* *Euripides not more tender of Prieſts.*

Τὸ μαντικὸν πᾶν σπέρμα φιλότιμον κακόν. Iphigenia *in Aulide.*

Achilles in the ſame Play (the Sobriety of whoſe Character Mr *Collier* is much in love with) threatens *Calchas* the Prophet before ſpoken of, and breaks out into this exclamation; *What are Prophets? Fellows that by gueſs ſometimes tell truth, but generally Lies.*

——τίς δὲ μάντις ἔστ' ἀνήρ.
Ὃς ὀλίγ' ἀληθῆ, πολλὰ δὲ ψευδῆ λέγει,
Τυχών. Ibidem.

Pentheus in the *Bacchæ* uſes *Tireſias* very ruggedly. He charges him with being Mercenary, and an Impoſtor, with ſeducing the People, and introducing a new false ſuperſtitious Worſhip, and orders the Seats from whence he took his Augural Obſervation to be pull'd down, with abundance of other Menaces, and hard words. Theſe may ſuffice for *Euripides* at this time.

Seneca *meddles little with Prieſts.*

Seneca makes little uſe of the Prophets, or Prieſts; *Tireſias* appears twice in his *Oedipus*, and *Calchas* once only to deliver an Oracle. *Oedipus* charges *Tireſias* with confederating with *Creon*, and charging a falſe crime upon him, and traiterouſly endeavouring to ſupplant him in his Throne. Theſe Inſtances ſufficiently demonſtrate, that the *Antients* were not afraid to make their Perſons of the *Drama* ſpeak pertinently to their Character, tho they ſhould thereby happen to bear hard upon their Prieſts. Nay, they thought it no offence to make 'em ſpeak things inconſiſtent with Piety, and the Religion of their Country.

Ajax Antigone *and* Philoctetes.

The Inſtances of this are innumerable. The Rants of *Ajax*, *Creon* , and *Philoctetes* in *Sophocles* are extravagant. This Tragedian affords abundance, but to make a collection of ſcattered expreſſions, would require more room than

than we can at present ſpare; however, *Euripides* and *Seneca* afford divers ſo very remarkable, that I can't paſs 'em over abſolutely without notice. In the *Hecuba*, *Talthybius* exclaims at a ſtrange rate upon the Conſideration of the turn of *Hecuba*'s fortune. *O Jupiter! what ſhall I ſay? ſhould mankind addreſs themſelves to you: Or have we been cheated with a ſham Story of Gods, and Providence, while Chance governs all things?*

Euripides *and* Seneca *full of prophane expreſſions.*

Ταλ. Ὦ Ζεῦ, τί λέξω; πότερά σ' ἀνθρώπους ὁρᾷν;
Ἢ δόξαν ἄλλως τήνδε κεκτῆσθαι μάτην
Ψευδῆ δοκοῦντας δαιμόνων εἶναι γένος,
Τύχην δὲ πάντα τἀν βροτοῖς ἐπισκοπεῖν.

Hecuba.

Polymeſtor is much ſuch another ſort of a Comforter, he cries out in the ſame Play, and upon the ſame occaſion, *Oh what a ſlippery thing is Human Grandeur, which is never ſecure. The Gods perplex and harraſs Mankind, that our Ignorance may ſupport their Altars, and Worſhip.*

Φεῦ, οὐκ ἔστιν οὐδὲν πιστὸν, οὔτ' εὐδοξία,
Οὔτ' ἂν καλῶς πράσσοντα, μὴ πράξειν κακῶς.
Φύρουσι δ' αὖθ' οἱ θεοὶ πάλιν τε καὶ πρόσω,
Ταραγμὸν ἐντιθέντες, ὡς ἀγνωσίᾳ
Σέβωμεν αὐτούς.

Ibidem.

Electra,

Electra, for a ſhort one has a very pithy Ejaculation. *O Nature, what a curſe art thou upon Mortals.*

Oreſtes. Ὦ φύσις ἐν ἀνθρώποισιν ὡς μέγ' εἶ κακόν.

Her Brother *Oreſtes* is allied to her in Principles as near as in Blood; he can't tell what to make of the Gods, any more than the two Gentlemen before. Yet he *ſerves* 'em whatever they be.

Ibidem. Δουλεύομεν θεοῖς, ὅ τι ποτ' εἰσὶ θεοί.

All that he knows of 'em is, that *they are naturally dilatory.*

Ibidem. Μέλλει. Τὸ θεῖον δ' ἐστὶ τοιοῦτον φύσει.

Troades. *Hecuba* is much of his mind; ſhe thinks the *Gods but bad Friends*, κακοὺς συμμάχους. The *Cyclops* tell *Ulyſſes*, That *Riches were the wiſe mans only God, and that he did not care a fart for Jupiter; but thought himſelf as great a God as he.*

'Ο πλȣτος, ἀνθρωπίσκε, τοῖς σοφοῖς θεός.
Ζηνὸς δ' ἐγὼ κεραυνὸν ȣ φρίσσω ξένε.
'Ουδ' οἶδ' ὅτι Ζεὺς ἐς' ἐμȣ κρείσσων θεός. Cyclops.

In the *Ion*, which is pretended to be a *Moral* Play, *Creusa* addresses herself directly to *Apollo*, and cals him κακὸς ευνάτωρ, *lewd Whoremaster*. Her Servant afterwards calls him Rascal, and advises her to set fire to his Temple. With such Flowers as these *Euripides* abounds, which I leave for others to gather. Ion.

Seneca is as full of 'em as he, but I shall refer the Reader only to the *Chorus* of the second Act of his *Troas*, which being spoken by the *Chorus* looks more like the Poet's own Opinion, than if it had come from any other Person of the *Drama*.

Post mortem nihil est, ipsaq; mors nihil, Troas.
Velocis spatij meta novissima.
Spem ponant avidi, soliciti metum.
Quæris quo jaceas post obitum loco?
Quo non nata jacent.
Tempus nos avidum devorat, & chaos.
Mors individua est noxia corpori,
Nec parcens animæ. Tænara, & aspero
Regnum sub Domino, limen & obsidens

Custos

Cuſtos non facili Cerberus oſtio,
Rumores vacui, verbaq; inania,
Et par ſolicito fabula ſomnio.

Which is thus tranſlated by the *Earl* of *Rocheſter.*

After Death nothing is, and nothing Death,
The utmoſt Limits of a Gaſp of Breath.
Let the Ambitious Zealot lay aſide
His Hopes of Heaven (whoſe Faith is but his Pride)
Let ſlaviſh Souls lay by their Fear,
Nor be concern'd which way, or where,
After this Life they ſhall be hurl'd,
Dead they become the lumber of the World.
And to that Maſs of Matter ſhall be ſwept,
Where things deſtroy'd with things unborn are kept.
Devouring Time ſwallows us whole,
Impartial Death confounds Body and Soul.
For Hell, and the foul Fiend that rules
The everlaſting fiery Goals,
Deviſ'd by Rogues, dreaded by Fools,
With his grim griezly Dog that keeps the Door,
Are ſenſeleſs Stories, idle Tales,
Dreams, Whimſeys, and no more.

Ano-

Another exception, which Mr *Collier* makes to the Stage is, that *they treat the Nobility rudely*. I must confess 'tis no complement to make a Fool of a Lord. But if Birth or any other Chance shou'd make a Lord of a Fool, I suppose the rest of that Noble Order wou'd not think themselves accountable for his Follies, or abus'd in his Picture. Shou'd the Poets presume to make such a one the Representative of his Order, and propose him as a common Standard, by which the Endowments of Quality in general were to be measur'd, their Insolence wou'd deserve the severest chastisement that cou'd be given. Or shou'd any one of 'em dare to characterize too nearly and particularly any of those Noble Persons, no doubt but he wou'd soon feel the weight of his Resentments, and smart sorely for his sawcy Liberty. But while the Poet contents himself with feign'd Persons, and copies closely after Nature, without pressing upon her in her private recesses, and singling out Individuals from the herd, if any Man, of what Quality or Employment soever, fancies himself concern'd in the representation,

Rude treatment of the Nobility a false charge.

let

let him ſpoil the Picture by mending the Original. For he only is to be blam'd for the Reſemblance. If Men of Honour and Abilities cou'd entail their Wiſdom and Virtues upon their Poſterity, then a Title wou'd be a pretty ſure ſign of Perſonal Worth, and the Reſpect and Reverence that was paid to the Founders of honourable Families ought to follow the Eſtate, and the heir of one ſhou'd be heir of t'other. But ſince Entails of this kind are of all kinds the moſt liable to be cut off, 'tis not abſolutely impoſſible but there may be ſuch a thing in the world, as a Fop of Quality. Now if there be ſuch a thing, it does not appear to me, that becauſe the Perſons are great, and elevated by their Dignity above the reſt of Mankind, and draw the Eyes of the People upon 'em, more than other men do, that therefore their Faults or Imperfections will be leſs viſible, or leſs taken notice of, or that the Splendour of their Figure is an infallible Antidote againſt the Infection of their Examples. Unleſs it be ſo, it is convenient that ſome reaſonable Expedient ſhou'd be allow'd to prevent

prevent the Miſchief of Imitation, and that thoſe who are too big to be aw'd out of their Follies, may be ſham'd out of 'em. But this is only Hypothetically offer'd. Mr *Collier* perhaps will tell us, that there are no ſuch Perſons, that a Fool of Quality is a meer Poetical Animal, and ought to be rank'd amongſt the *Harpyes*, *Hippogryphs*, *Centaurs*, and *Chimæra's* of Antiquity. If he proves this, my *Hypotheſis* in this point falls to the ground, otherwiſe I think it may ſtand in oppoſition to any thing that has yet been ſaid.

If theſe and abundance of other Paſſages in the *Antient* Poets were compar'd with thoſe, which Mr *Collier* produces out of the *Moderns*, the comparative Rudeneſs and Prophaneſs of the latter wou'd vaniſh. But he preſumes upon the lazineſs, or ignorance of the Majority of his Readers, and does not expect that any of 'em ſhou'd be at the pains to confront his arbitrary, and unfair accounts, with genuine quotations. But 'tis time to have compaſſion upon the Reader, who has run the Gauntlet thro a tedious Refutation ; in which if his ſatisfaction equals his Patience, the Author thinks his pains ſufficiently recompenc'd.

FINIS.